THE MICROSOFT NETWORK
VISUAL EXPLORER

THE MICROSOFT NETWORK VISUAL EXPLORER

Luanne O'Loughlin

CORIOLIS GROUP BOOKS

Publisher	*Keith Weiskamp*
Editor	*Ron Pronk*
Proofreader	*Kirsten Dewey*
Cover Design	*Anthony Stock*
Interior Design	*Bradley Grannis*
Layout Production	*Michelle Stroup*

Trademarks: All brand names and product names included in this book are trademarks, registered trademarks, or trade names of their respective holders.

Distributed to the book trade by IDG Books Worldwide, Inc.

Copyright © 1995 by The Coriolis Group, Inc.

All rights reserved.

Reproduction or translation of any part of this work beyond that permitted by section 107 or 108 of the 1976 United States Copyright Act without the written permission of the copyright owner is unlawful. Requests for permission or further information should be addressed to The Coriolis Group, 7339 E. Acoma Drive, Suite 7, Scottsdale, Arizona 85260.

Library of Congress Cataloging-in-Publication Data

O'Loughlin, Luanne
    Microsoft Network Visual Explorer / Luanne O'Loughlin
        p. cm.
    Includes Index
    ISBN 1-883577-66-7 : $19.99

Printed in the United States of America

10 9 8 7 6 5 4 3 2 1

To Michael

The little angel who started this book with me, but escaped to join the other angels.

Contents

INTRODUCTION   XXI
    Glimpsing the Future with MSN   xxii
    How to Use This Book   xxiii

ACKNOWLEDGMENTS   XXV

Part 1   MSN Centerfold: A Visual Tour of the User Interface   1

STARTING UP   2

THE FRONT PAGE   4

HOME BASE   6

EXPLORER VIEW   8

APPLES & ORANGES   10

LAYERS OF CONTENT   12

REVEAL UNDERCOVER ANSWERS   14

SPEEDY SHORTCUTS   18

EXCLUSIVE VIEWS   20

PRIZE DOWNLOADS   22

ON THE MENU   24

MAIL CALL   26

BUNDLES OF MAIL   28

SORTING THE MAIL   30

MAIL POWER TOOLS   32

SYSTEM TREASURE HUNT   34

PANNING FOR GOLD   36

WONDERS OF THE WEB   38

THE TOOLCHEST   40

RANDOM CHATTER   42

PROCEED WITH CAUTION   44

Part 2   Mastering MSN: A Q & A   47

GENERAL   49

What Does It Cost to Be an MSN Member?   49

Will I Pay Phone Charges, Too?   50

What's Available on MSN?   50

How Do I Save $$$ Using MSN?   50

Why MSN?   51

How Does MSN Differ from the Other Major Online Services?   52

Will It Be Difficult to Learn How to Use MSN?   52

Why Do Businesses Like Being on MSN?   52

Does Everyone Have the Same Access to Content on MSN?   53

Does Microsoft Keep Profiles of Their Customers, and What Do They Do with the Profiles?   53

How Many Family Members Can I Have on My Account?   53

How Do I Keep My Kids from Getting into Areas with Adult Content?   54

*How Do I Get My Member Information in MSN's
   Address Book?* 55
How Can I Change My Access Number? 56
What Is a Guidebook? 56
What Is a Title? 57
Can I Omit the Screen for MSN Today? 57
What Is a GO Word? 57
Where Do I Get a Current List of GO Words? 58
What Is the Find Function for? 58
Is There a Global File Search on MSN? 59
What's the Big Deal About Rich Text? 59
What Is Shareware? 59
What's the Best Way to Navigate on MSN? 60
*Somehow I Clicked through All My Screens and
   I'm Left Looking at My Desktop. How Do I Navigate Now?* 61
*It Seems So Tedious to Have to Use the Pull-down Menus.
   Any Other Ideas?* 61
What's a Shortcut? 62
How Do I Add to Favorite Places? 62
How Many Things Can I Do at Once on MSN? 63
What Is an ICP? 63
What Is an EForm? 63
How Do I Find Help? 63
Is It Safe to Use Credit Cards to Make Online Purchases? 64
Can I Find Out If a Friend Is Online when I Am? 65
Where Do I File Complaints or Suggestions? 65
How Do I Reach the Execs at The Microsoft Network? 65
*If MSN Isn't Working Right and I'm Wasting Time in Paid Areas,
   Who Do I Contact for a Credit?* 66
My Best Friend Has a Mac—Can She Get on MSN? 66
Where in the World Is MSN Available? 67
Do I See the Same MSN Screens as Those Seen in Germany? 68

ELECTRONIC MAIL   68

   What Do I Need to Know About E-mail?   68

   How Do I Send Internet E-mail?
     Is It Different from Sending MSN Mail?   68

   How Do Friends Send Mail to Me?   69

   How Do I Send Mail to Friends?   69

   *How Long Does It Take for Internet Mail to
     Reach Other Services?*   69

   How Do I cc Myself on Internet Mail?   70

   What's the Simplest Way to Include a File with My E-mail?   70

   Can I Send Attachments with Internet Mail?   70

   Can I Put Shortcuts in My E-mail Messages?   70

   Can I Put Icons in My Word Processed Documents?   71

   Can I Send a Message from My Word Processor?   71

   *What Can Friends Do when They Receive the
     Messages with the Icons?*   72

   *Can I Send E-mail Containing an Icon to Someone Who Doesn't
     Have Windows 95?*   72

   Help! How Do I Make Sense Out of the Mail in My Inbox?   72

   Does MSN Have Any Tools to Help Organize My E-mail?   73

   Can I Send the Same Message via E-mail and Fax?   73

   How Do I Keep Backup Copies of My Correspondence?   73

   *Why Do Some of the Messages in My Mailbox
     Have Exclamation Points?*   73

   What Does the Envelope Icon Mean?   74

   Can I Compose Mail Offline?   74

   Can I Access and Read Mail Offline?   74

   How Can I Avoid Junk Mail?   75

   How Do I Know If I Have Mail Waiting when I Sign On?   75

   Can I Permanently Save My E-mail?   76

   Can I Check on the Status of Mail that I've Sent?   76

   How Do I Know If My Boss Got the Mail I Sent?   76

How Do I Locate Members from Other Countries? 76
What Do I Do When I Have a Mail Problem? 76

FORUMS, BULLETIN BOARDS,
FILE LIBRARIES, AND CHATS 77
What Is a Forum? 77
What Is a BBS? 78
What Is a Kiosk? 78
What Happens to the Messages I Post? 78
Who Can Delete My Messages? 78
I Can't Find a Message I Posted. Was It Deleted? 78
Where in the Forum Can I Find the GO Word? 79
*XYZ Is My Favorite Forum . . . Sometimes the Chat Button
Is Missing. What's Going on?* 79
Can I Save All the Text from an Online Session? 79
Can I Read the Message Boards Offline? 80
How Do I Know Who Is in a Forum or Chat Room? 80
Can I Write E-mail from within a Forum? 81
Can I Have Two Forums Open at the Same Time? 81
How Do I Start a Download? 81
Can I Download Files at the End of My Online Session? 81
Oh Where, Oh Where, Do My Files Go? 82
How Do I Open Archived Files? 83
Will MSN Compress Files for Me? 83
What Are GIFs, PICTs, JPEGs, and What Do I Do with Them? 83
How Do I Listen to Sounds/Waves on MSN? 84
*Is There Shareware That Will Help Me Make
the Most of My Time on MSN?* 84
Are There Any Printing Tips from MSN? 84

INTERNET 84
Am I Charged for Internet Access? 84
Is My Internet Access Restricted in Any Way? 85

How Do I Know If I Am Still in MSN or If I Have Jumped to an Internet Site? 85

What Are Usenet Newsgroups? 85

What Is the World Wide Web? 86

How Do I Get to the World Wide Web? 87

What Is HTML? 87

What Does It Mean to FTP a File? 87

What Is a Listserv or Mailing List? 88

How Do I Find Good Internet Sites? 88

Part 3 A Five Star Tour of The Microsoft Network 89

ARTS & ENTERTAINMENT 91
- *Jazz Central Station* 91
- *Mr. Showbiz* 92
- *Court TV* 92
- *TV Host* 93
- *Cinemania Connection* 93
- *Music Central Connection* 94
- *Music Central Newsstand* 94
- *Village Voice* 95

BUSINESS & FINANCE 96
- *Mainstream Career Center* 96
- *Winning Resumes* 97
- *Small Office Home Office* 97
- *Ubiquitous FedEx* 98
- *Big, Basic Brown* 98
- *Hoover's Business Resources* 99

Decision Point   100
Fidelity Online Investor Center   101

COMPUTERS & SOFTWARE   102
Software Companies   102
Newsbytes   103
PC World Communications   104
NewMedia   104
ZD Net Magazines   105
MIDI & Electronic Music Forum   105
Multimedia & CD-ROM   106
Computer Games Forum   106
Desktop Publishing Forum   107
Maxis   107
Shareware   108
Microsoft Knowledge Base   109
Microsoft Windows 95   109
Komputer Klinic   110
Online Service Providers   110

EDUCATION & REFERENCE   111
Encarta Encyclopedia   111
Bookshelf Forum   112
The Princeton Review   112
Kaplan Online   113

HEALTH & FITNESS   113
Medicine Forum   114

HOME & FAMILY   115
Theme Parks!   115
Best Friend AnimalNet   116
Photography   116
Splash Kids   117

KidStar Online   118
Ingenius Online   119
Gardening Delights   119
In the Kitchen   120
Pathfinder's Kitchen   120
Parenting   121
Children First   121
Lanier Guides   122

INTERESTS, LEISURE & HOBBIES   123
Arts & Crafts   123
Automotive Forum   124
Collecting   125
Games   125
Creative E-Mail   126
Gourmet GiftNet   126
Magic and Illusions   127
Astrology   128
Alien Encounters   128
Travel   128

NEWS & WEATHER   129
MSN News   130
The WeatherLab   130
USA TODAY   131
NBC Supernet   132

PEOPLE & COMMUNITIES   133
Genealogy   133
People to People   134
New Age Forum   134
DisAbilities Forum   135
SeniorNet   136
Inspiration from the Mind Garden   136

Friends of Europe Forum   136
History & Archaeology   137
Women's Wire   138
Public Affairs   138
Armed Forces Forum   139
NET political Network   140
GoverNet   140

SCIENCE & TECHNOLOGY   141
  Astronomy & Space   142
  ScienceFair   142
  Smithsonian and Air & Space   143

SPECIAL EVENTS   144

SPORTS & RECREATION   144
  ShaqWorld Online   144
  Online Games, Inc.   145
  Martial Arts Network   146
  Scuba Online   147
  Sports Media   147
  ESPN SportsZone   147
  @Play   148

INTERNET CENTER   148

MSN PASSPORT   149

CHAT WORLD   150

Part 4   You, Too, Can Be an Internet Dynamo   153

WHAT'S THE DIFFERENCE BETWEEN MSN AND THE INTERNET?   155
  What in the World Is the World Wide Web?   156

Making the Connection   157
Internet Encounters   159
What Are the Boundaries of MSN? The Internet?   160
When Do You Need the Browser?   162
Must I Use Microsoft's Browser?   162
When Do I Need Internet E-mail?   162
Mailing Lists   163
How Do I Subscribe to a List?   163
How Do I Find Interesting Mailing Lists?   164
What's a Newsgroup?   165
Tantalizing Telnet   167
The Three Caballeros   168
Pssst...What Is FTP?   168
How Do You Find Out Where Files Are Stored on FTP Sites?   170
Searching for Gopher   170
What Are All Those Addresses I See in the Newspaper That Begin with http://?   171
Any Tips for Keeping Track of URLs?   171
What's the Fastest Way to Navigate?   172
How Do I Read a URL?   172
How Does the Web Differ from the Internet?   173
What's HTML?   175
What's on a Web Page?   175
Can I Create My Own Web Page on MSN?   176
Webbish Features   176
The Silken Web   176
Treasures of the Web   176
Internet Couch Potato Headquarters   177
At the Movies   177
Bookish Webbish Reads   178

Bring on the Locusts 178
A Walkman for your Computer 179
Bucky Bison 180
Daily Dilbert 180
The Imperative Informer 181

Part 5   Ten Fun but Useless Web Sites That Actually Work   183

Bill's House 185
San Diego Bay Cam 185
Trojan Room Coffee Machine 186
Foam Bath Fish Time 187
Talk to My Cat 188
What's in My Desk Drawer 189
CD Player Gateway 189
RIT Computer Science House Drink Machine 190
Cams Around the World 191
Steve's List of T-Shirts 192

Part 6   Webs of the World   193

AFRICA   195
  Cape Town 195
  Johannesburg 195
  Witwatersrand 195

ASIA AND OCEANIA   195
  Australia 195
  Beijing 195

Hong Kong   195
India   195
Japan   195
Korea   196
New Zealand   196
Singapore   196
Taiwan   196
Thailand   196

EUROPE   196
Austria   196
Belgium   196
Croatia   197
Czech Republic   197
Denmark   197
Estonia   197
Finland   197
France   197
Germany   198
Greece   207
Hungary   208
Iceland   208
Ireland   208
Italy   209
Latvia   209
Lithunia   209
Luxembourg   209
Netherlands   209
Norway   210
Poland   211
Portugal   211
Russia   212

Slovakia 212
Slovenia 212
Spain 212
Sweden 212
Switzerland 213
Turkey 215
United Kingdom 215

Central America   221
Costa Rica 221

North America   221
Alberta 221
British Columbia 221
New Brunswick 222
Nova Scotia 222
Ontario 223
Mexico 224
Puerto Rico 225
United States of America 225

Appendix   227
Independent Content and Solution Provider Directory for the Microsoft Network 227

Glossary   233

Index   245

Introduction

The fact that you've bought this book probably means you're also an early adopter of the hot new technology found within Windows 95 and The Microsoft Network (MSN). Being an early adopter of software is a lot like being a pioneer. It's adventurous and exciting, but you're also dealing with stuff that's still a bit rough around the edges. There are times when excitement gives way to confusion.

I should know. Much of this book was prepared while Windows 95 and MSN were still in beta. Betas aren't meant to be perfect—if they were, they wouldn't be betas. Without the challenges of the beta, I would have had an easier time in writing, but you would have a less interesting book in your hands. The beta's challenges helped me to identify and smooth over many potential bumps you might otherwise encounter on MSN's superhighway, and to polish up some of the murky areas of the MSN help screens and other documentation.

Through the pages of this book, I'll share the *way things work* on MSN today. Sometimes, features work differently from the way MSN's online instructions describe, which can be frustrating. At this writing, MSN is still a work in progress. I suspect that Microsoft wanted to ship MSN, right at the outset, with Windows 95—for several (mostly sensible) marketing reasons. But I also suspect that, if the developers of MSN had their druthers, they'd druther have waited a few more months to do a bit of smoothing and polishing of their own.

However, I do think Microsoft Network represents the wave of the future. And I'm speaking as someone who's also a Macintosh fan. Mac fans aren't supposed to like Microsoft, but I stand in awe of their marketing prowess, programming skills, and drive to reach goals.

With Windows 95, Microsoft Office, and Microsoft Network, the gang at Microsoft has developed a seamless family of products that can help you in your work and play (and your kids' education, too). For instance, you'll soon be pasting MSN shortcuts into your MS Word documents and copying the document icons into your email, thus sending the documents as attachments through Microsoft Exchange and The Microsoft Network. Sounds complex? No, it's really easy. The Microsoft way will become the easy way.

Whenever I tell friends and associates about my work on this book, they ask for my opinions about how likely and how difficult it will be for MSN to succeed. Specifically, they know of the books I've written on America Online and CompuServe, and wonder whether I think Microsoft's online service can succeed amidst an already crowded market.

In my view, just like with Windows 3.1, the initial surge will be worth watching, but not quite earth-shattering. Then, suddenly, a larger surge will occur and the Win95-MSN-Office trilogy will become the definitive communication system for office, email, and entertainment. In fact, I believe the next surge of burgeoning growth of the Internet will become a Microsoft-based phenomenon. As tens of millions of users upgrade to Win95, computer users worldwide will experiment online. Many will venture out onto the Internet and may even switch to a direct Internet service provider. But many more will stay with MSN as their preferred content provider, and will use MSN as their gateway to the Internet.

Glimpsing the Future with MSN

The developers of MSN have learned well from the powers that brought us America Online, CompuServe, GEnie, Prodigy, Delphi, and e-world. They've taken the best highlights and features from these other services and woven them into the finer fabric now called The Microsoft Network. They also went a step further (perhaps several steps further). Since so many businesses depend on Microsoft software, Microsoft is in an enviable position. They took their strengths in software, marketing, and customer service and expanded on them with MSN, which serves as both a focal point and transfer point for information—one that people will come to use on a daily basis.

With MSN, not only can you make great discoveries, you can share those discoveries with your friends. By claiming your Favorite Places and sending shortcuts to friends, you'll be building a communications network among your friends and associates. Microsoft is thrilled (and laughing all the way to the bank) because you and your associates will be increasing your activities with Microsoft products.

Do you remember how your Mom (or maybe it was you) first used the microwave only for reheating last night's dinner? Seemed like a waste of technology, huh? Of course, now she can cook entire meals with just the touch of a few buttons. Or how about your early experiences with your VCR? First, you only watched movies that you rented from Blockbuster, but now you can program without fear. (Actually, an awful lot of very intelligent people *still* can't program their VCRs, but that's another matter....)

Very shortly the Windows 95-Microsoft Network-Microsoft Office way will cease being novel and will instead become t*he way things get done*. I'm in awe of Microsoft and its products, and I suspect that their slogan "Where do you want to go today?" will take on increased meaning as more and more users realize that the answer is: "Anywhere. Just fire up MSN and let your imagination be your guide."

How to Use This Book

Are you planning to read this book from cover to cover? I doubt it. How's that for honesty? This book is a browser's paradise, and I'm well aware of that. Eventually, though, I expect that you'll leaf through most of the pages as you refer to various questions, screen shots, and prime areas on MSN. So here's a quick orientation to help you get the most from the different sections in this book.

Using the MSN Centerfolds

We begin with the centerfolds—a tease of a name. Each centerfold will entice you into the seductive back alleys and dazzling forums of The Microsoft Network. You would undoubtedly find it boring if I were to walk you through every possible command and pull-down menu, so instead I've focused on the major features that you can use to get online and productive in as short a time as possible. Be sure to read the centerfolds before you begin your journey on MSN.

Mastering MSN: A Q&A

By using a friendly question-and-answer format, I hope to help you solve some of the more perplexing problems about navigating and using MSN. If you want to know how to solve your mail problems, save online time, and stay connected when MSN seems to encourage you to do otherwise, you'll find the answers here. The Q and A format is fun, too. I hope it proves to be your guide to maintaining your sanity online.

Using the Five Star Tour of MSN

This third section is my favorite because I love exploring online systems. Even on days I'm not working, I have to check my e-mail and favorite message boards and newsgroups. I can spend hours online on my days off. Sometimes I think I have more faceless e-mail friends than real friends with faces.

Even now, MSN continues to fascinate as I prowl and troll through layers of new folders. MSN is continually adding forums—or maybe I should say that the Independent Content Providers (ICPs) are putting up their forums on MSN in continually increasing numbers. In any case, I'm always on the lookout for new stuff. I've tested a myriad of GO Words to see if they'll lead me down some new, exciting path. It's kind of like being one of the first to try a new ride at Disneyland. On MSN, even when I'm not successful, I still enjoy devising potential GO Words to see what forums are in work. I get a real thrill when I try a GO Word and receive a message saying that I'm not authorized to enter. That little goodie means another forum is under construction.

On the Five Star Tour, I'll take you to my favorite sites as well as to those that might soon be on the top of your list. I wish I could say that this tour provides a definitive list, but given MSN's new presence, I know that many more forums will be up and running by the time you read this. It's my hope that this tour will whet your appetite for exploring on your own.

You Too Can Be an Internet Dynamo

Are you ready for the Internet? Absolutely. If you've got The Microsoft Network, then you've also got immediate access to the Internet. The folks at MSN have made it possible for you to sail effortlessly onto the 'Net. But once you're there, you might find it a little tricky to navigate such a vast network of sites and information. So, I'll try to help you stay on course by answering frequently asked questions about using the Internet. And of course, I'll cover such perplexing Internet-related terms like World Wide Web, UUENCODED, Usenet Newsgroups, Gopher, HTML, and FTP. I'll even give you a quick tour of some great Web sites. With the help of MSN and this book, I suspect you'll be surfing the 'Net like an old pro in a matter of days (well, weeks maybe).

Ten Fun But Useless Web Sites That Actually Work

You can master the Internet and enrich your social conversations with a quick tour of Useless Web Sites That Actually Work. I had great fun prowling for these gems of the Internet. Once your friends discover that you know the locations of both fabled and not-so-famous sites, they will be dazzled by your vast Web-surfing proficiency.

You'll soon be trading shortcuts the way kids trade baseball cards. What do you mean by that? Well, with MSN you can send (to your friends) the URLs for these favorite places, in the form of shortcuts. Sure the sites are silly—they typify the creativity found on the Net. Can you think of a better way to demonstrate your knowledge of the far corners of the Internet?

Glossary

In the back of the book you'll find a handy glossary of the terms I've used in this book. Of course, where *else* does one find the glossary? Keep this indispensible guide close by to help you over those little ruts in the language of Windows 95, MSN, and the Internet. A quick scan serves to remind us of such tidbits as *what used to be a directory is now a folder.*

As you head off into the world of MSN and the Internet, you'll be well equipped to share in the intelligent interaction, lively debate, and fascinating finds of this electronic frontier.

Acknowledgments

The writing of this book has encompassed a very eventful period of my life. I'll probably always remember this time as the "MSN phase." In time, I hope this comes to be known as "MSN Phase 1" as revised editions of the book are printed.

In any case, when this book was conceived, I was living in a comfortable cul-de-sac of suburbia between Baltimore and Washington, D.C. By the time I was ready to gear up for the actual writing of the book, I found myself in another suburb—adjacent to Los Angeles. In fact, most of the research, writing, and editing were conducted from my new home base in Southern California. (I think it's now time to get out and meet the neighbors.)

The profound change of locale makes me appreciate those who helped keep life on an even keel through the tumult of moving and the simultaneous planning of a book that loomed on the horizon. Of course, Tom and Carly are the first to be thanked for their patience during this tumultuous summer. Tom also gets credit for the fun and games involved in installating the beta version of Windows 95 and MSN. I also spent five weeks on "modified bedrest" and appreciate the friends and relatives who helped out when all I was allowed to do was type at the computer with my feet elevated.

My superb editor, Ron Pronk, once again fielded my numerous questions by phone, fax, and mail as we defined and shaped the content of the book. Our daily bantering—with a good dose of humor—evolved into this guide. We were challenged along the way by the work in progress now known as *The Microsoft Network*.

As always, publisher Keith Weiskamp is to be commended for his interest in the online services, and I thank him for allowing me to do this third book for Coriolis Group Books.

There's a strong team at Coriolis—and there are many who've worked on this book. Ron tag-teamed with Joanne McClintock and Jenni Aloi to work through the editing of the manuscript, Kirsten Dewey did a painstakingly thorough job in proofreading the typeset galleys, and Michelle Stroup did a wizard-like job designing and typesetting the book. What you hold in your hands is largely a product of her inventiveness. And finally, Brad Grannis and Anthony Stock combined their vast artistic and design skills to create a wonderful cover.

Speaking of hands, I must also thank those at Coriolis who are responsible for encouraging you to actually put this book in your hands: Publicist Shannon Bounds and Marketing Director Tom Mayer. They've spread the good word and carried the online religion—and the Coriolis message—to your favorite bookstore.

At Microsoft, Naveen Jain found the time in his hectic schedule to answer my technical questions about MSN. I'd also like to thank Telle Zeiler from Waggener Edstrom for her numerous contributions and guidance along the Microsoft way.

I owe a debt of gratitude to the members of MSN, who are pioneers in shaping a new online community. From the beta testers to the paid members, there are many who contributed to the content of this book and the testing of MSN's functions.

My online friends, spanning the globe, have provided support and inspiration. I'm almost embarrassed to admit how many times a day I check my E-mail in the midst of writing. Julie, Mike from Alaska, CK, Jane, Linda B., Susan, Jillann....and many more—thanks for keeping me at the computer!

If you'd like to share your thoughts on this book or about MSN in general, you can reach me at LuanneO@coriolis.com.

Luanne O'Loughlin
San Pedro, California

PART 1

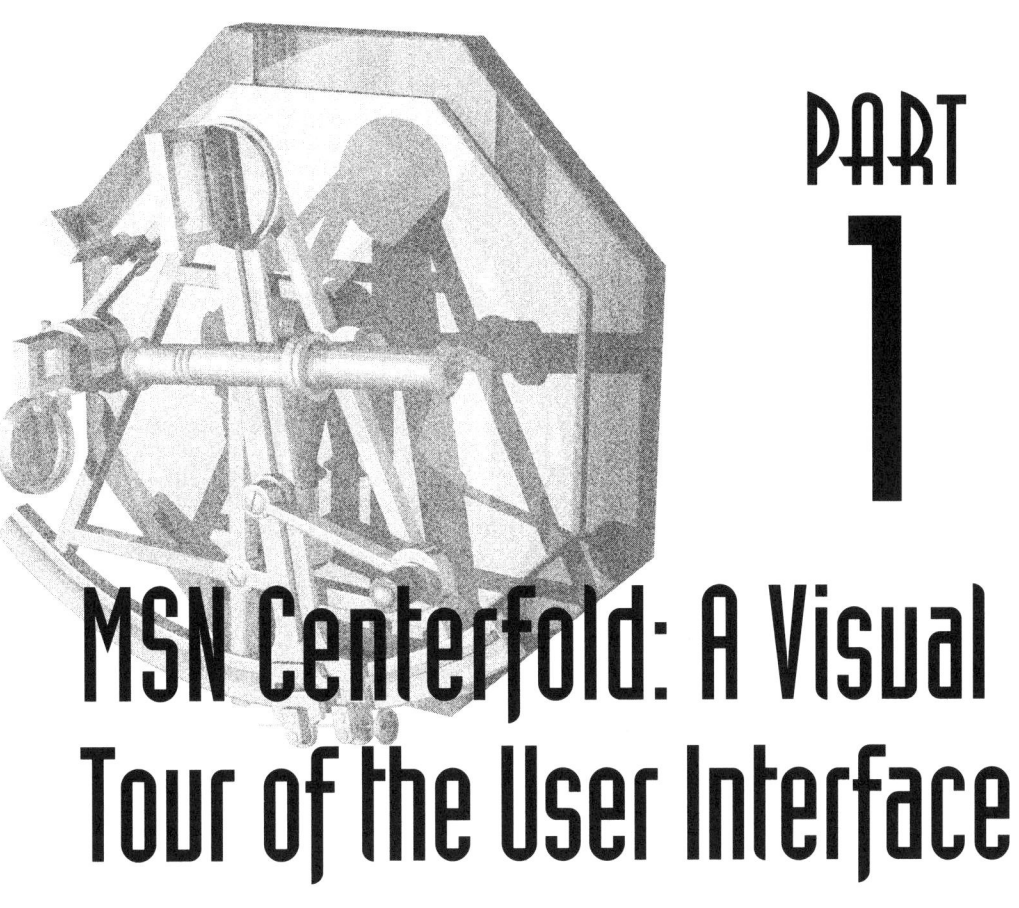

MSN Centerfold: A Visual Tour of the User Interface

It's easy to jump into MSN once Windows 95 is installed on your desktop. Just give that desktop icon a quick click and you'll sail into the seductive interface of MSN, where there are few restraints aside from the limits of your credit card. Once your screen lights up with the colorful images of MSN, you may begin to wonder—how do I find whatever it is I'm looking for, and how do I get back out?

The Centerfold is a quick tutorial on MSN's features and tools. Here I'll show you the basics of the screens and the directional tasks necessary for you to accelerate through the twists and turns of this electronic mountain road.

I like the term Centerfold because it conveys a seductive tease into dark corners, quiet rooms, and exciting floorshows. For all of its captivating features, MSN might as well be Las Vegas!

The Centerfold pages illustrate the screens you'll see on MSN. I hope I've done my best to simplify this mesmerizing system. Whether you're here to work or play, I want you to experience the joys of membership, rather than the tedium of navigation.

2 MSN Centerfold: A Visual Tour of the User Interface

Starting Up

MSN Centerfold: A Visual Tour of the User Interface

With a click of MSN's icon on the desktop, you'll immediately notice that the world is literally at your fingertips. (Remember Microsoft's slogan: "Where do you want to go today?" On MSN, the answer is a resounding "anywhere.") You're within a local phone call of communicating on a worldwide network that contains information on topics ranging from esoteric arts to today's hard and graphic news.

The Microsoft Network icon takes you to the MSN service itself, plus the World Wide Web—as long as you've installed the Internet browser—from thethe Plus! Pack or from an MSN download.

Without the browser, the MSN icon will convey your electrons to and from the basic service of MSN, including Internet newsgroups and mailing lists. With the browser, you gain World Wide Web access. If you don't have that access now, you'll soon want it to expand your online experience.

To reach the Web and bypass MSN, select The Internet icon from your desktop. If you don't have an Internet icon now, go ahead and install the Internet browser.

The Front Page

MSN Today is the welcoming screen you'll see each time you begin your adventure on MSN. Here you'll find the day's highlights. This screen, with its featured events, comes up each time you sign on, unless you know how to request otherwise. I like to compare this screen to the front page of a daily newspaper with its continually changing stories and daily surprises—except the surprises on MSN tend to be a lot more pleasant than the surprises in my newspaper.. Each picture represents a link to a topic or a forum within MSN. Further navigation can be conducted via the topics that are featured in the picture of the globe on the left side of the screen. This screen is jam packed with bits and bytes to tease you into the deeper layers and folders of MSN. Fifteen links are quickly apparent, with dozens more choices behind each of these selections. Your best bet is to open this window and then **minimize** it so you can quickly refer back to it whenever you need to.

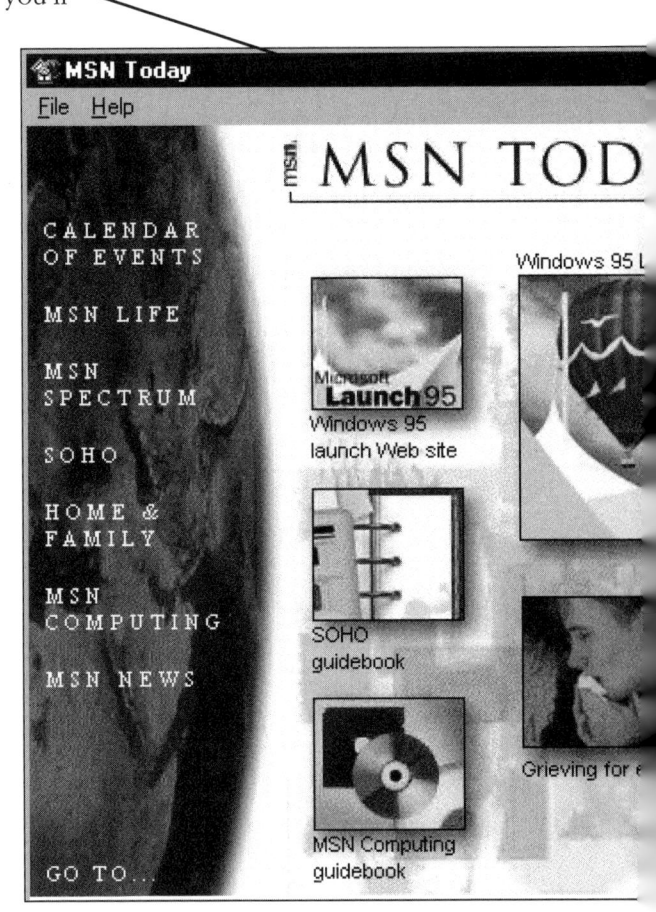

Hint: To prevent MSN Today from appearing on startup, select Options from the View Menu. Select the General tab and make sure the statement Show MSN Today on Startup is unchecked.

MSN Centerfold: A Visual Tour of the User Interface   5

The icons in the upper right corner indicate that Microsoft Office, which was loaded on start-up, is ready and available.

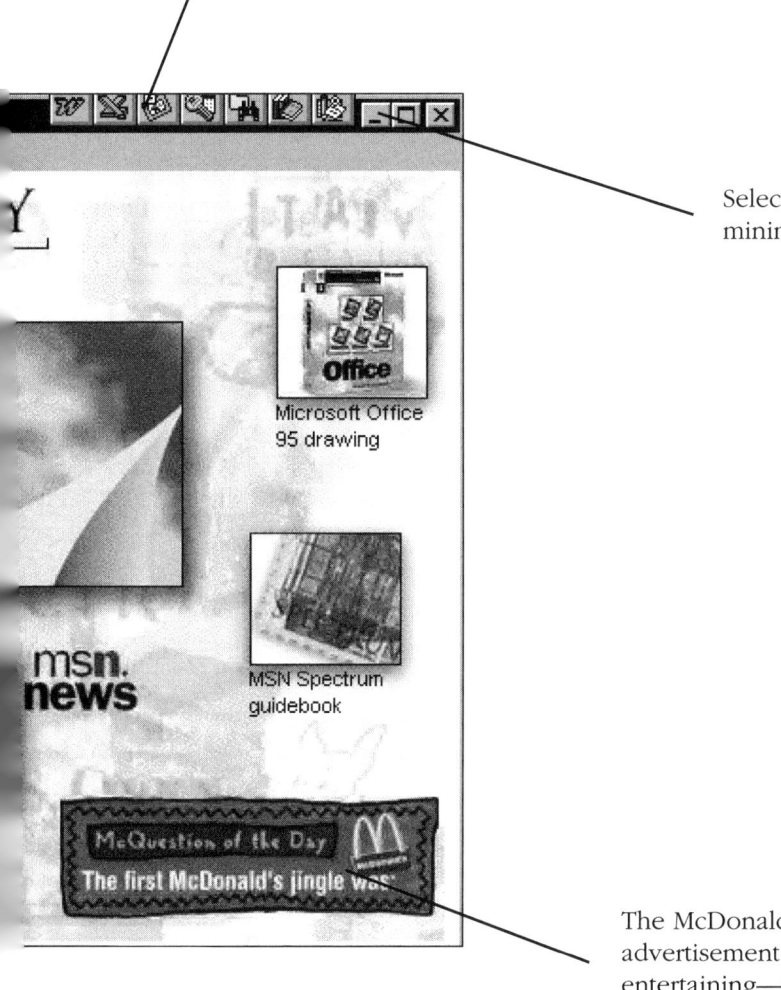

Select to minimize

The McDonald's link is representative of a paid advertisement on MSN. These ads are usually entertaining—they have to be in order to keep people visiting them. Click on this space to review the ad of the day.

MSN Centerfold: A Visual Tour of the User Interface

Home Base

MSN Central is your jumping off point—the center of basic navigation. It's your home base guide to MSN. Anywhere you want to go, you can get there from here.

Take a look at what lies behind each of these pull-down menus; it'll help speed you on your way to becoming an MSN maven.

From the Tools menu, you can choose to add or delete the icons for your preferred navigational style. With MSN you can modify the environment so that it works best for you. And with Options (left), you can choose to omit the MSN Today screen from startup.

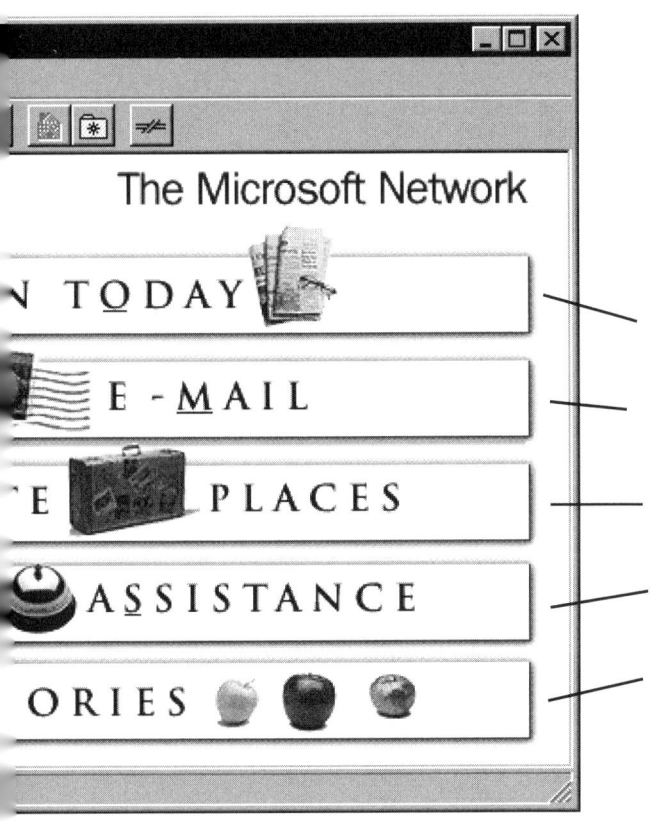

MSN Today—each day's online news and events.

E-Mail—Your personal mailbox, based in Exchange.

Favorite Places—Add your favorites to this site for fast navigating.

Member Assistance—Questions, Answers and Resources online.

Categories—Your starting point for exploration online.

At any point in the system, you can return to MSN Central with a right click on the MSN icon located in the status bar.

MSN Centerfold: A Visual Tour of the User Interface

Explorer View

If you're already familiar with the Explorer in Windows 95, you may prefer the Explorer view of MSN. If you like to see folders and what used to be called directories, Explorer will be your preferred view. Since I am also a Macintosh user, I prefer to navigate by icon and without Explorer.

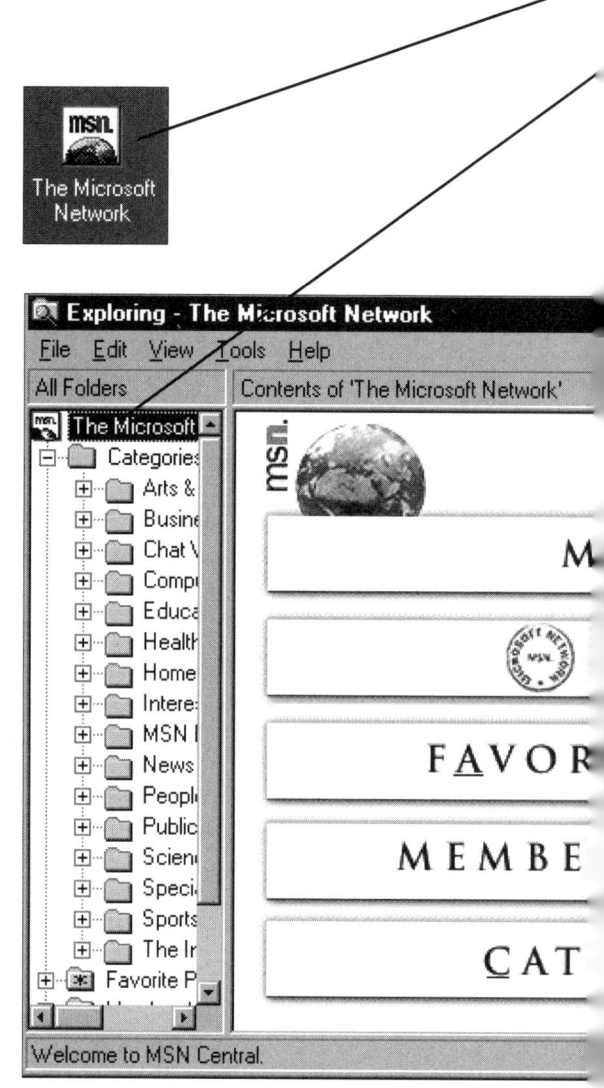

MSN Centerfold: A Visual Tour of the User Interface   9

Take another look at MSN, this time viewed through Windows 95's Explorer. To view MSN with Explorer, right click on the MSN icon on your desktop. Select Explorer and MSN will launch in the Explorer mode.

Explorer grants a hierarchical view of the system and allows you to see relationships between levels.

Take the world view with Explorer. Just as Columbus and Magellan led the exploration of the New World, you can travel through Microsoft's online world with Explorer.

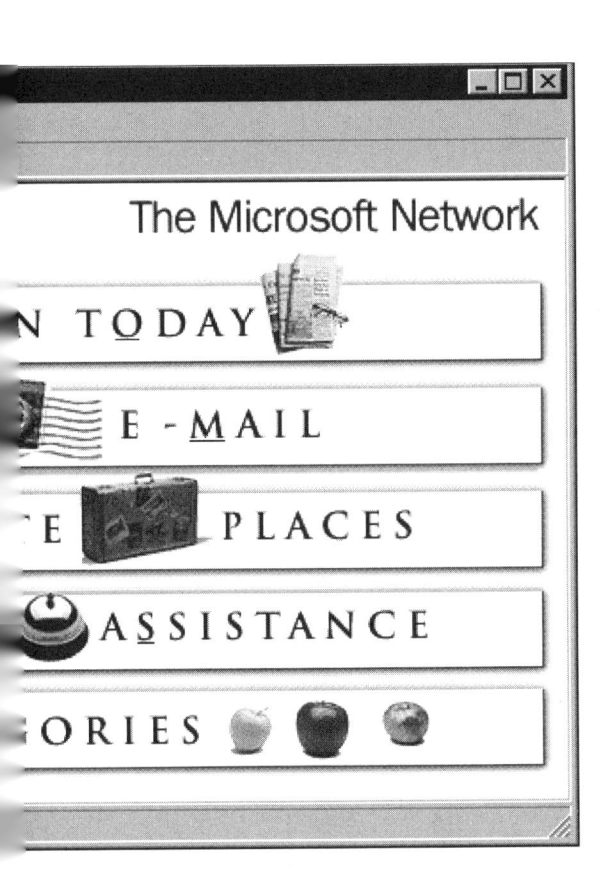

The Microsoft Network

N TODAY

E - MAIL

E   PLACES

ASSISTANCE

ORIES

Apples & Oranges

The Categories screen reveals the wealth of creativity and content that went into the creation of MSN. All content can be found from here—in one location or another.

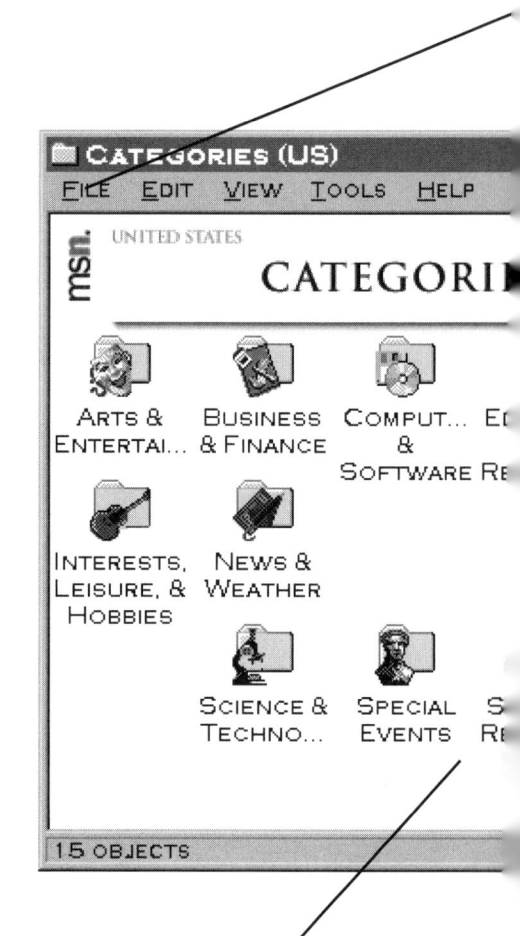

Categories was established to be flexible. It's easy to see that additional categories can be added swiftly, as needed.

Jeopardy it's not, but you can create a Jeopardy-like game with the surplus of forums and information waiting to be discovered behind Categories.

Go to
Categories

MSN Centerfold: A Visual Tour of the User Interface   11

As you find sites to return to, pull down the File Menu and choose Add to Favorite Places or use the menu to create a shortcut to expedite your return. That's the best way to save time and maneuver without confusion.

As the starting point to exploring MSN, Categories is the home base for content. There's no clearer topic than Categories.

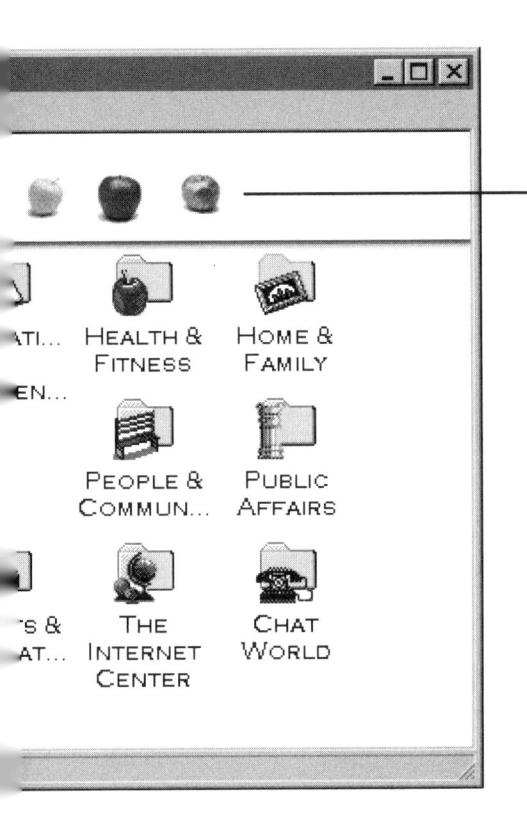

The fruit motif serves as a friendly reminder that all types of apples, oranges, and varieties of information can be found here.

Layers of Content

Within each category, multiple choices are available for further exploration. Here, you'll begin to discover the forums. MSN is as deceptive as the skin of an onion. Peel back one layer, and you'll find another. Peel back that layer, and you'll find yet another. Just a few mouse clicks can seductively lead you into hours of online exploration.

From Categories, the first place to check—if you are experimenting by investigating through sequential layers—is Arts & Entertainment. This is but one example of the depth and levels of content you'll find in each category on MSN.

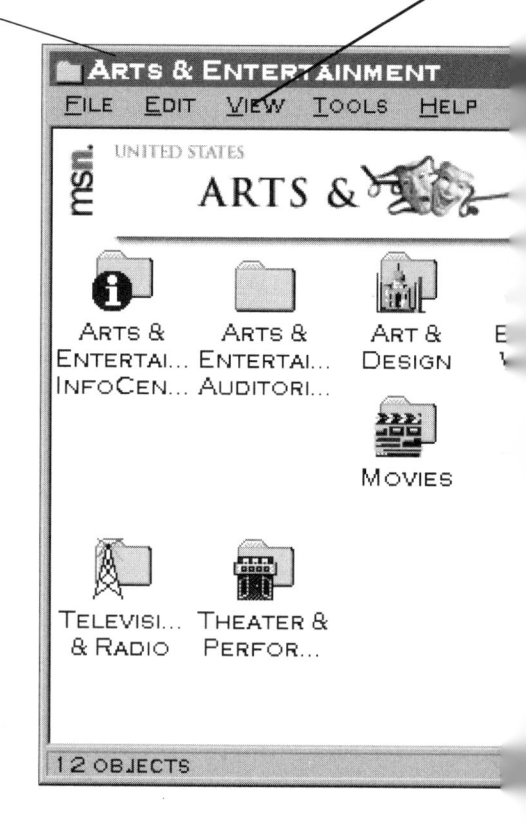

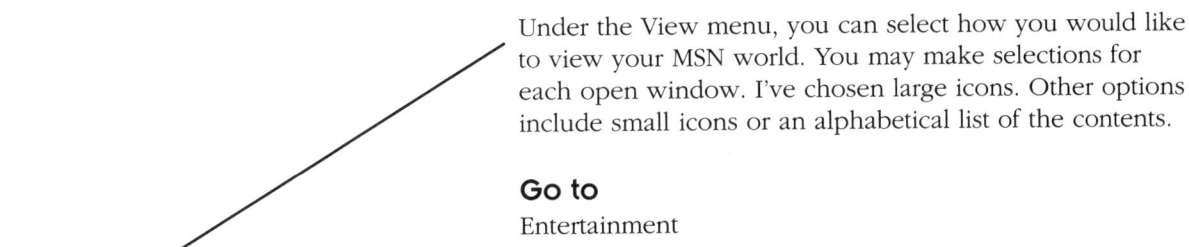

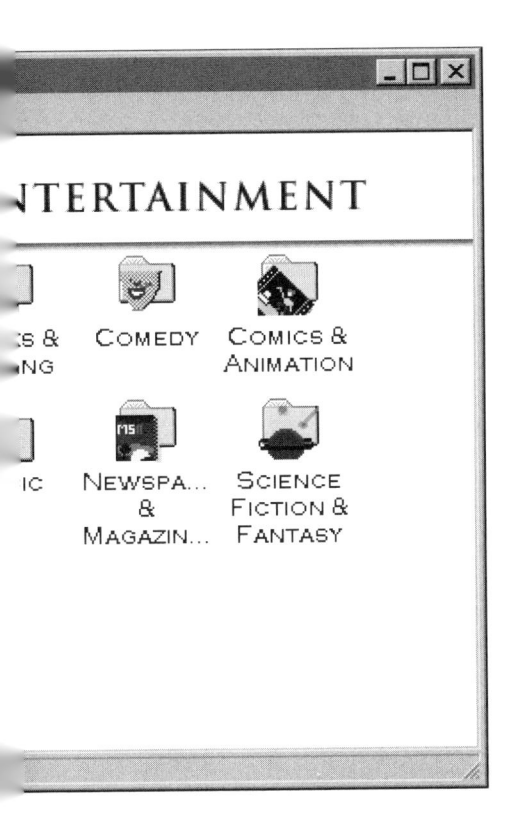

Under the View menu, you can select how you would like to view your MSN world. You may make selections for each open window. I've chosen large icons. Other options include small icons or an alphabetical list of the contents.

Go to
Entertainment

14 • MSN Centerfold: A Visual Tour of the User Interface

Reveal Undercover Answers

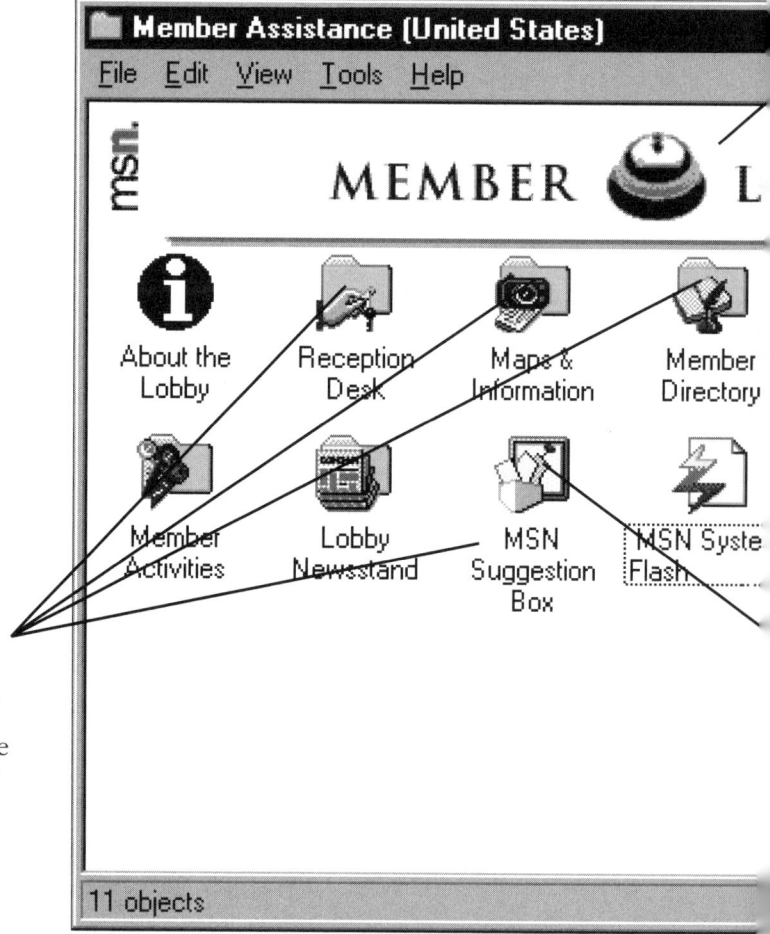

System Maps, the Member Directory, Member Support, and the MSN Suggestion Box provide the best reasons for getting to know this area.

Member Support's Bulletin Boards are shared by advanced and novice MSN users. Here, you can ask questions about MSN and get answers from experienced users. Due to the high volume of participation in this area, you can be assured that your question will be answered in a matter of hours. Some members have commented that you'll get a more timely answer here than from an official request at the MSN Suggestion Box.

Go to
Lobby

Starting from home base—MSN Central—Member Assistance leads you to sources for all information pertaining to MSN. For a reason that remains a mystery to me, Member Assistance becomes Member Lobby when you leave MSN Central.

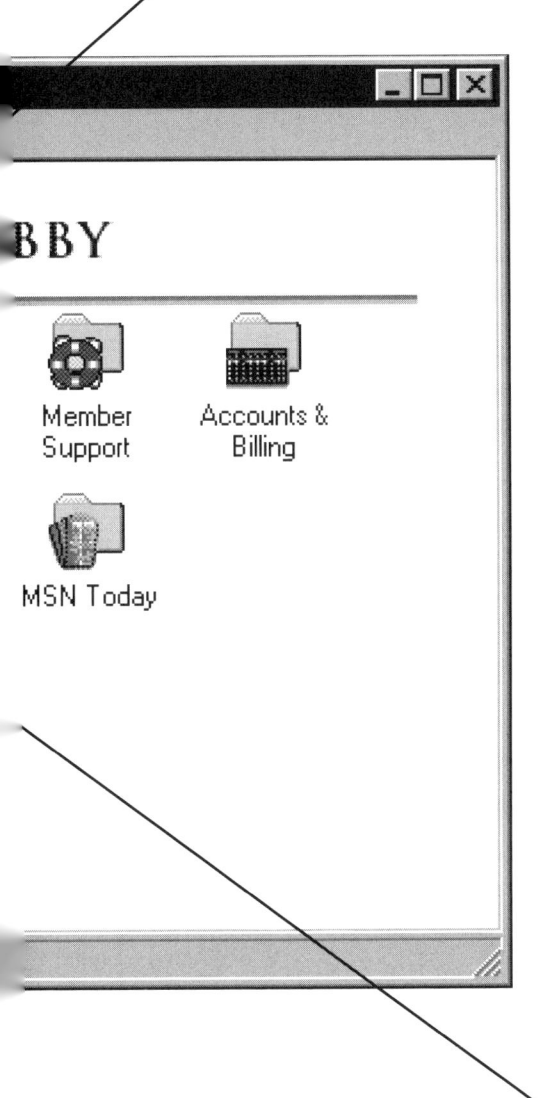

Even if you don't have questions, you can learn a great deal by perusing the Member-to-Member topics. A great number of tried-and-true solutions can be uncovered here. I check this area every time I sign on!

MSN Guidebooks are mostly editorial and somewhat advertorial features provided by Microsoft. Each is designed to teach a good deal more about the online systems and its features—presented in a magazine style format. Several guidebooks are available, including MSN Life, MSN Spectrum, MSN SOHO (Small Office, Home Office), MSN Home & Family, MSN Computing, MSN Sports & Recreation, MSN Kids & Co., and the Microsoft Guidebook.

Go to
MSNmaps

Go to
MSNguidebooks

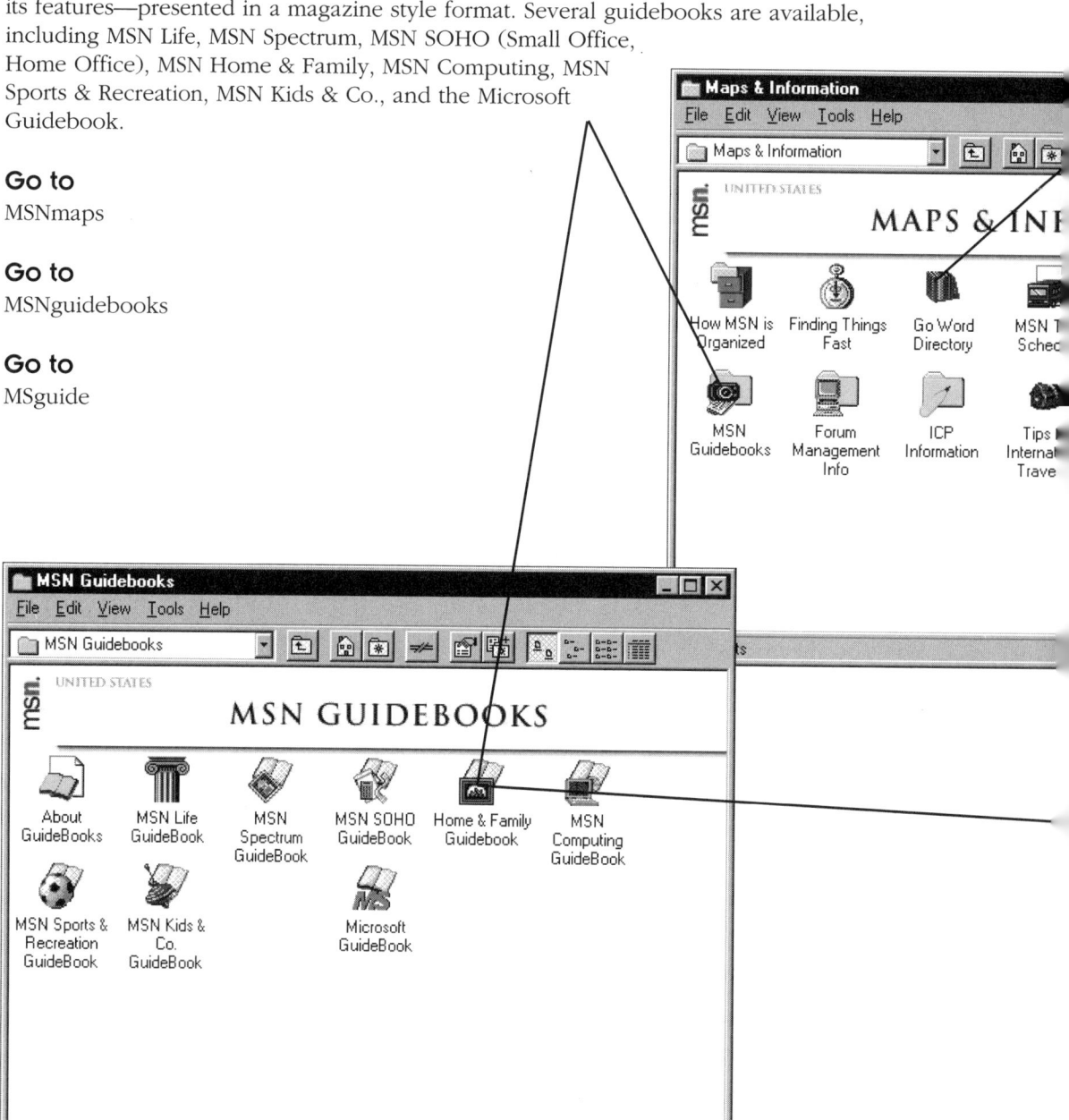

Go to
MSguide

MSN Centerfold: A Visual Tour of the User Interface   17

The GO Word Directory has been added to help you learn these speed demon tools, but unfortunately it is not yet printable.

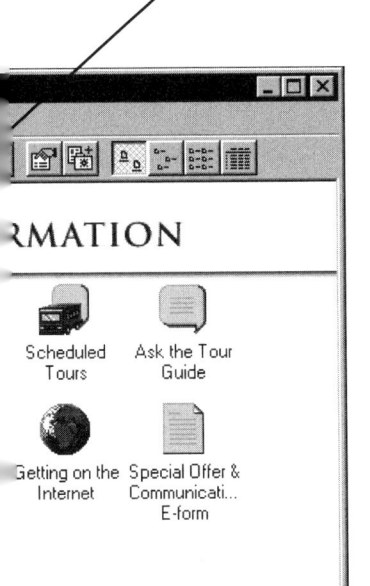

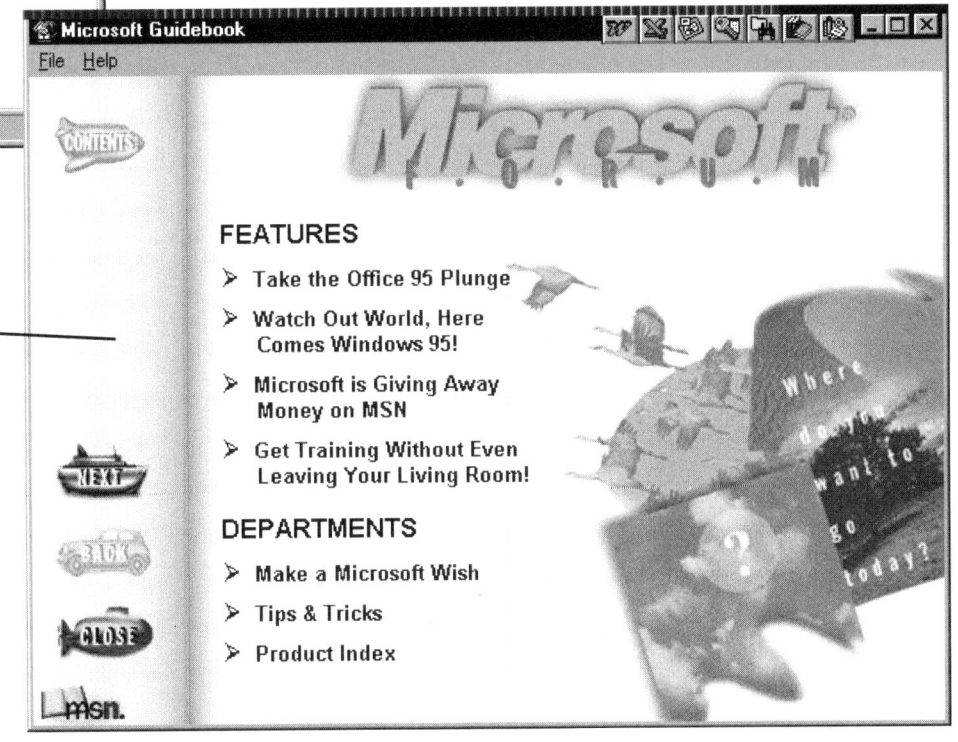

18 MSN Centerfold: A Visual Tour of the User Interface

Speedy Shortcuts

You may prefer Favorite Places as the designated spot for your preferred choices.

Hint: Practice creating a shortcut and join me in the Theme Parks! Forum.

Go to
Travel

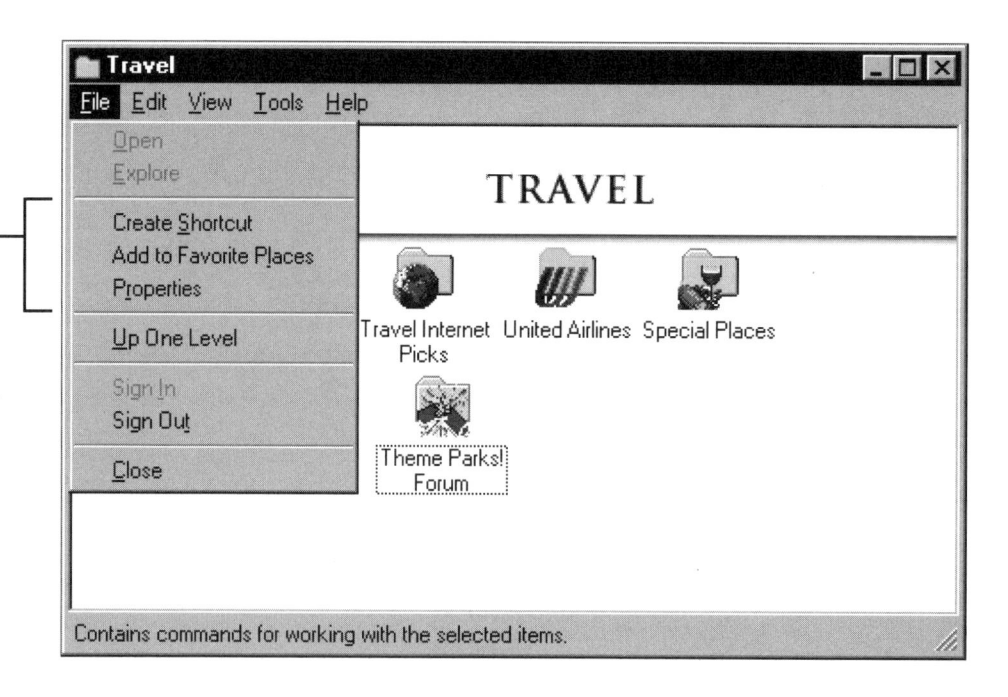

When I discovered the Travel Folder, it was like finding Fantasyland and Tomorrowland rolled into one great place. That said, I was thrilled to find the Theme Parks! Forum, and you can bet I quickly created a shortcut to ensure a fast return.

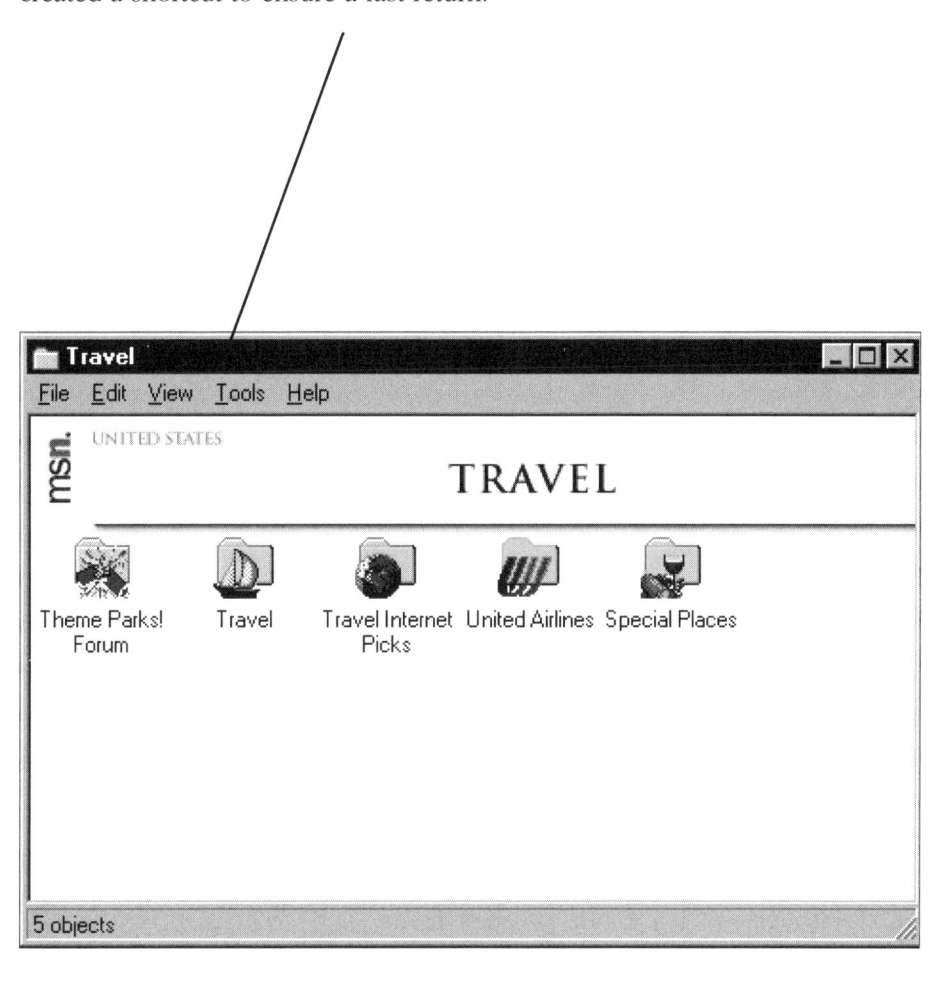

20 MSN Centerfold: A Visual Tour of the User Interface

Exclusive Views

It's the happiest place on earth, and you can view it any way you want. You certainly don't need an E-ticket for this ride. I'm partial to the cute personality of large icons, but you may find it easier to view the small icons. It's a small world after all, isn't it?

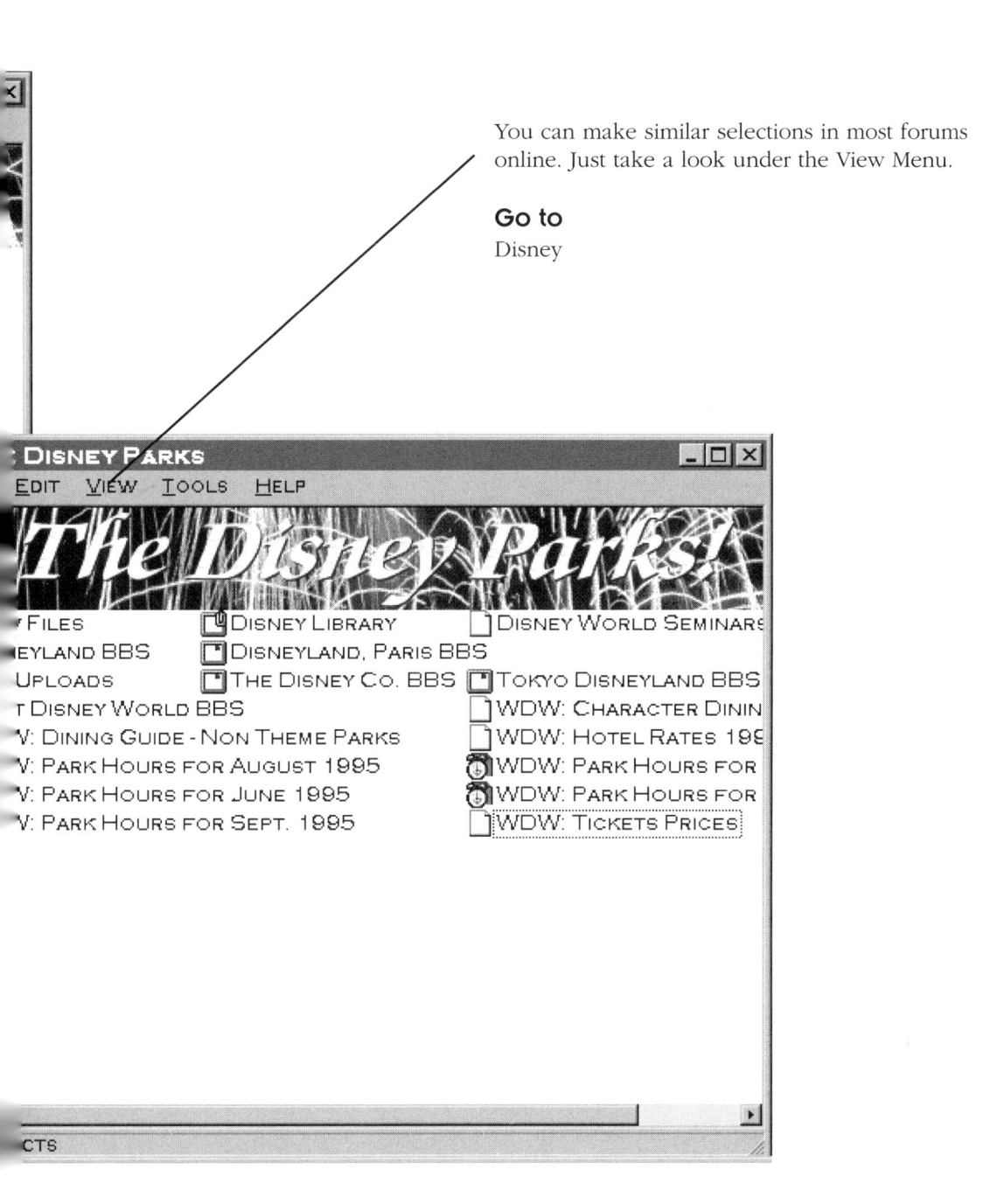

MSN Centerfold: A Visual Tour of the User Interface   21

You can make similar selections in most forums online. Just take a look under the View Menu.

Go to
Disney

22   MSN Centerfold: A Visual Tour of the User Interface

Prize Downloads

In the WDW Magic Kingdom folder, every message includes a downloadable file. The highlighted paperclip is another sign that there attachment to the message. Of course, in this case, the attachment is a downloadable file.

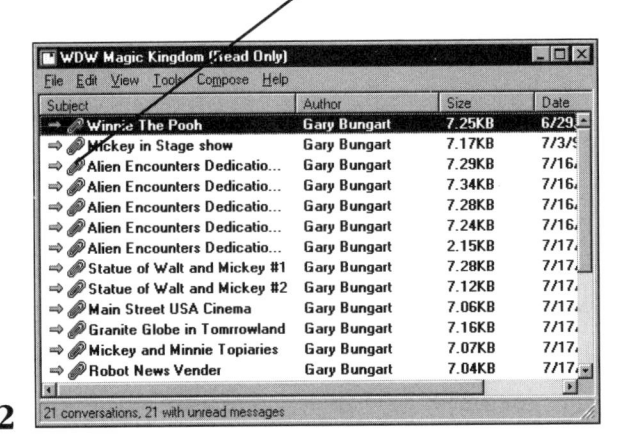

1

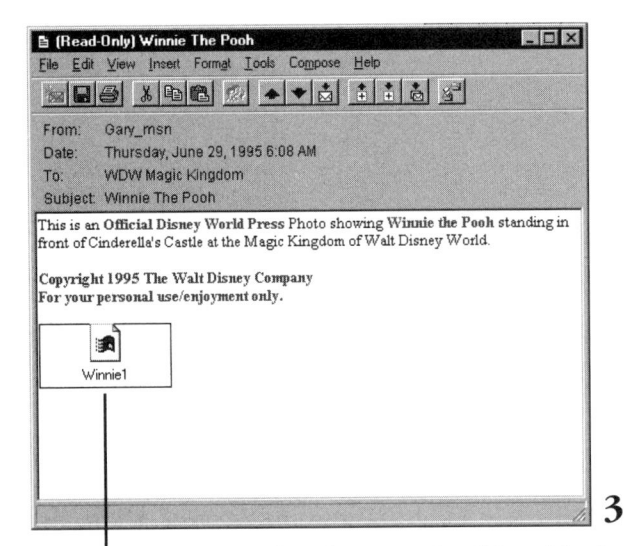

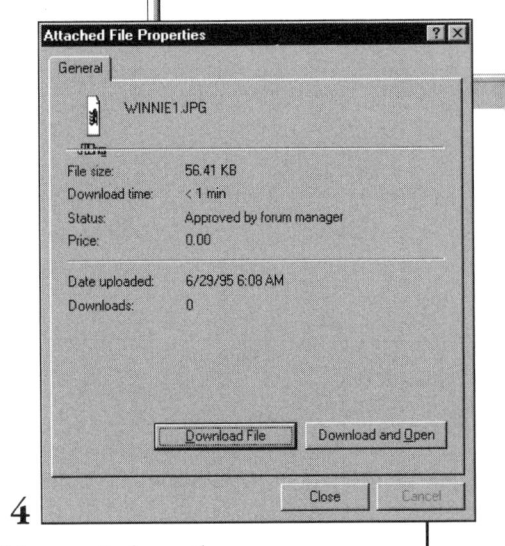

2

3   **4**

Rather than wonder if I grabbed a good image, I chose the Download and Open option. This uses a few seconds more online time, but I can't resist the wonders found online.

In the Disney Library and the BBSes, you can be assured of finding super fans of Walt, Mickey, and the parks.

The steps to a download of Winnie the Pooh provide a great tour of the fun to be found online—even without the Electric Parade.

5 Here comes Winnie!

6

Tip: If you look carefully at the image of Winnie the Pooh, you can see that the screen is representative of the browser. Until the image was built, it was transparent to me that this image did not reside on MSN, but instead was transmitted from a source on the World Wide Web.

Go to
Theme Parks

On the Menu

Layered over my favorite places are the File, Edit, View, Tools, and Help menus. You may be familiar with the general operations of each from your experience with Windows 95, but they merit further attention on MSN.

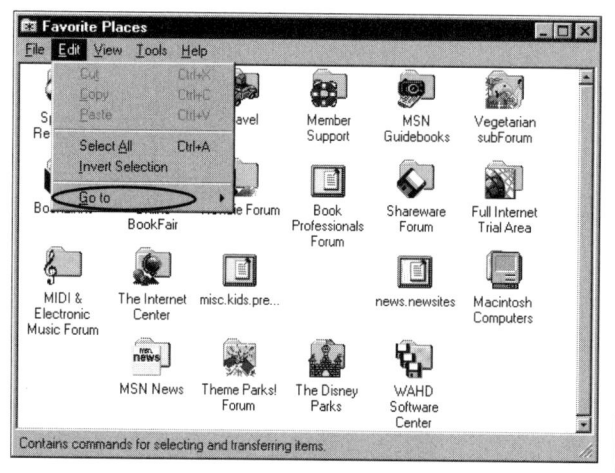

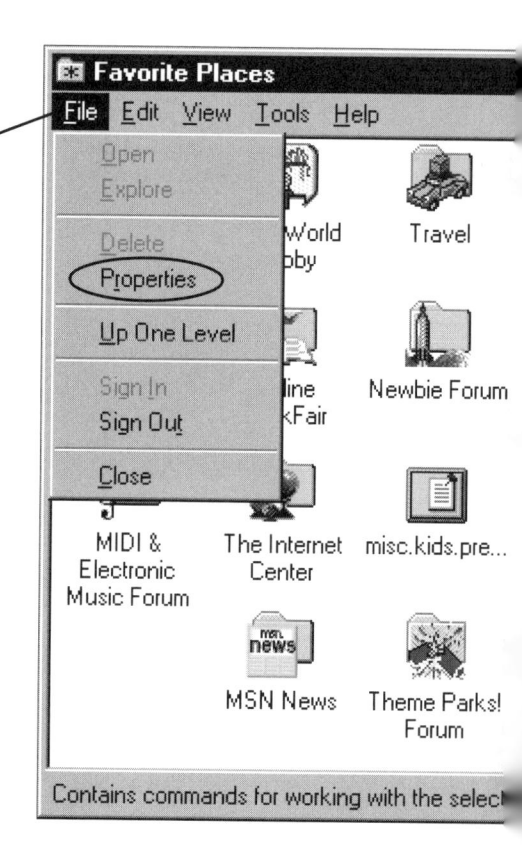

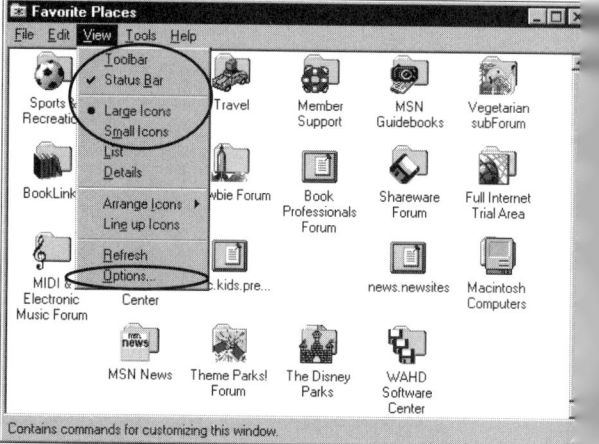

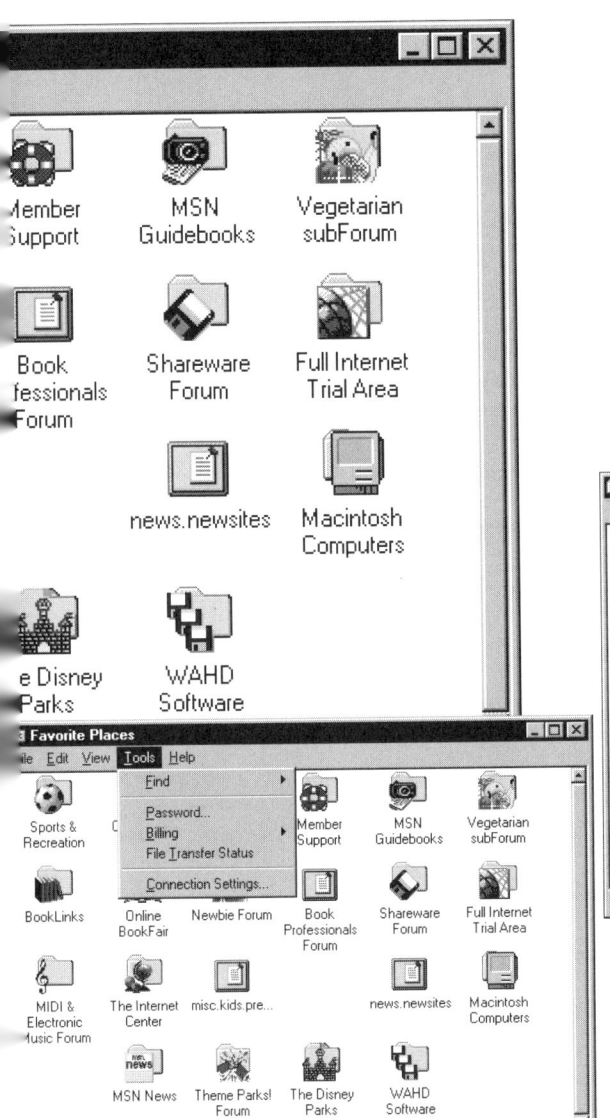

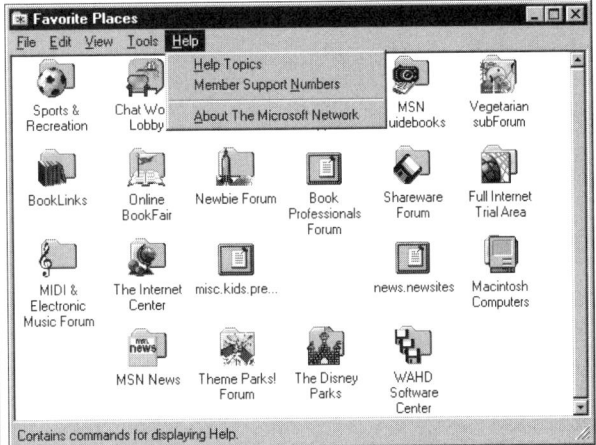

MSN Centerfold: A Visual Tour of the User Interface   25

Don't vegetate—investigate! Take a few minutes to experiment with the features of each command. I've circled those you shouldn't miss.

Mail Call

Microsoft Exchange is your personal mailroom. With its organizational tools, it is much more than a mailbox.

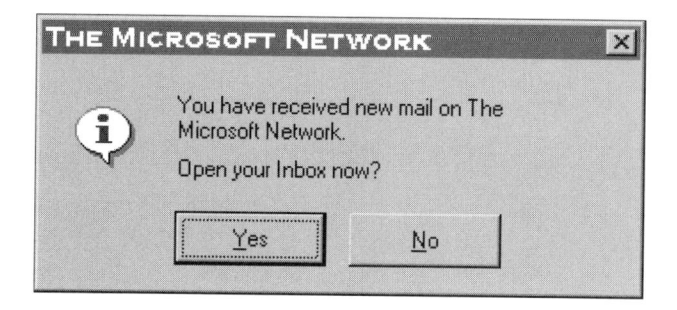

Folders can be added to and deleted from the personal folders. I've added Read Mail to mine. I tend to get a lot of mail and it's easier for me to transfer mail that I've read from my inbox to the Read Mail box. To make my move, I choose Select All from the Edit menu, and then Move from the File menu. Then I designate the Read Mail folder as the destination. You may prefer additional folders for your mail organization, so add them to your heart's delight...mail from spouse, mail from significant other, mail pertaining to work.

Hint: When you sign on, MSN will notify you of incoming mail. Be sure to check again before you sign off. Wouldn't you hate to miss an email?

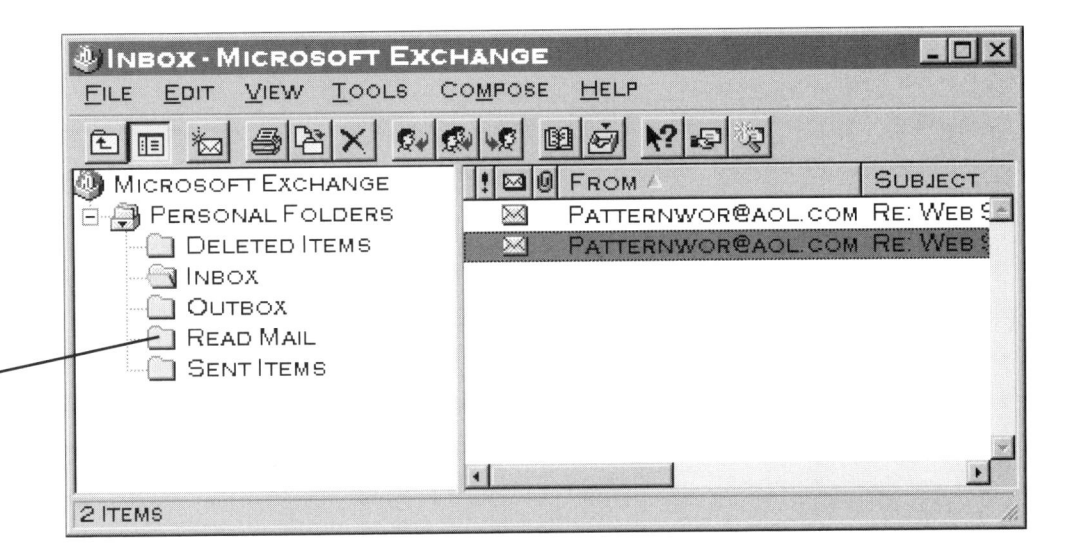

MSN Centerfold: A Visual Tour of the User Interface   27

Bundles of Mail

My friend Mark, a true friend of MSN, calls himself a paladin of MSN—perhaps *the* paladin. In this single piece of mail, he has included two additional sources of information.

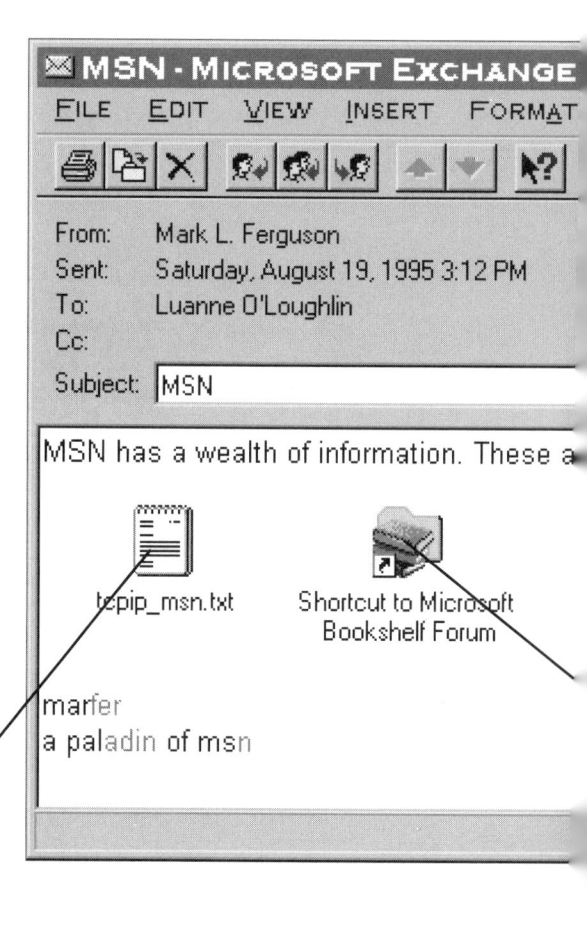

Mark has included a text file, shown here as tcpip_msn.txt, and a shortcut to the Microsoft Bookshelf Forum. When I double click on the text file, it will open in my associated text reader—I've designated MS-Word for this purpose. I can open the file from its position within the mail piece or I can move it to another location.

The same goes for the shortcut. I can access it where it resides or I can move it to the desktop for ready reference.

MSN Centerfold: A Visual Tour of the User Interface

Sorting the Mail

This has been sorted by subject, in alphabetical order.

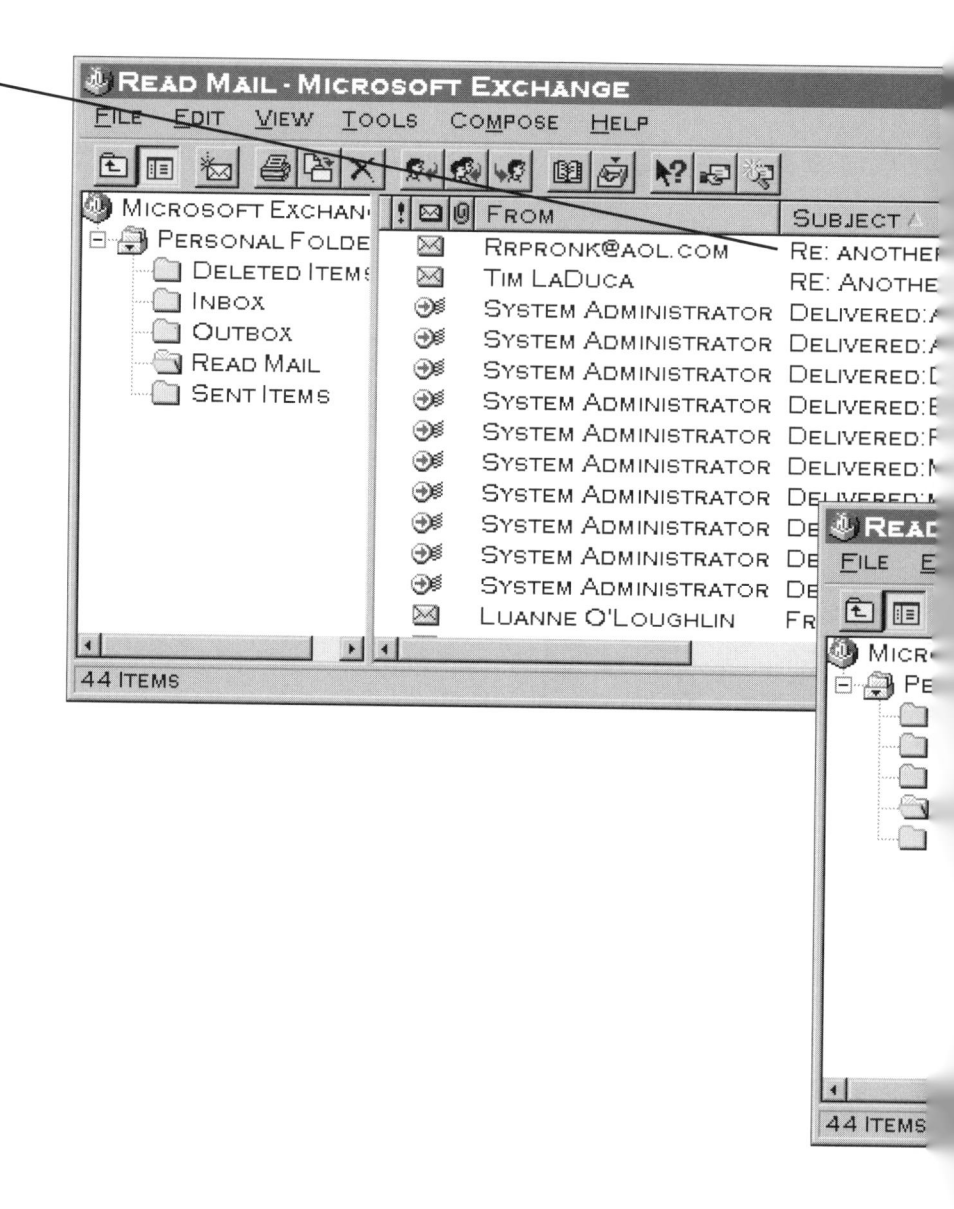

MSN Centerfold: A Visual Tour of the User Interface   31

All of the mail folders can be sorted according to your liking: to/from, subject, sent/received, and file size. Within each of these selections, there are further choices you can make. For instance, lists can appear in ascending or descending order. Click on the column head (Subject, Received, and so on) to specify how you want your messages sorted.

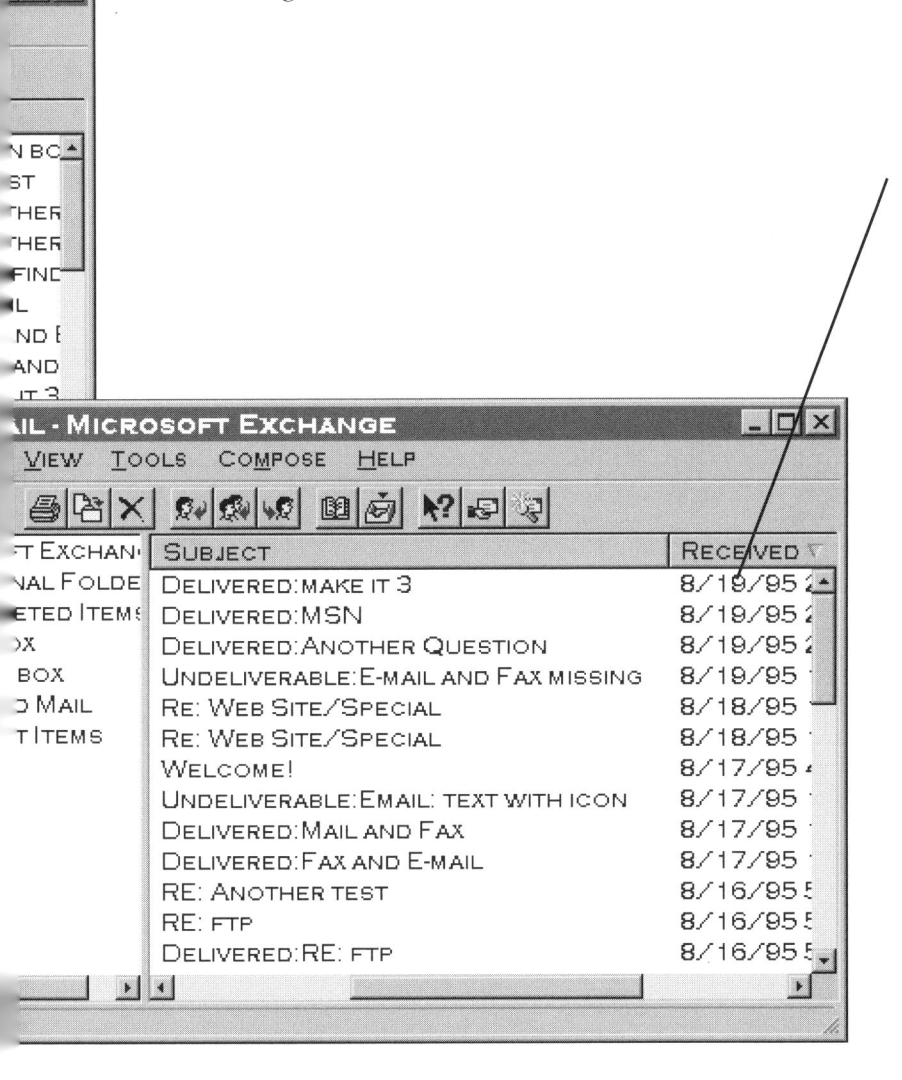

This time I've chosen to review my Read Mail by date—with the most recent date appearing first.

Subject	Received
Delivered: make it 3	8/19/95
Delivered: MSN	8/19/95
Delivered: Another Question	8/19/95
Undeliverable: E-mail and Fax missing	8/19/95
Re: Web Site/Special	8/18/95
Re: Web Site/Special	8/18/95
Welcome!	8/17/95
Undeliverable: Email: text with icon	8/17/95
Delivered: Mail and Fax	8/17/95
Delivered: Fax and E-mail	8/17/95
RE: Another test	8/16/95
RE: FTP	8/16/95
Delivered: RE: FTP	8/16/95

Mail Power Tools

Did Santa Claus get your letter? Do you need to know whether Bill Clinton is taking your latest suggestions? In this case, how can I be sure Russell Siegelman has received my ideas about his master project, MSN?

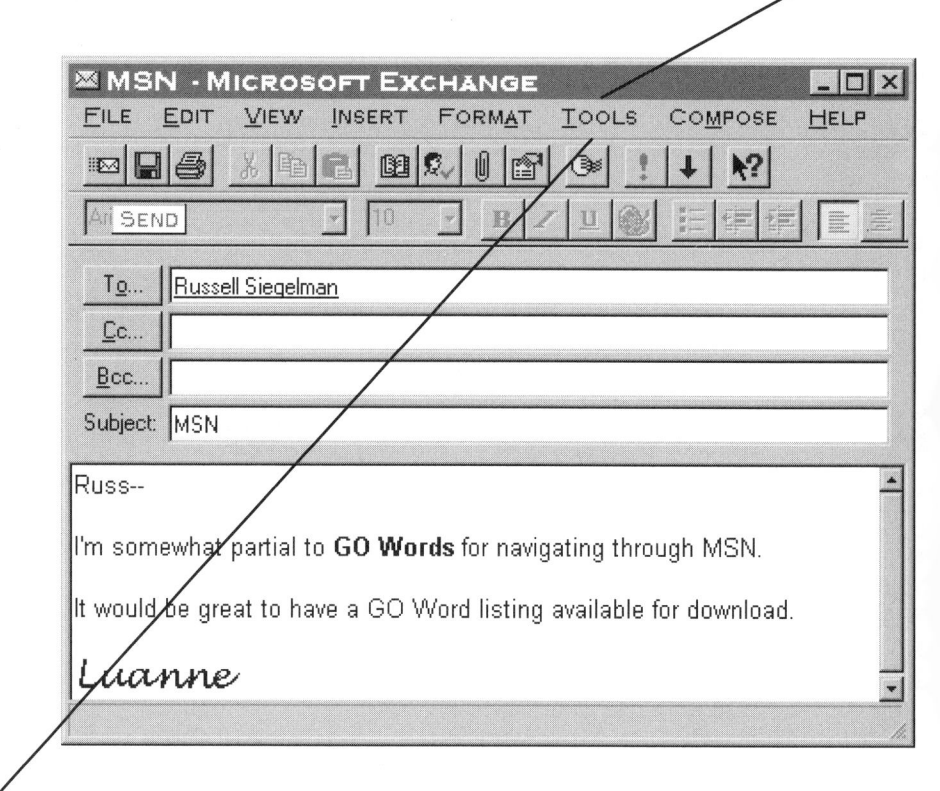

You can request a receipt on any piece of mail...To review your receipt options, select Options from the Tools Menu, followed by the Send tab. There you can select to receive a receipt when the mail is received or read.

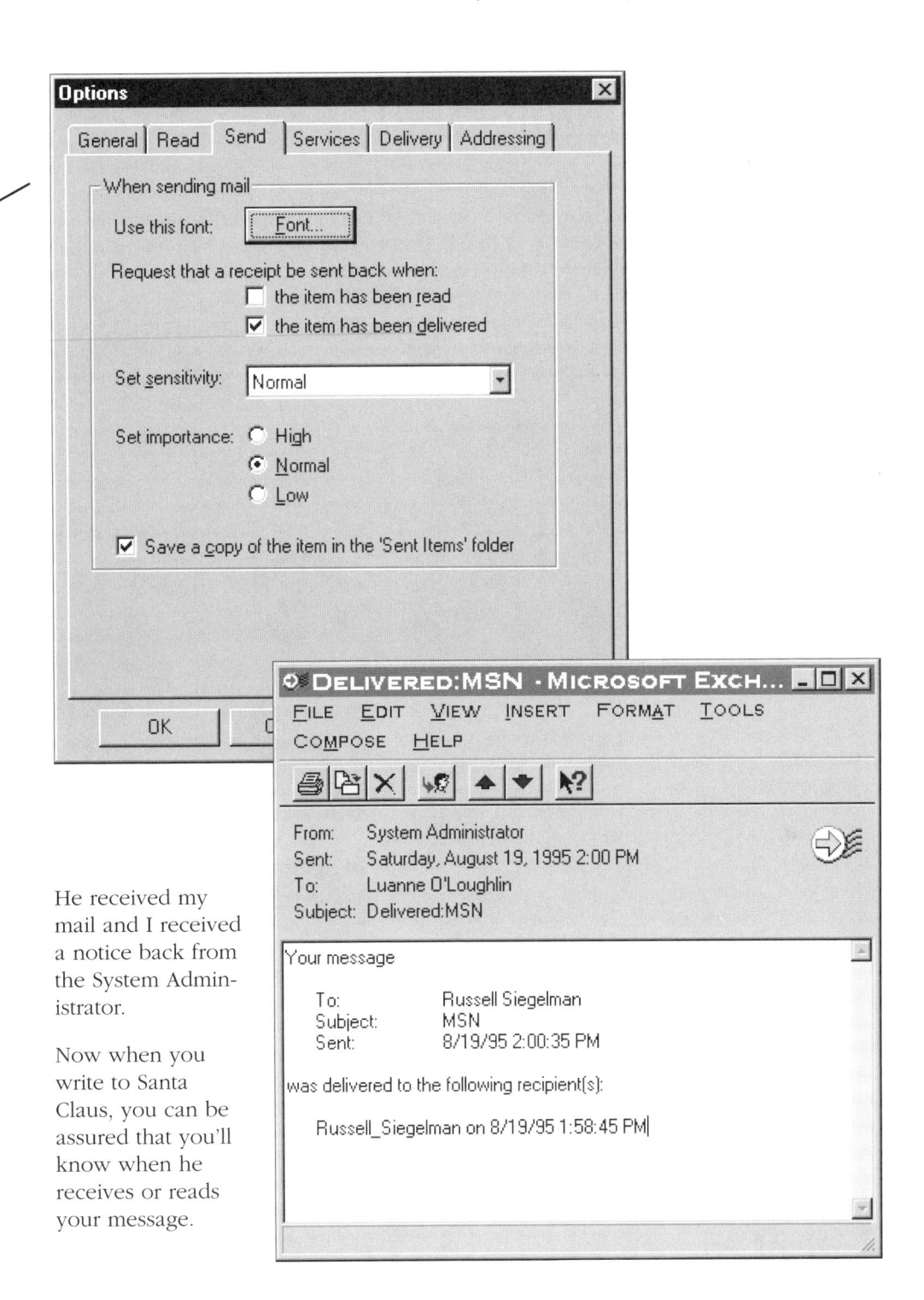

He received my mail and I received a notice back from the System Administrator.

Now when you write to Santa Claus, you can be assured that you'll know when he receives or reads your message.

System Treasure Hunt

There's nothing quite like MSN's global index. It works just like the Find function on Windows 95. When MSN is open, you can choose to find files on your computer or topics on The Microsoft Network. Of course, I'm not interesting in sifting through the muck on your hard drive (especially if it needs a cleaning like mine).

This is a great place to try all those buzzwords that include your favorite topics and hobbies. The Find function serves as a system-wide searcher for just about anything you can think of.

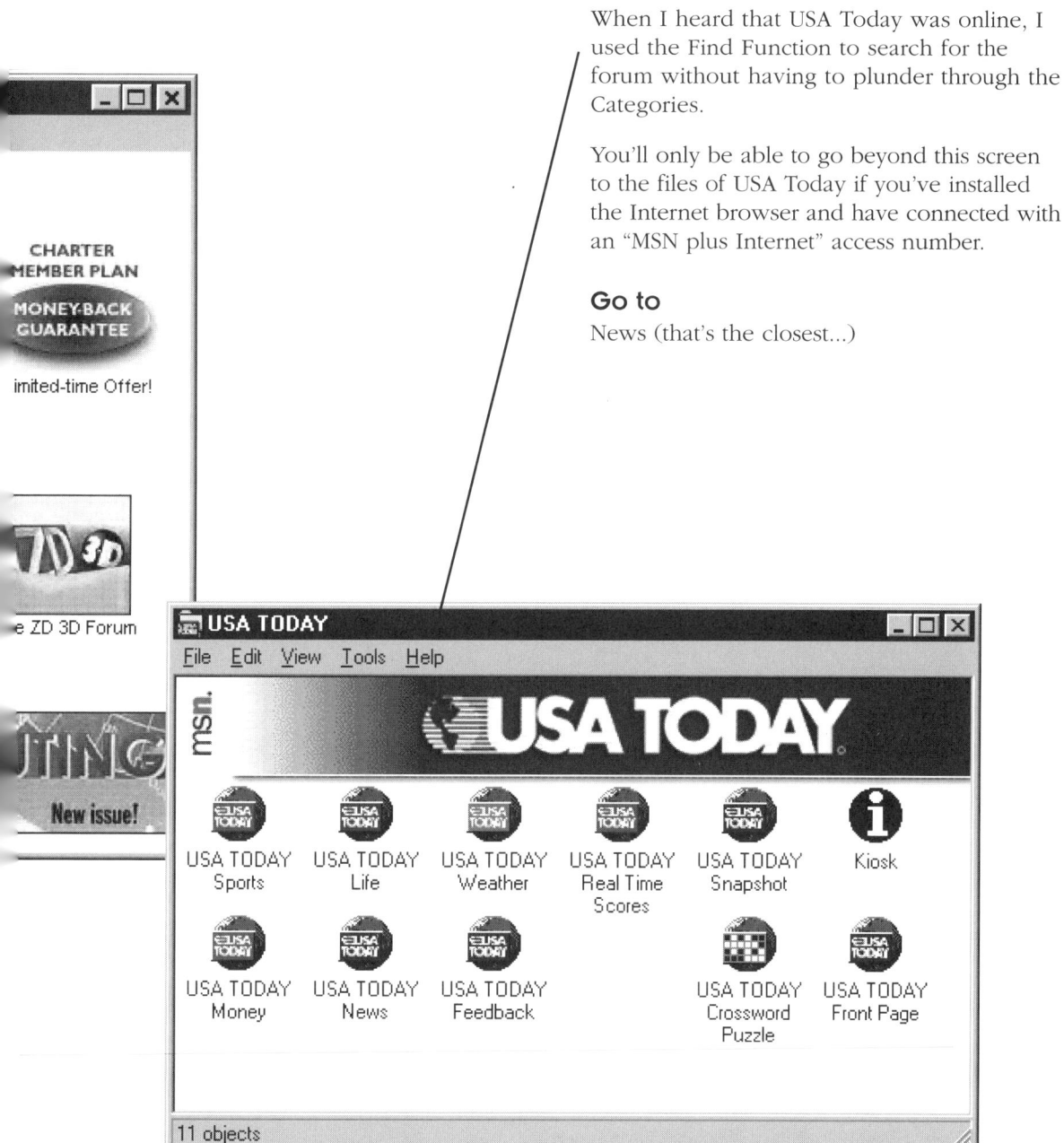

When I heard that USA Today was online, I used the Find Function to search for the forum without having to plunder through the Categories.

You'll only be able to go beyond this screen to the files of USA Today if you've installed the Internet browser and have connected with an "MSN plus Internet" access number.

Go to
News (that's the closest...)

PANNING FOR GOLD

From the Help Menu, multiple aids are available to facilitate your search for online how-tos.

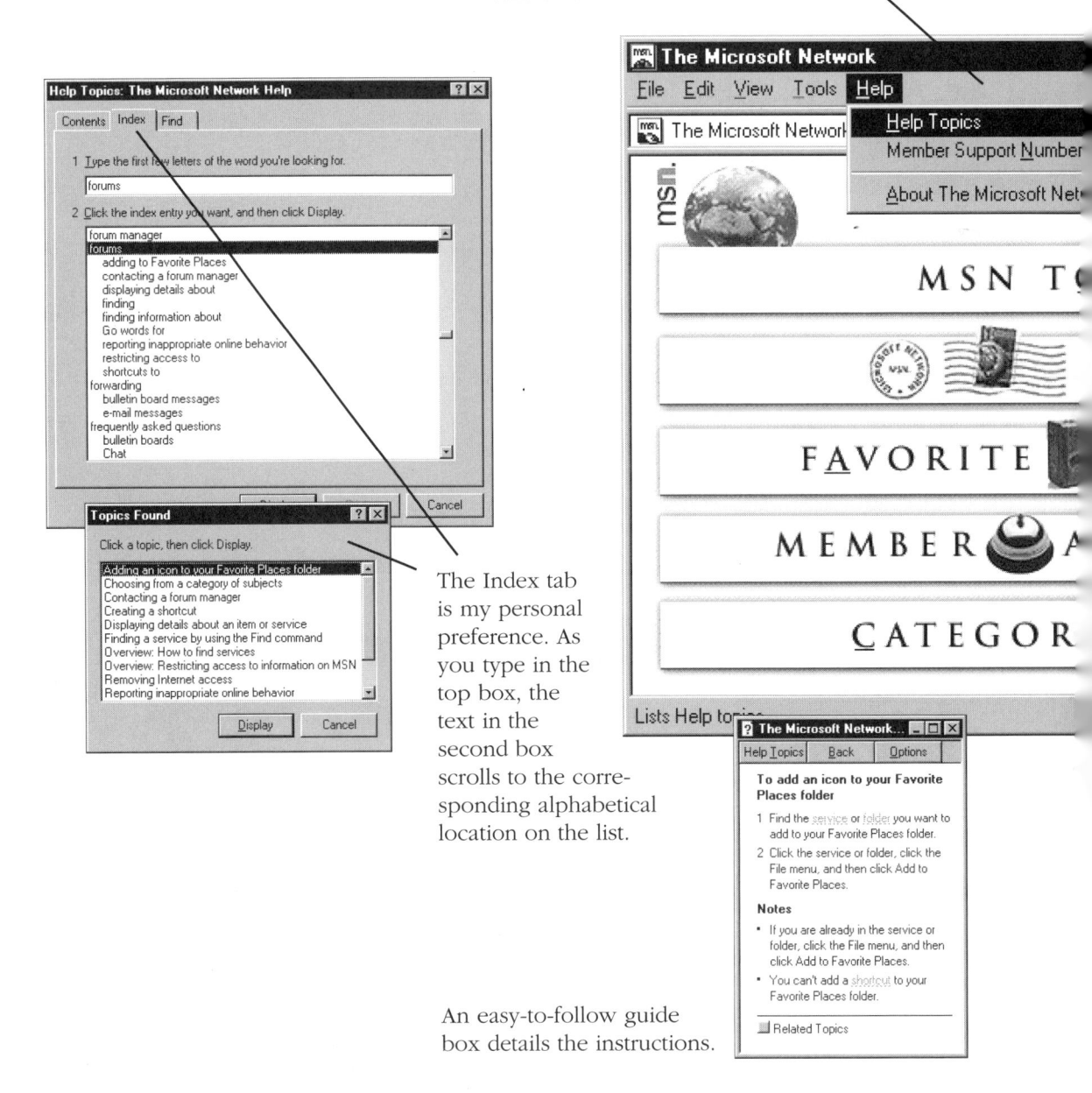

The Index tab is my personal preference. As you type in the top box, the text in the second box scrolls to the corresponding alphabetical location on the list.

An easy-to-follow guide box details the instructions.

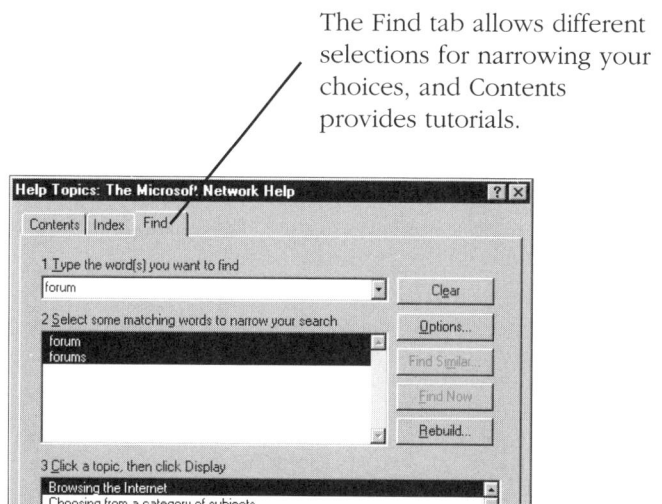

MSN Centerfold: A Visual Tour of the User Interface   37

The Find tab allows different selections for narrowing your choices, and Contents provides tutorials.

The Contents Tab leads to solid tutorial files. Make it a point to review these to build your skills on MSN. These are printable files, so load the printer with paper!

38 • MSN Centerfold: A Visual Tour of the User Interface

WONDERS OF THE WEB

Store your favorite places here. That works much better than typing all those URLs (lengthy addresses, like http://www.acs.oakland.edu/oak/SimTel/win3/capture.html).

Launching the browser from your desktop sends your electrons straight to msn's home page.

There are 10 hotlinks on this home page. Simply click on one and another Web page will arrive at your screen.

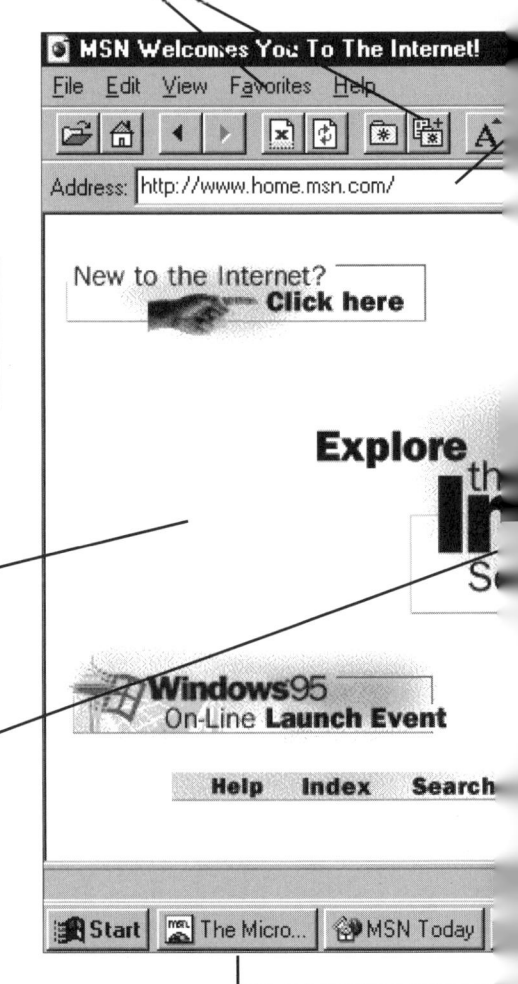

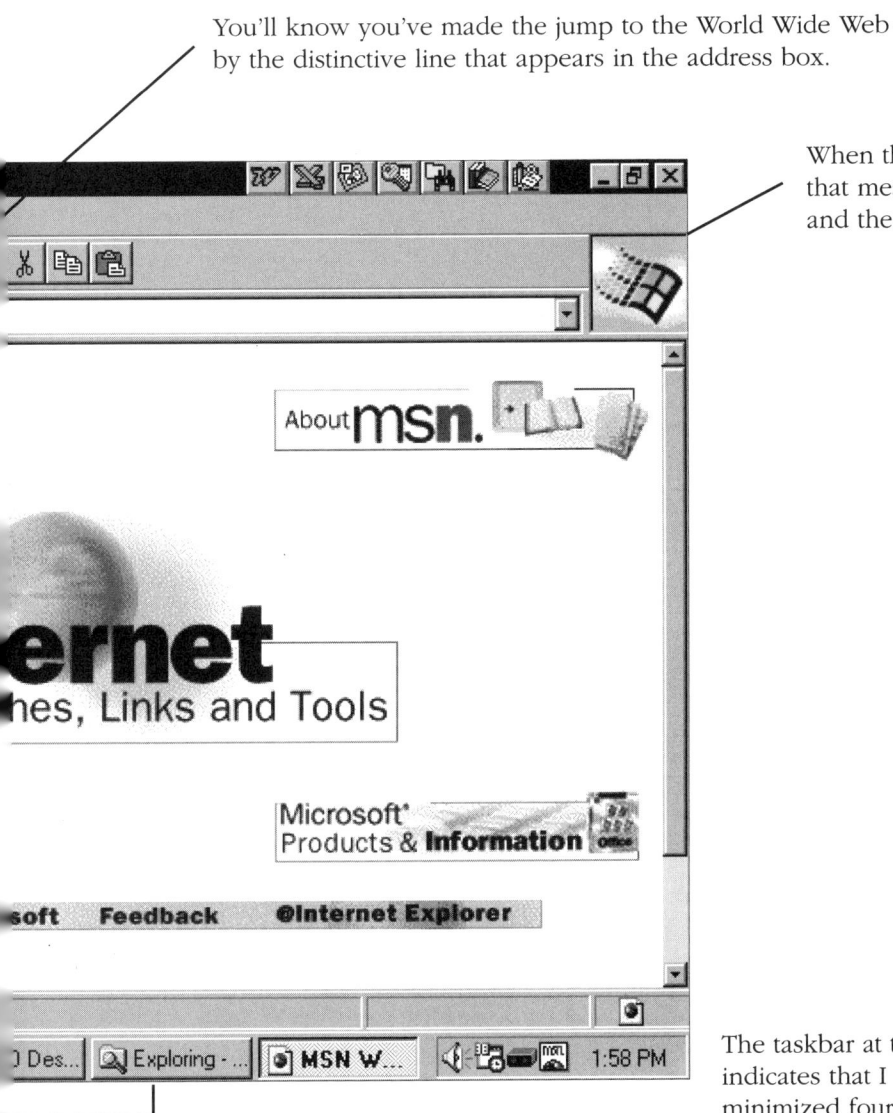

MSN Centerfold: A Visual Tour of the User Interface   39

You'll know you've made the jump to the World Wide Web by the distinctive line that appears in the address box.

When the clouds are moving, that means the link is active and the page is building.

The taskbar at the bottom of the screen indicates that I already opened and minimized four screens or programs prior to accessing the Web site.

Go to
WWW

THE TOOLCHEST

There are scores of tools available on MSN. Whether you are posting to a BBS, conversing in a chat, or surfing the Web, these are the tools of choice.

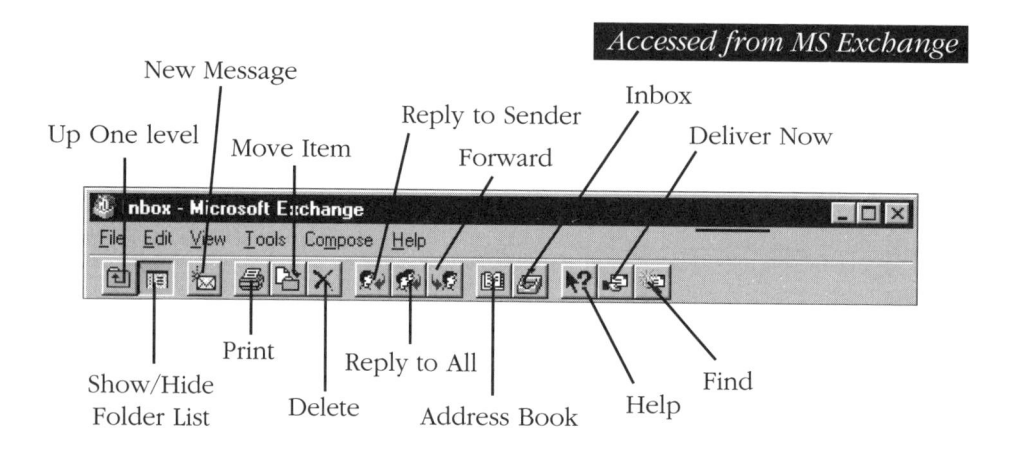

Accessed from MS Exchange

- Up One level
- New Message
- Move Item
- Reply to Sender
- Forward
- Inbox
- Deliver Now
- Show/Hide Folder List
- Print
- Delete
- Reply to All
- Address Book
- Help
- Find

Accessed from MSN Central

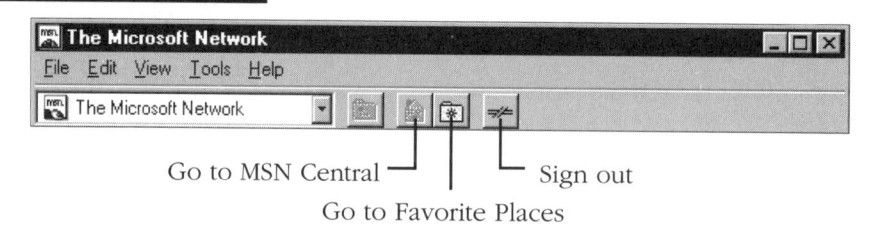

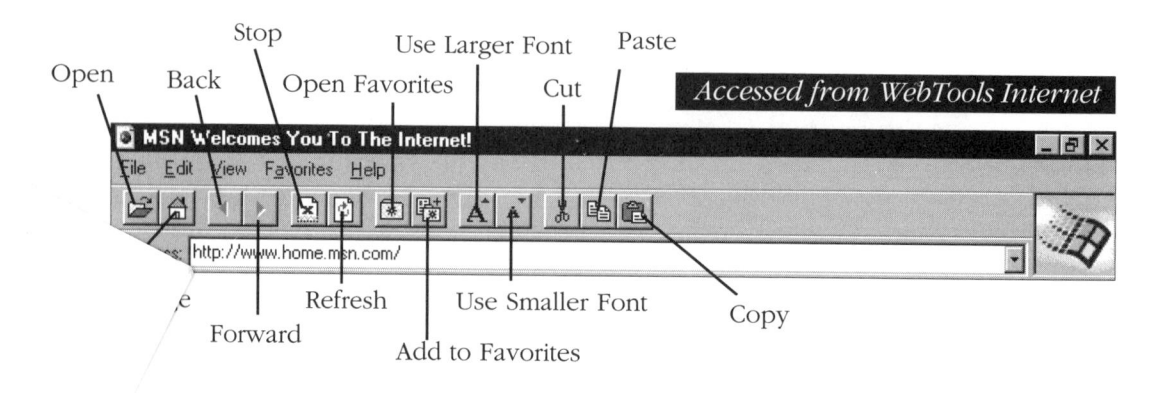

- Go to MSN Central
- Go to Favorite Places
- Sign out

Accessed from WebTools Internet

- Open
- Back
- Stop
- Open Favorites
- Use Larger Font
- Cut
- Paste
- Forward
- Refresh
- Use Smaller Font
- Add to Favorites
- Copy

MSN Centerfold: A Visual Tour of the User Interface   41

Category Tools

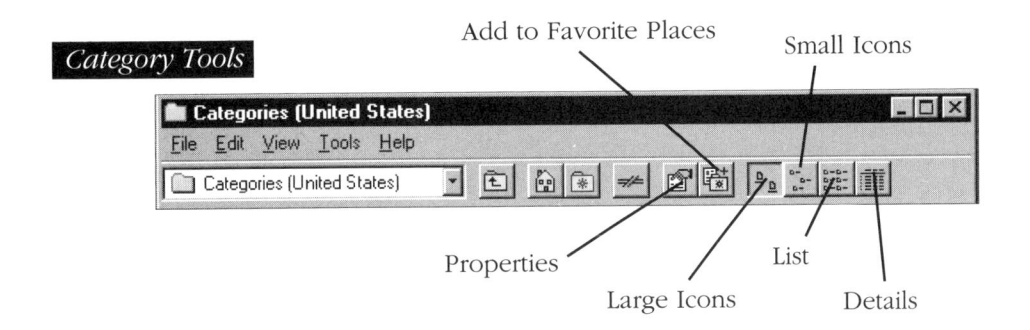

Categories (United States)
File Edit View Tools Help

- Add to Favorite Places
- Small Icons
- Properties
- Large Icons
- List
- Details

Chat Tools

CW Lobby
File Edit View Tools Help

- Save
- Add to Favorite Places
- Copy
- Cut
- Paste
- Show Spectators
- Ignore (Member)
- Member Properties

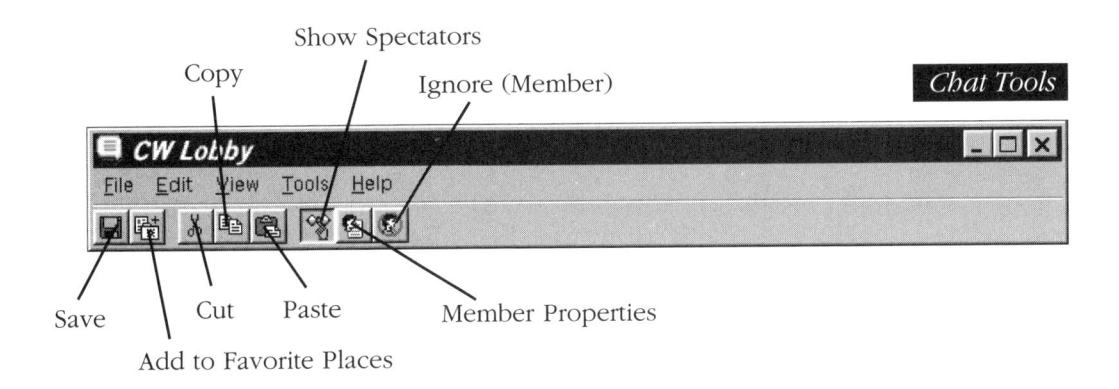

BBS or Message Board Tools

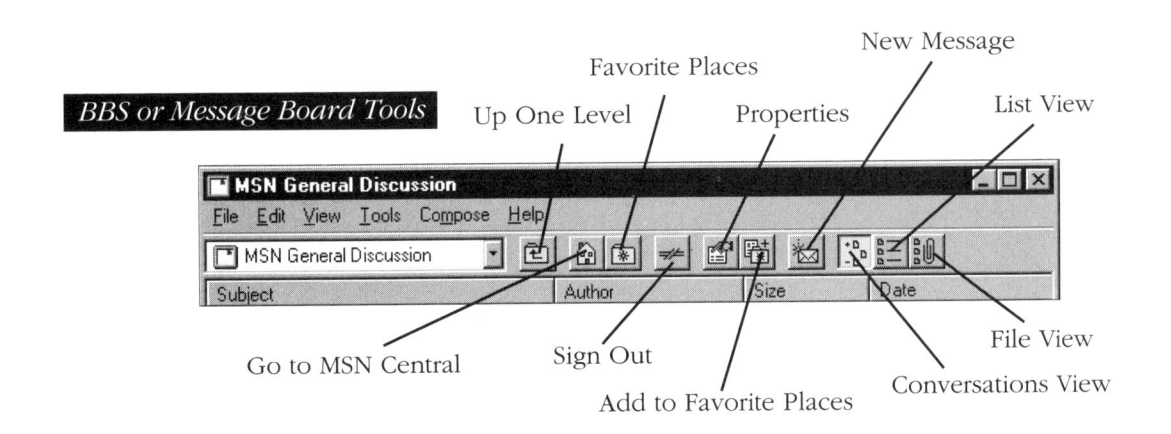

MSN General Discussion
File Edit View Tools Compose Help

Subject | Author | Size | Date

- Up One Level
- Go to MSN Central
- Favorite Places
- Sign Out
- Properties
- Add to Favorite Places
- New Message
- List View
- File View
- Conversations View

Random Chatter

Each chat has a life of its own. Nowhere is online etiquette more clearly needed than in a chat room.

Don't use all caps. That's the online equivalent of shouting.

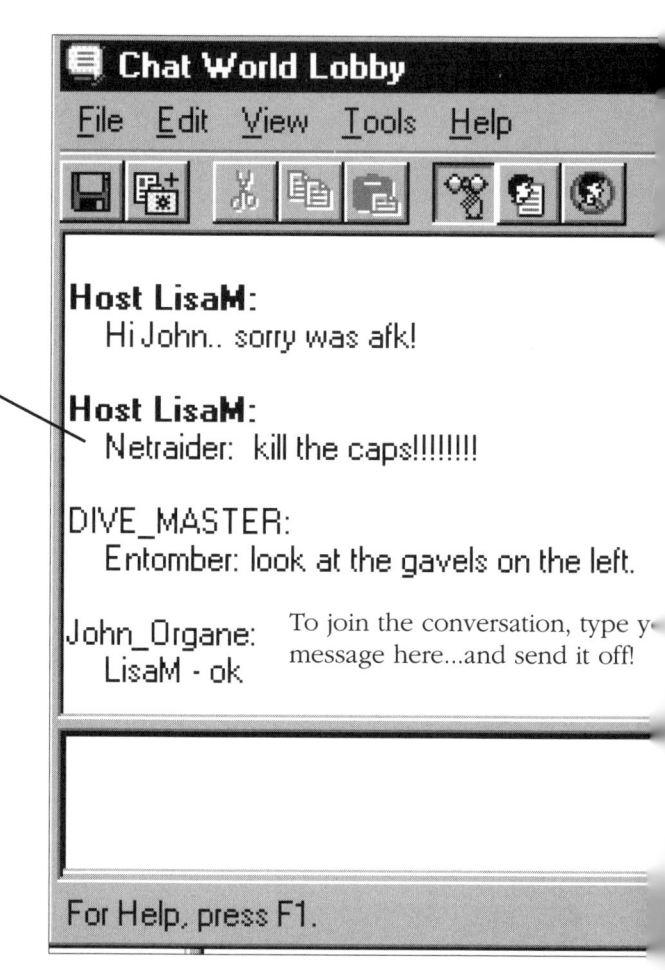

Chat World Lobby

File   Edit   View   Tools   Help

Host LisaM:
Hi John.. sorry was afk!

Host LisaM:
Netraider: kill the caps!!!!!!!!

DIVE_MASTER:
Entomber: look at the gavels on the left.

John_Organe:
LisaM - ok

To join the conversation, type your message here...and send it off!

For Help, press F1.

Hint: Always read the guidelines so you won't be embarrassed by adding boorish behavior.
Are boors ever embarrassed? Please make every effort to be polite—save the locker room conversation for offline pursuits.

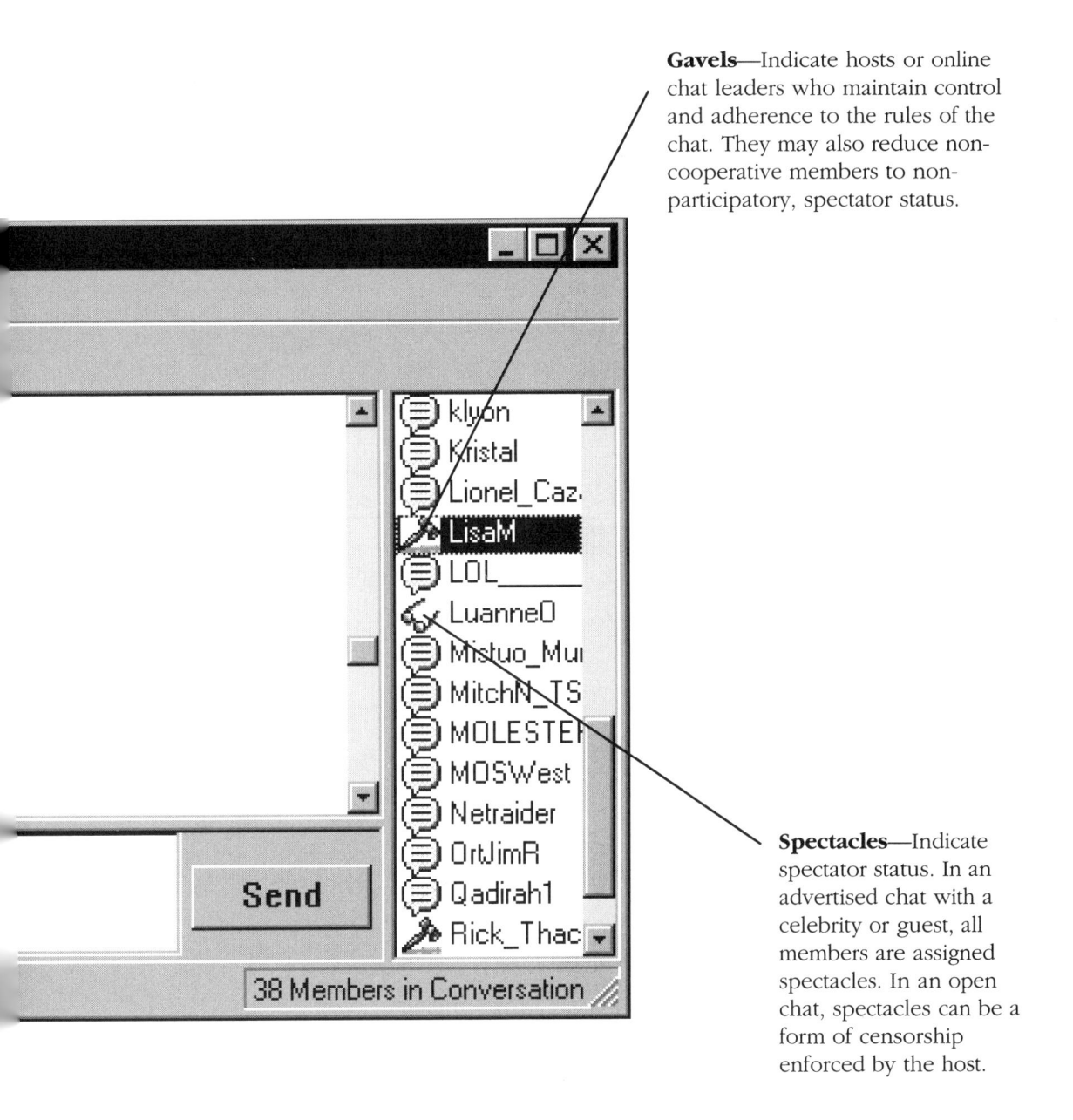

MSN Centerfold: A Visual Tour of the User Interface   43

Gavels—Indicate hosts or online chat leaders who maintain control and adherence to the rules of the chat. They may also reduce non-cooperative members to non-participatory, spectator status.

Spectacles—Indicate spectator status. In an advertised chat with a celebrity or guest, all members are assigned spectacles. In an open chat, spectacles can be a form of censorship enforced by the host.

Proceed with Caution

Every now and then, electronic glitches and witches confound us all. This page carries a selection of error messages and the reasons why you may receive each one.

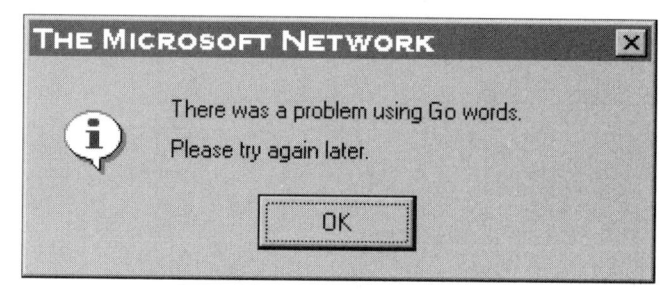

> **The Microsoft Network**
> There was a problem using Go words. Please try again later.
> [OK]

This signifies a technical problem at MSN.

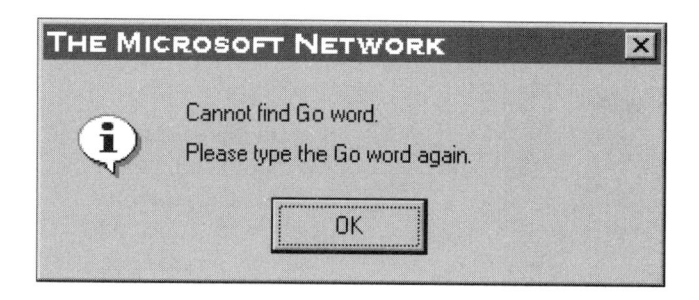

> **The Microsoft Network**
> Cannot find Go word. Please type the Go word again.
> [OK]

The Go Word you used is not valid.

MSN Centerfold: A Visual Tour of the User Interface   45

The Microsoft Network

This task cannot be completed at this time. Please try again later.

OK

This signifies a technical problem at MSN.

This signifies a technical problem at MSN.

Online Viewer

This service is not available at this time. Please try again later.

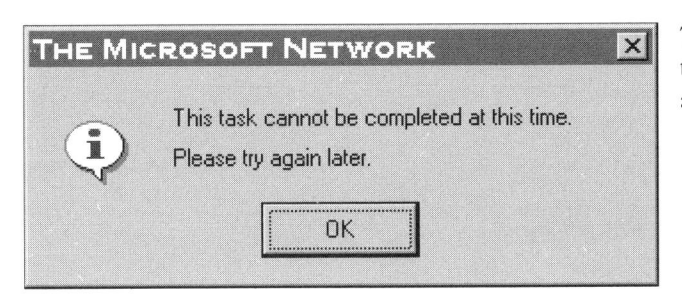

OK

The Microsoft Network

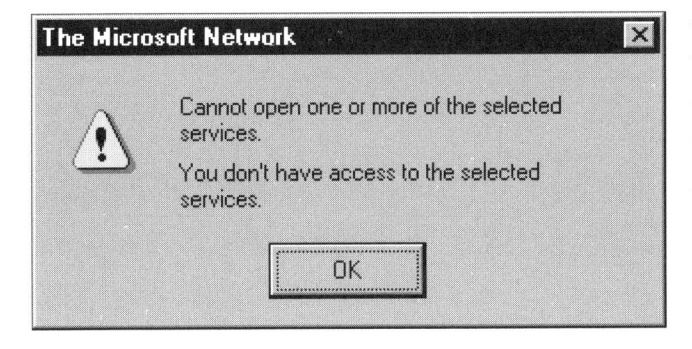

Cannot open one or more of the selected services.

You don't have access to the selected services.

OK

You used a Go Word for a private forum or tried to gain access to a forum that is not yet open to the public.

PART 2

Mastering MSN: A Q&A

Competition among online providers is really starting to heat up, but it hasn't always been that way. In the beginning (and the beginning was only about a dozen years ago), there was just CompuServe, which at the time seemed out of reach of the average user because its interface had an ogre-like disposition. Today, being part of the online community is commonplace—even trendy. CompuServe has given its interface a, well, facelift. America Online has come online and is as popular as ever; Prodigy is still going strong, and the Internet is experiencing explosive growth. Now, with the introduction of The Microsoft Network (MSN), getting online is as easy as clicking your mouse on a big, friendly Start button, or, in this case, the icon on your desktop that arrived with the installation of MSN. By including MSN (in most cases) with Windows 95, Microsoft hopes to capture a large number of home computer users who own modems but have never bothered installing any of the other online services. So getting online with MSN is simple—just install Windows 95 (which in itself is often easier said than done).

Now that you've sailed or grumbled through the installation of Windows 95, it's time to get started with MSN. Be prepared to take some time getting up to speed with this program, though. It's not going to be a breeze, mainly because MSN, although powerful, is still a work in progress. But it won't take long before your light bulb will click on and you'll get to that point where you're comfortable enough to solve the challenges you encounter without feeling overwhelmed.

And that's my plan—to get you to the point where you are comfortably proficient.

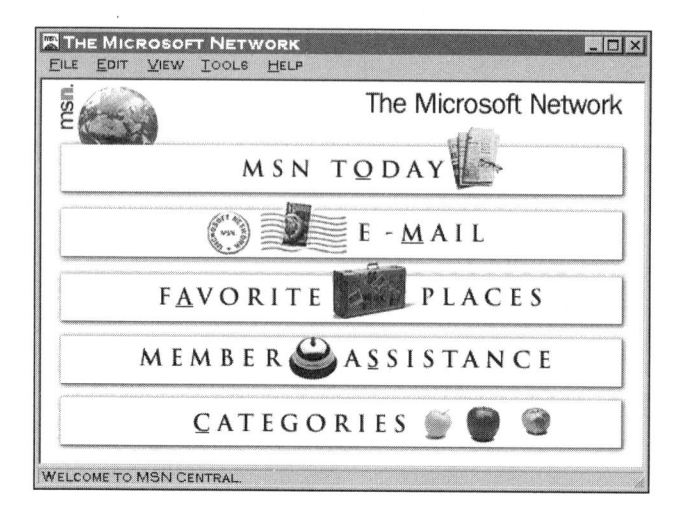

If you feel a bit lost now, don't think twice about it. In fact, I think learning MSN is one of those experiences where the novice has an advantage over more experienced online system users. In my case, I am constantly comparing MSN to America Online and CompuServe, where I have spent hundreds of hours in the past three years. At times, I expect MSN to present features in a way that's similar to the other services, and in many cases, that's exactly the case. But Microsoft often behaves like a maverick, presenting features in a way that bears little if any resemblence to the other services. Sometimes I understand why MSN marches to its own drummer, sometimes I don't.

If you are already experienced with another commercial online service, you, too, will find comforting similarities and bothersome differences between them and MSN. My best advice to you is to evaluate MSN based on its own merits.

General

What Does It Cost to Be an MSN Member?

MSN offers several subscriptions to its service, allowing you to select the option that best fits your needs. But if you haven't been online, how do you know which option is best for you?

Will you use MSN from work or from home? Do you have any free time now? When I'm not working on a book, I generally spend two hours a day online. I check my e-mail and favorite message boards at the beginning of the day and again at the end of the day. My e-mail friends span the globe, yet we can easily remain in touch. Beyond that, I find the online services to be extremely addictive, so I can only recommend that you inflate your initial use estimate. It is very common for online members to generate bills in the range of $20 to $30 each month. My usage of two hours per day could easily run $150 per month with the Standard Monthly Plan. Given my usage levels, I am the perfect candidate for the Frequent User Monthly Plan. I do hope that you are able to demonstrate more restraint than I do.

MSN offers a variety of membership plans, ranging from annual to monthly, for the U.S. and international markets.

In the United States, Microsoft offers three membership plans: the Annual Plan, the Frequent User Monthly Plan, and the Standard Monthly Plan.

Plan	Cost	Includes	Each Additional Hour
Annual	$49.95 per year	3 hours per month	$2.50
Frequent User Monthly	$19.95 per month	20 hours per month	$2.00
Standard Monthly	$4.95 per month	3 hours per month	$2.50

I just can't walk away without criticizing the Annual Plan, which saves a whopping 79¢ per month over the Standard Monthly plan. Ahem (excuse me for clearing my throat), but I don't see the advantage of endowing the coffers of Microsoft to save less than $1 per month. That's like getting one free cup of coffee each month . . . yippee.

Not mentioned in the membership fees are the additional fees you will encounter in forums sponsored by independent content providers. In Microsoft's courtship of third-party content providers, the premise has been that providers are not limited in the ways in which they realize revenues for their services. Those fees may include an hourly surcharge, a cover charge for entry to the forum, or even a fee for each download.

Will I Pay Phone Charges, Too?

In most parts of the United States, MSN members will be able to dial in on a local call. Members in rural areas may find that there is no local number in their area. In that case, they should check with the local phone company to see if there is a special calling plan that can assist in controlling costs. Find the closest number for your area and call the phone company. Tell them that you expect to make 10 or so (you pick the number) calls per month to a specific number that is beyond your free calling area. For a flat rate you may be able to add that one number or exchange to your "free" calling area. These special calling plans may not be listed in the front of your phone book, so go ahead and make your request known.

At the time of this writing, those members signing up for MSN Plus Internet service had fewer access number choices than those desiring just MSN access. I am in the major metropolitan area of Los Angeles. In my case, the MSN access call incurs no toll charge. But if I needed to call the next closest number for MSN Plus Internet access, I would pay 4¢ for the first minute and 1¢ for each additional minute. If you are in an area that has a "free" MSN number and a toll charge for MSN Plus Internet, you can switch between the two access numbers depending on which service you need.

What's Available on MSN?

MSN membership provides Internet access, including an e-mail account, thousands of newsgroups, and access to the World Wide Web (where available). Whether your interests are in sports, science fiction, or the weather, you'll discover hundreds of special-interest bulletin boards with download libraries. The multimedia reference centers and the hot news of the day are yours—as it happens. Rounding out the coverage is a wide spectrum of content and services from hundreds of independent content providers (ICPs). Many ICPs will also offer value-added services for an additional fee. That means you'll find more commercially recognized names providing their services with surcharges.

How Do I Save $$$ Using MSN?

The best tip for saving money is to make sure that you use your online time efficiently. You can use Microsoft Exchange—it came with Windows 95—to read and write your e-mail offline. You will only be connected (and paying) for the duration it takes to deliver your mail.

Microsoft has provided a number of tools to allow you to customize how you work with MSN. In the next few pages we'll get into using shortcuts, GO Words, and Favorite Places to speed your online time. With these tools, you can minimize the time you spend navigating between your special interest areas.

You can also set MSN to disconnect when your system has been inactive for a period of time. Set this time to be as short as possible, so if you get distracted by your spouse, child, or significant other, you won't continue to incur online charges.

From time to time, you will find annoying slowdowns on the system. It happens on all the commercial online services, and it is likely to happen during peak periods of use. I am quite sure that Microsoft is working hard to keep the system running efficiently, but neither you nor I need to pay to accomplish a task in 10 minutes that can normally be accomplished in 5 minutes. When you hit one of these slow periods, log off to save your time, money, and patience.

To be a smart online consumer, you also need to know how MSN calculates online charges. MSN usage time is rounded to the nearest minute based on 30-second increments. For example, two minutes, 30 seconds will be counted as two minutes, while two minutes, 31 seconds will be counted as three minutes.

Why MSN?

The Microsoft Network is truly the online system of the future—here today. With the release of Windows 95, millions of people are a single mouse-click away from joining this revolutionary system, which extends the Windows-based PC beyond desktop communication and file sharing to a worldwide community of people, ideas, and information. With MSN, you also have easy and clear access to the tangled World Wide Web, and you are able to communicate at a level never before possible from your PC. When fully operational (several enhancements are already planned), MSN will provide the setting for a worldwide electronic marketplace of products and services that cuts across multiple industries and all types of businesses.

Would an example of Microsoft's integration help? I am a member of a cooking club that gathers once a month for a scrumptious tasting session. As the group coordinator, I also send a little newsletter to our group members each week. Of course, we all have MSN accounts. This week, I sent a pasta carbonara recipe, in the form of an attachment. That attached file, created in MS-Word, was added by clipping the file's icon and pasting it in the e-mail message. To take this a level further, the Word file included an Excel spreadsheet that allowed for quick recipe adjustments. I have also found a terrific new pasta recipe collection in the file library and I've included the shortcut to the file library in my e-mail message.

When Jenni, Carol, and Suzanne received my e-mail message, they quickly reviewed the pasta recipe and were able to adjust it for the number of guests they expected at dinner. Using the shortcut I included, they were transported to MSN to view and retrieve the collection of pasta recipes.

How Does MSN Differ from the Other Major Online Services?

The MSN technology is extremely fascinating, yet terribly simple. It all comes down to one word, *integration*. I'm sure it comes as no surprise to you that the Microsoft family of products integrates seamlessly with MSN. Sit back and imagine that you're e-mailing a letter to your brother Bob, telling him about the great up-to-the-minute sports statistics you've found on MSN; you can simply include a special *shortcut* symbol in your e-mail or in the attached MS-Word document. When he receives your mail, he can click on the shortcut, get connected to MSN, and be taken directly to the sports scores forum. But let's not get ahead of ourselves. He will, of course, have to have a setup similar to yours—with Windows 95, MSN, and Word

There's no better computer-based source, with as many tools, for efficiently communicating with others.

Will It Be Difficult to Learn How to Use MSN?

The great thing about MSN is that MSN acts just like Windows 95. As you learn a new technique or skill applicable to Windows 95, you gain knowledge that will improve your skills on MSN. You'll find easy, consistent, and graphical functionality. Windows 95 allows your files—and MSN—to be browsed using Explorer or from an icon-based view. Downloading can be activated and accomplished by drag-and-drop. Shortcuts, enabling personalized and efficient navigation, can cross from MSN to your desktop. E-mail, Exchange, and word-processing functions (MS-Word or WordPad) carry through with the same interface for core communications.

Why Do Businesses Like Being on MSN?

Aside from Windows, Microsoft's success has been built on providing software applications for business. Where would your office be without Microsoft Word and Excel? In developing MSN, Microsoft has developed an online system that brings together the needs of businesses and consumers. Microsoft has capitalized on what they have learned from providing customer support to millions of users. With their enviable expertise, they have designed MSN to help other companies reach their business customers and consumers.

The success of MSN will depend in part on its ability to support the symbiotic relationship between businesses and customers. The customer profiles will aid businesses by generating targeted online members for their forums. Further on, you'll read more about customer profiles.

Microsoft's expectation and goal is a computer on every desk and in every home. With the expected dominance of Windows 95, MSN is the answer that can integrate the communication needs of businesses and consumers.

Does Everyone Have the Same Access to Content on MSN?

I think this is one of the most interesting questions you've asked. You did ask it, didn't you? Believe it or not, everyone does not have the same access. In this scenario you run a tire store and you buy your inventory from the Square Wheel Rubber Company. As long as I'm fabricating this story, I'll add that the Square Wheel Rubber Company has a forum on The Microsoft Network. Square Wheel has arranged for you to see their icon—and access their forum—on MSN. If you are in their top tier of designated customers, you may even have access to pricing information and discounts that are not available to run-of-the-mill dealers. The tire-buying consumer cannot see the icon, and they don't even know that Square Wheel has a forum on MSN. You could say, they don't know what they're missing. Is that corny?

Does Microsoft Keep Profiles of Their Customers, and What Do They Do with the Profiles?

Is Big Brother lurking? Anyone who knows me, knows that health topics are my favorite hobby research area. The Microsoft Network knows that I have a lot of hits (accesses) in health and fitness areas—they can count each visit I make—and they can customize my screens so that I see the icons for new health or related areas. MSN can personalize the content based on my online use profile.

Try to forget about the Big Brother aspects and think about the possibilities these profiles present. Pertinent and interesting articles are automatically highlighted; shopping catalogs can be customized to your taste and sizes; and weather reports, street maps, and calendars of events can be localized to your area.

Think of it this way. After you've used MSN for a period of time, you won't have to go looking for new "favorites"; they'll find you. And you won't miss out.

How Many Family Members Can I Have on My Account?

Each MSN account is an individual account, just for you. And, one account equals one member ID. You can set up additional accounts on your computer for other family members, but each will be billed separately. To use two or more accounts and use both from the same PC, all you need to do is type the appropriate member ID and password for the account you want to use.

So how do you get another member ID? You need to run sign-up again to create a new and separate account. Don't forget that each account will show up on your credit card bill. You can refer to your online statement to see which family member is generating each bill. Let's just hope you can track those accounts on your family budget—or in Microsoft Money. The more account holders, the more memberships, and the more fees MSN can generate.

How Do I Keep My Kids from Getting into Areas with Adult Content?

No one has access to the adult content areas, such as the Sexuality Forum (GO TO sexy), until they apply for and receive a token. The application asks you to verify that you are over 18 years of age. Once the token has been granted, it is good for all adult/restrictedcontent on MSN. If you let your child use your MSN account—or if you leave your password around—Johnny or Susie will be able to access the restricted content.

Please note that each MSN account holder is supposed to be 18 years of age or older.

Anyone with an MSN account can request a token for adult content. There's no requirement to prove one's age. You merely have to check a box that says you are over 18. From what I remember of my teenage years, I think there's a significant number of minors who have the ability to check that box.

America Online (AOL) has established a system that allows parents to control a family membership. With AOL's parental controls, the master account holder can control or limit the access of the other family members' accounts. America Online has put the controls in the hands of the family. Since Mom or Dad allows or restricts the access, she or he must take the blame if Johnny or Susie ventures somewhere beyond the family's morals. It seems to me that Microsoft's rule that each member is supposed to be 18 is merely designed to relieve them of responsibility and provide comfort to their lawyers. It does not provide a tool for parents to use in guiding their children. Certainly with Microsoft's programming prowess, it could have developed a more appropriate solution.

I am especially concerned because the list of content providers includes several with programming oriented toward young children. MSN is a family-oriented service, and it is unrealistic to expect parents to watch every step their children make online. I have a three-year-old and I know that it is impossible to watch her every single second, even though we often sit at computers in the same room. Software-based parental controls are a better solution.

I am hopeful that MSN will come forth with a system of parental controls in the near future. No system of parental controls will be 100-percent safe, and all require attentive parents. But good software tools can help us do our parenting jobs, too.

For now, parents, you have two options. First, check your child's online MSN access as often as you can. Weekly is not unreasonable. Second, send an e-mail to **Russell_Siegelman@msn.com** to express your concern regarding the need for better control of minors' access on MSN. And, if you find objectionable material in an area that is not labeled as an adult area, include that information in an e-mail to Mr. Siegelman, with a copy to the forum's manager.

> *Anyone with an MSN account can ask for a token for adult content. There's no requirement to prove one's age. You merely have to check a box that says you are over 18.*

How Do I Get My Member Information in MSN's Address Book?

When you first signed on to The Microsoft Network, you answered a few questions that formed the basis of your listing in MSN's Address Book. Your membership information comprises three tabbed pages: General, Personal, and Professional. The first page, General, was completed when you signed on to MSN the first time. You may wish to add or delete information from your profile. MSN allows you to minimize the content of your profile by deleting all information except the member ID. Every member ID is included in the directory. You can run, but you can't hide.

To open the Address Book for your own profile, follow these directions:

- Go to MSN Central.
- Click E-Mail.
- On the Tools menu, click Address Book.
- Select Show Names from the Microsoft Network.
- On the Tools Menu, click Find (or the magnifying glass icon).
- Type in your member ID.
- Double-click to select your name.
- Change or delete any information except member ID.

How Can I Change My Access Number?

From the Sign In screen, do the following:

- Click Settings.
- Click Access Numbers.
- Click Change Number for Primary Number.
- Select Country.
- Select State/Region.
- In Access Numbers box, select the number.
- Click OK until you return to Sign In.

You can also use this method to change the backup number.

MSN regularly updates the access numbers, so you should check on a regular basis to make sure you are using the most cost-effective access number for your location, modem (baud rate), and the number from which you are calling.

What Is a Guidebook?

MSN Guidebooks (GO TO: MSNguidebooks) provide shortcuts to information on a variety of subjects. They provide editorial content about MSN and its online features and can be thought of as a help file to be viewed online or downloaded. In Member Assistance (GO TO ussupport) you'll find Guidebooks under the Maps and Information icon.

What Is a Title?

Simply put, a title is a screen. Microsoft has added this Hollywood-type language, calling each screen, like MSN Today, a title. The rest of us peons call them screens. After all, it's what you see on your screen. I suppose you could also call them windows.

Can I Omit the Screen for MSN Today?

Omitting the screen for MSN Today is like throwing out the front page of *USA Today!* Why wouldn't you want all that color and excitement? OK, all that color and excitement takes a few minutes to download to your PC and it delays your rapid movement to other forums. At the MSN Central screen, you can select View and then Options to omit the MSN Today screen. There you'll find a box indicating Show MSN Today Title on Startup. Omit the checkmark and MSN Today will not appear on sign-in.

What Is a GO Word?

A GO Word is a direct link to a service. When you memorize and use GO Words, you can speed your navigation through MSN. You'll no longer have to navigate from MSN Central through the various levels. If you've ever used another online service, you'll recognize that MSN's GO Words parallel America Online's Keywords or CompuServe's GO Words.

In each forum, you can obtain the GO Word by checking the "Properties" listing under the File menu. The Find feature does not list GO Words. If you'd like to keep a list of GO Words, you should keep a WordPad document open to store a list of GO Words. Alternatively, you can move a shortcut to your desktop for easy access or add the site to your Favorite Places list.

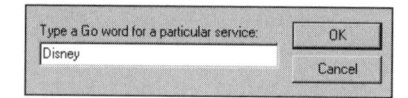

If you are good at memorizing trivia, start with the GO Words. If you'd rather tuck away icons for quick reference, you'll want to take advantage of Favorite Places.

Where Do I Get a Current List of GO Words?

When I last checked, a list of GO Words was not being maintained by the service. You can use the Find command to locate areas by name, similar to an index function, or you can look at the Properties for each forum to find the GO Word. I am confident, though, that a crafty and innovative MSN user will shortly compile and maintain a list of GO Words, and the first place I'd look for that list would be in the Member Assistance area.

In addition to the method described in the previous question, you can also determine a forum's GO Word before entering that forum. Simply right click the forum's icon, and then left click on Properties to bring up the Properties sheet. The GO Word is indicated on the Properties sheet. You must make note of this GO Word. It can't be used automatically by (intuitively) clicking it. You can use your right mouse button again to select the MSN icon on the status bar. From there, select GO TO and type the GO Word you see on the Properties sheet.

Like many MSN functions, there is yet another method for using GO Words. Click on the Edit menu, select Go To, and then click Other Location. At this point type the GO Word for your intended destination.

For a list of GO Words, use the Find function. Type **Go Word Directory** in the "containing" box. It will appear on the list below. Select Go Word Directory and you will be transported to a BBS where you can download the list in alphabetical or category order. At this writing, the Go Word Directory is neither extensive nor comprehensive, but I am hopeful that it will be improved over time.

What Is the Find Function for?

The Find function creates an index based on the word or words you specify. You can use the Find function to discover new areas on MSN or to speed your way to specific forums. Find only locates the exact word you type in. To find variations of the word, you'll need to use wildcard characters. For example, you'll need to use **craft*** to find all variations including craft, crafters, and crafting. You can also use the Boolean terms "and" and "or" in search strings. Perhaps you'd like to try **Windows and 95**.

From Find, you can double-click on the found items to launch them. This will carry you straight to the designated forum, folder, or file. From Find, when in doubt, use Open Containing Folder (from the file menu). I was looking for news services and when I tried to look up Reuters, I was charged $.10 because the only reference that came up was one of Hoover's detailed financial reviews. If I had used Open Containing Folder, I would have known better. I would have seen that *that* Reuters reference took me to Hoover's database.

Is There a Global File Search on MSN?

MSN 2.0 will feature a unified MSN and Internet Find function. From one source, you will be able to find/retrieve services, titles, web pages. Future search functions will include W*hat's Popular on MSN* and *What's Popular with My Peers*.

What's the Big Deal About Rich Text?

Rich text allows you to communicate with a more precise message. Just as a magazine cover grabs your attention with various fonts and colors, you can express or delineate your words with color and fonts—and add charts and pictures. If your message is sent to someone who doesn't use Windows 95, they will receive a plain text version of your e-mail. Which of the messages below would you rather read?

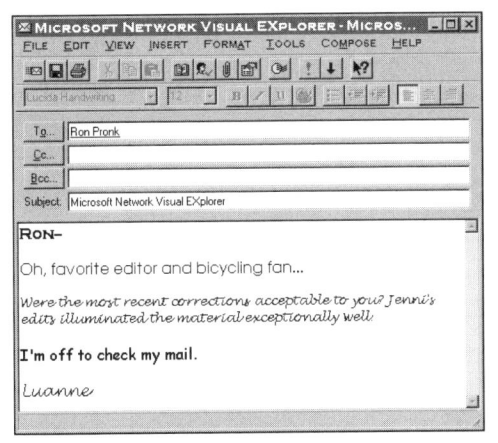

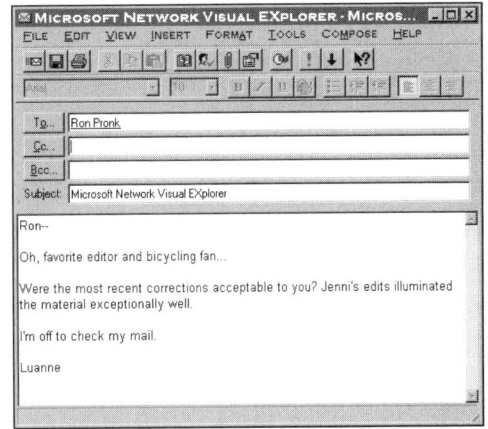

What Is Shareware?

Shareware is software that you can *try before you buy*. You'll find shareware in dozens of forums on MSN, but the most prominent is the Shareware Forum (GO TO shareware). The forum or MSN may charge a download fee, but you only owe money to the software's author if you decide to keep the program. Many of the files you will find in the download libraries include shareware.

The libraries also include macros for popular software, GIF (image) files, utilities, financial programs, children's software, and hundreds of other categories.

Try before you buy is the definitive premise of shareware. Distributed on an honor system, shareware is provided for evaluation for a defined period of time before purchase. Generally, the shareware package is complete, but more often users are given incentives (other than their integrity) for registering. Payment of the registration fee may entitle the user to upgrades and future editions, notices of "fixes," and even enhanced versions. Shareware is distributed with disclaimers and conditions that users must adhere to, and I encourage you to promptly pay the authors and developers so they can continue to provide valuable and useful software at a reasonable cost.

You'll also find commercial demo files among the download libraries. Commercial demos may be disabled in some way—perhaps allowing only 10 records in a database, or making it not printable—but you'll still be able to interact with the program to determine if it possesses the attributes you require. A number of shareware files are also called demos by their authors.

What's the Best Way to Navigate on MSN?

From MSN Central: From the View menu, click Toolbar. A checkmark will appear. Now, when you navigate, a yellow box with an up arrow will appear on each window's toolbar. Clicking this will take you up one level.

If the toolbar doesn't stay that way, go to My Computer, select the View menu, and put a check on the toolbar.

From the File menu: Choose Up One Level.

From most screens: Use the backspace key. It will take you up one level to the prior level. This won't work if you are reading a message-board posting. In that case, the backspace key has an editing purpose.

Use the Explorer mode: From the desktop, right click on the MSN icon and select Explore. In the left windowpane, double-click any icon (or shift-click the plus sign) to expand the navigation tree. In the left pane, you can single click any icon to open that folder. In the right pane, double-click any icon to open any folder, file, or chat.

From the MSN icon: After opening any instance of MSN, you can open others by double-clicking on the MSN icon on the desktop. Then manage multiple screens.

From the Edit menu: Each Edit menu has a Go To Other Location that lets you use a GO Word. Right clicking on the MSN icon on the taskbar gets you the same

GO TO option. You can also open second (and third, and so on) windows with the GO TO option.

From My Computer: Open My Computer on your desktop; select the View menu, followed by Options and then the Folder tab. Check the radio button that says "Browse Folders Using Separate Windows for Each Folder." This lets you leave windows open as you navigate.

The best thing about these navigational tools is that you can use one, some, or all. Each one will aid your navigation on MSN, and together they will make you the speed demon of the network.

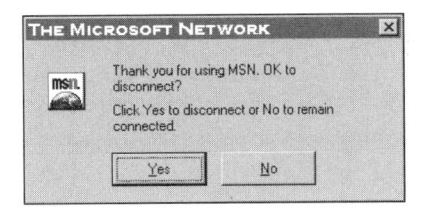

Somehow I Clicked Through All My Screens and I'm Left Looking at My Desktop. How Do I Navigate Now?

You may have already found out that if you don't navigate the Microsoft way, you may suddenly find yourself looking at the desktop with a message asking if you want to sign off MSN.

That's so frustrating! If you're like me, you want to get back on, but you're still a bit confused. At this point, click No, then right click on the MSN icon on the status bar. With another click you can return to the MSN Central window.

That's the simplest way to get back to where you were going. As you become more comfortable, you will find one of the navigation tips in the prior question to be perfect for your online style. You may prefer shortcuts or Favorite Places. It's your choice. Once you know your options, you can design your own paths to your favorite areas and forums.

It Seems So Tedious to Have to Use the Pull-down Menus. Any Other Ideas?

Of course, there are GO Words, but they require memorization. Some, like, GO TO Internet, are easy to remember, while others are a bit more cumbersome. Just as in

Windows 95, there are a number of shortcuts to help you. The underlined letters in menus can help: Press ALT + the underlined letter to speed you on your way. That seems to work most of the time.

SHORTCUT TO THE INTERNET CENTER.MCC

What's a Shortcut?

Shortcuts are OLE links to services that you can use to jump immediately to specific areas within MSN. You'll frequently find shortcuts while reading the message boards. If you double-click on a shortcut, you will be transported directly to the appropriate area. If you are not logged on to the system, MSN will be launched, and you will be prompted for your password. You can create your own shortcuts—and customize your environment—by incorporating the shortcuts for any folder, forum, bulletin board, or file library.

The most used shortcuts can be added to your MSN Favorite Places folder or placed anywhere on the desktop. Because shortcuts are OLE objects, they can be moved around as easily as files. For example, if you find interesting information in a particular location, you can share the "find" with friends by sending a shortcut by e-mail or by posting the shortcut on a bulletin board.

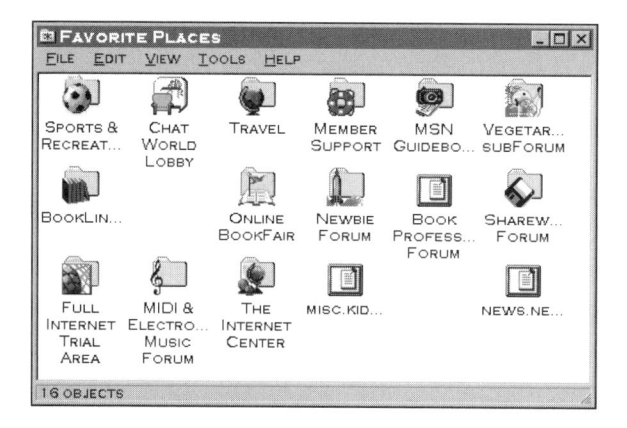

How Do I Add to Favorite Places?

My Favorite Places online include sites from travel, health, computing, and MSN's Member Support area. When you find a site that you would like to add to your collection of Favorite Places, there are two ways to proceed. (1) If you are in the forum, use the File menu and select Add to Favorite Places. (2) If you have not yet entered the forum—and can see the forum's icon—select the icon to highlight it; then, from the File menu, choose Add to Favorite Places.

You have easy access to your Favorite Places—at all times—with a right click on the MSN icon on the status bar in the lower right corner of your screen.

How Many Things Can I Do at Once on MSN?

You can drink a cup of coffee, eat a donut, and even watch TV.

I think what you are really asking about is multitasking, right? Windows 95 provides multithreaded multitasking capabilities, and MSN takes advantage of that feature. While a file is being downloaded, you can still browse around, read e-mail, participate in a chat room, or do anything else online. Just start the download and continue checking your favorite message boards and chat rooms. You may find some delays as your download continues in the background, but it's better than just staring at a status bar to see if it is filling up.

One other multitasking fact: While you are downloading in the background and viewing a BBS on your screen, the MSN client software may be updating automatically by downloading new software components in the background.

What Is an ICP?

An ICP is an Independent Content Provider. The Microsoft Network has contracted with providers who develop and present two types of services. The basic services are really provided by MSN, but they may be contracted services under the MSN label. ICPs can more often be thought of as commercial providers. Generally, their services are in extended areas and they may be known as name brand forums. Two examples that fall into the ICP category are Eddie Bauer and NBC.

What Is an EForm?

Just like the "e" in "e-mail," the "E" in "EForm" refers to an online, electronic form. You will encounter EForms throughout MSN, and they are frequently used to request permission for entrance into a forum. If you request the token to access the adult content on MSN, you will make your request through a standardized EForm. Another EForm is the MSN Suggestion Box EForm at GO TO English_help.

How Do I Find Help?

Wherever you see a Help menu on the menu bar, you can access terrific help documents from MSN. The Help files provide details on MSN from A to Z. If you need more information on accessing newsgroups, replying to messages, Internet access, or hundreds of other tips, make friends with the Help files.

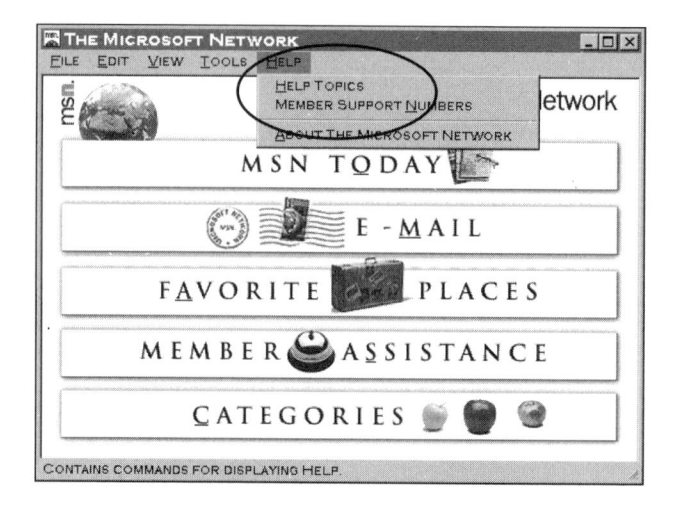

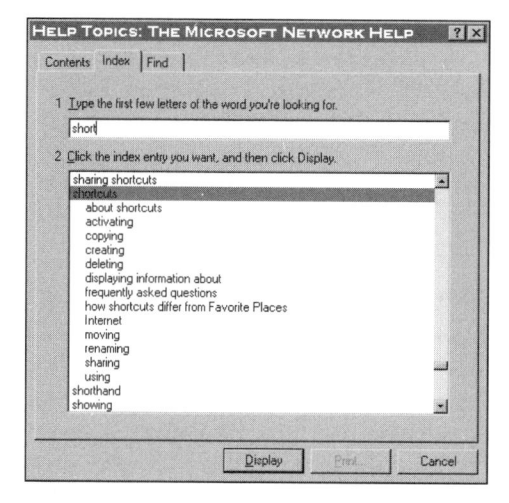

In the above example, you can see how the Help File's index function speeds your search and directs you straight to the information you need.

Is It Safe to Use Credit Cards to Make Online Purchases?

I think it's easy to say that it is as safe as using your telephone to purchase a red mesh knit polo shirt from Lands' End. When you use the phone, you need to make sure that you are using a hard-wired phone and a not a portable or cellular phone. That way, without a wire-tap, no one can hear your credit card number.

Similar safety measures have been developed for online commerce. While MSN will transfer your order to the online retailer, the data is encrypted with public and private keys to ensure security to the financial transaction. Planned security enhancements will soon improve the security beyond the name-brand catalog level with which you are familiar.

Can I Find Out If a Friend Is Online When I Am?

This feature, available on other online services, is not available on MSN. If this is a feature that is important to you, go ahead and request it. In the meantime, you will have to rely on e-mail or make new friends in the chat rooms.

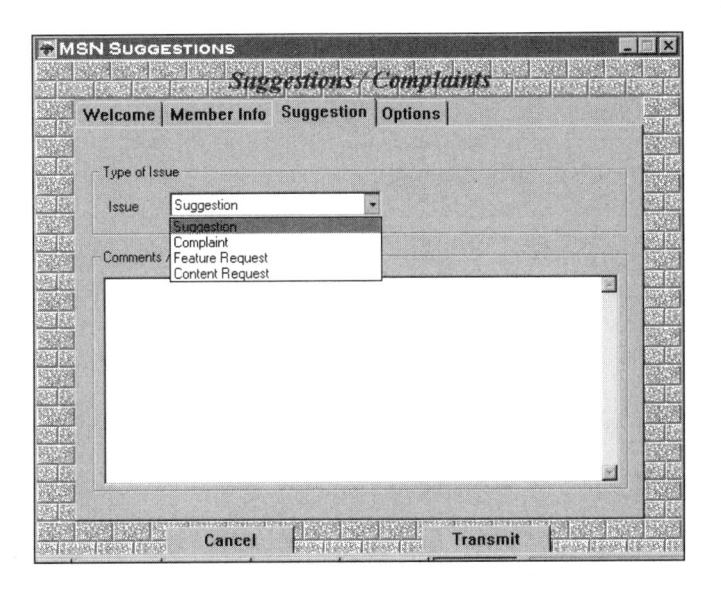

Where Do I File Complaints or Suggestions?

In the Member Lobby, you'll find the MSN Suggestion Box, where you can submit comments, complaints, and kudos. The Member Lobby is located behind the Member Assistance area. You can get there from MSN Central or use GO TO English_help.

How Do I Reach the Execs at The Microsoft Network?

Russell Siegelman is the general manager of The Microsoft Network, and you can send e-mail to him at the following address:

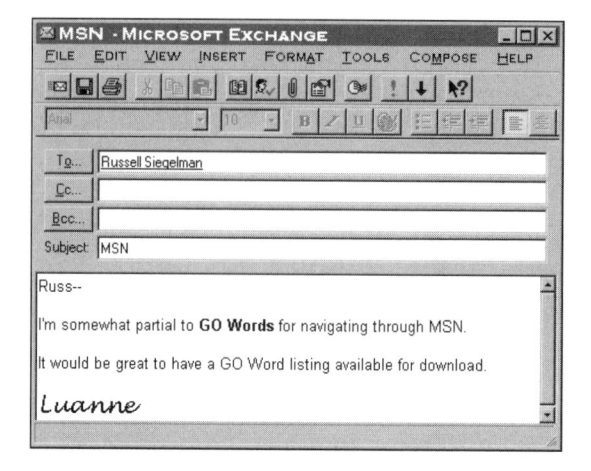

```
┌─ MSN - MICROSOFT EXCHANGE ──────── _ □ × ┐
│ FILE  EDIT  VIEW  INSERT  FORMAT  TOOLS  COMPOSE  HELP │
│ [toolbar icons]                                        │
│ [formatting toolbar]                                   │
│ To...   │ Russell Siegelman                          │ │
│ Cc...   │                                            │ │
│ Bcc...  │                                            │ │
│ Subject:│ MSN                                        │ │
│ ┌────────────────────────────────────────────────┐  │
│ │ Russ--                                         │  │
│ │ I'm somewhat partial to GO Words for navigating through MSN. │
│ │ It would be great to have a GO Word listing available for download. │
│ │ Luanne                                         │  │
│ └────────────────────────────────────────────────┘  │
└──────────────────────────────────────────────────────┘
```

Russell_Siegelman@MSN.com

It's his job to make MSN the best it can be, and it's your job to let him know what works and what doesn't.

Do you frequently encounter busy signals at your local access number? Do you think you've found a bug in the software? Do you have an idea for an enhancement in the next update? These are all reasons to send e-mail to Mr. Siegelman.

If MSN Isn't Working Right and I'm Wasting Time in Paid Areas, Who Do I Contact for a Credit?

Just file a complaint along with a request for a time credit in the MSN Suggestion Box in the MSN Lobby. If you don't get a reply, send an e-mail message to Russell Siegelman at the address in the question above.

My Best Friend Has a Mac—Can She Get on MSN?

At the launch, access for traditional Macs was not available. PowerMac owners with Insignia's SoftWindows 2.0 will have the first Macintosh look at MSN once Windows 95 is installed. (Insignia has said that SoftWindows 2.0 will run Windows 95, although somewhat slowly. However, the beta version of SoftWindows 2.0 that I tested did not include Windows 95 access.) Direct Macintosh access is planned for the second half of 1996. Until that time, Mac Internet users will be able to access only MSN's Web site (http://www.msn.com). For a real look at MSN, your friend may have to share your PC . . . if you are willing to give it up for hours at time.

Where in the World Is MSN Available?

Access is available just about any place you'd like to travel or live. MSN access is available and local dial-up access is running in 52 countries. The MSN application has been adapted for 26 languages including English, German, French, Spanish, Swedish, Dutch, Italian, Norwegian, Danish, Finnish, Portuguese, Japanese, Chinese, Korean, Russian, Czech, Polish, Hungarian, Turkish, Greek, Arabic, Basque, Hebrew, Thai, Indonesian, and Catalan—and selected dialects. International users will find membership plans priced in 18 currencies. While the basic service is available around the world, Internet Web access, pricing, and the plans available vary by country.

Most countries have access to a local language tree. In many parts of the world, multiple languages are spoken. With MSN, users can switch among branches of the tree. The U.S. language tree includes French and German choices. This seems like a great way to practice those rusty language skills for those of us who are less than fluently bilingual.

To view the language tree available in your home country, select the View menu, followed by Options. Choose the General tab and look at Content View. The choices on my screen include: English (United States), French (Standard), and German (Standard).

Do I See the Same MSN Screens as Those Seen in Germany?

Not necessarily. MSN has been designed as a global communications service. Just minutes apart I took the screen shots of the US and Australian MSN Today screens and was surprised to see how differenct they were. To conduct your own investigation, use the Find function to seek MSN Today.

Electronic Mail

What Do I Need to Know About E-mail?

You can write e-mail online or offline, and you can correspond with other MSN members or over the Internet. You can simply send messages in plain text or enhanced with rich text. Your e-mail messages can be sent with or without attachments or shortcuts. Attachments are always represented as icons in messages. It is easiest to send e-mail when you are online, but the extra steps involved in offline mail preparation can reduce your online costs and keep your phone line open when you're waiting for calls.

How Do I Send Internet E-mail? Is It Different from Sending MSN Mail?

Internet mail addresses are necessarily longer and more detailed than MSN mail addresses. To send mail to a correspondent within MSN, you only need their member ID.

In your company, you only need simple addresses, but correspondence to another company requires a longer, and more detailed, address.

Further on in this section you'll find sample addresses for sending mail to other services and to Internet addresses.

In either case, the address must be precisely correct. Your small town postmaster may be able to deliver to the Smiths on Elm Street, but these darn computers expect you to be a good deal more precise in addressing e-mail.

You may have difficulty sending e-mail if the address has not been entered in your Personal Address Book. You can get around this by typing the following, including the brackets, in one of the address fields (to, cc, or bcc):

```
[MSNINET:user@domain]
```

Note that "user" and "domain" in the above example are italic, indicating they are variables.

How Do Friends Send Mail to Me?

My username is LuanneO, and depending on the service my friends use, they address mail to me as follows:

```
America Online    LuanneO@MSN.com
CompuServe        INTERNET:LuanneO@MSN.com
e-world           LuanneO@MSN.com
Internet          LuanneO@MSN.com
MSN               LuanneO
Prodigy           LuanneO@MSN.com
```

How Do I Send Mail to Friends?

Depending on the service my friend uses, I would address mail to him or her as follows:

```
America Online    friendname@aol.com
CompuServe        12345.6789@compuserve.com
e-world           friendname@eworld.com
Internet          friendname@domain
MSN               friendname
Prodigy           ABC123A@prodigy.com
```

Note that CompuServe and Prodigy use some combination of numbers or letters and numbers, respectively, instead of a name in their addresses.

How Long Does It Take for Internet Mail to Reach Other Services?

Generally, it only takes a few minutes for your Internet mail to reach its destination, but your letter to your old flame may get delayed at a few points. It is possible, but not likely, that there will be a delay leaving MSN. Mail is more likely to be delayed entering an online service, rather than leaving for its destination. If your mail is going to another online service, there may be at delay due to the volume on their servers.

But, trust me on this one, as long as it is addressed properly, it will always beat the U. S. Postal Service.

How Do I cc Myself on Internet Mail?

Try this:

yourscreenname%MSN.com@cunyvm.cuny.edu

Your mail will head to that server and bounce back so that you can verify that your e-mail message left MSN on its journey over the Internet.

What's the Simplest Way to Include a File with My E-mail?

Oh good, a simple question! You can drag a file's icon into a document or even drag a shortcut icon into a document or e-mail message. How's that for easy? The best way to be safe and sure is to use the paper clip icon or select the Insert pull-down menu. There are few limits to the files or attachments you can send with your MSN mail, but you may encounter restrictions in sending attachments to members of other online services.

Can I Send Attachments with Internet Mail?

UUENCODED Internet mail attachments can be delivered to your MSN mailbox. Any Internet mail with UUENCODED attachments will be converted to a standard MSN attachment for delivery to your mailbox. Likewise, outbound attachments will be UUENCODED for transmission.

From the e-mail composition window, use the Insert menu and select Object or File.

UUENCODING is an Internet standard process for transferring files over the Internet. You can send and receive Internet mail with attachments if the attachments have been UUENCODED. Your correspondents on other commercial online services may not be able receive or read your messages if their mail system does not support UUENCODED attachments.

Can I Put Shortcuts in My E-mail Messages?

You sure can. The shortcuts are represented by icons and can be transmitted in your e-mail. When your correspondent receives the mail, if equipped with Windows 95, he or she can click on the icon to go straight to the represented area on MSN.

Alternatively, you can include an icon representing a document, and the document will travel as an attachment with your mail. Generally, both of these features can be used only when both the sender and recipient have Windows 95 and are MSN members. It is possible that you can send a UUENCODED attachment to someone who has a non-MSN Internet account and Windows 95.

Can I Put Icons in My Word Processed Documents?

Just as in e-mail, you can put icons in your word processed documents, such as those created with MS-Word. Just think, your e-mail could include an icon indicating an attachment and then your attached document could include a shortcut for a favorite area on MSN. What you can do with icons and shortcuts is interchangeable.

Both the sender and recipient must have Windows 95.

Can I Send a Message from My Word Processor?

I tried this in Microsoft Word. First I wrote a document, and then I selected Send from the File menu. Microsoft Exchange opened and an e-mail form appeared on the screen. The Word document became an attachment within the message portion of the e-mail screen. From there, I addressed the e-mail message and sent it on its merry way.

What Can Friends Do When They Receive the Messages with the Icons?

The icons, shortcuts, and attachments are such a novelty that I suspect there will be great hordes of e-mail writers sending mail to each other just to include icons. Perhaps you've discovered a great message board (BBS) on frogs and lizards and you don't want your friends to get lost on the way to the site. By sending them the icon in the form of a shortcut, you can be almost assured that they'll join you. I say "almost" because they may not share your interest in frogs and lizards.

Can I Send E-mail Containing an Icon to Someone Who Doesn't Have Windows 95?

Go ahead and send it, but there's a good chance the icon will disappear and your friend will receive garbled text where the icon was. The text of your mail should be fine, but you may need to explain why the icon didn't make it.

The last time I tested this, I sent messages from my MSN account to my AOL account. The mail with the Internet shortcut (URL) transferred without a glitch. The same for the attached MS-Word file. I guess I was pushing the envelope when I tried to send a Microsoft Network shortcut to my PowerMac running AOL. That one didn't work.

Help! How Do I Make Sense Out of the Mail in My Inbox?

You can view your mail in the order it arrives (default mode), or you can organize it by subject, the name of the sender, date, or size of file. In the example, the mail has been sorted according to the name of the sender.

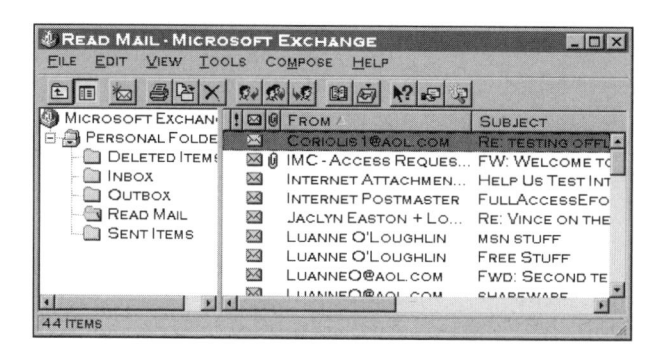

If you view the inbox by subject, you will create a conversation thread that keeps all related conversations together. All food messages will appear together if labeled as "Food," followed by all health messages if they are so labeled, and so on.

With the other options, your e-mail can be sorted according to the "From" field to quickly locate and track all mail from each of your correspondents. Messages from Andrew, Beth, Charlie, Diana, Edward, and Zoe will appear in alphabetical order in your inbox.

Given these examples, I trust you are wise and worldly enough to figure out to sort your mail according to file size or date.

Does MSN Have Any Tools to Help Organize My E-mail?

Microsoft Exchange allows you to customize folders for saving your mail. You can save both inbound and outbound mail. In addition, you can view your incoming mail list by author (the writer of the mail) or subject so that similar topics are listed together.

Can I Send the Same Message via E-mail and Fax?

With MSN and Microsoft Exchange, you can send the same message to different types of recipients. You can send a message simultaneously to Microsoft Mail, CompuServe, America Online, Internet, and fax users as long as Exchange contains profiles for the users at those destinations.

How Do I Keep Backup Copies of My Correspondence?

There are lots of reasons to keep copies of correspondence. The most common is to have a copy of what you actually sent and when you sent it in case an office controversy develops. These things happen.

You can print copies of the mail, instruct Exchange to save all copies of correspondence that you have sent, save a copy just before you send it, or send a blind copy to yourself.

I think you'll agree that having Exchange save a copy automatically or sending yourself a blind courtesy copy (bcc) are the best solutions.

Why Do Some of the Messages in My Mailbox Have Exclamation Points?

The exclamation point means that the message importance set by the sender is high. A blue down arrow means the sender has denoted it as low importance, and no sign means normal importance. Of course, every message to my editor, Ron, is accompanied by an exclamation point.

What Does the Envelope Icon Mean?

The envelope is the symbol for a mail message. The circle with the arrow is the symbol for a receipt or a message from the system administrator.

Can I Compose Mail Offline?

Just follow these directions to compose mail offline:

- Open Exchange from the Start menu or by selecting the Inbox icon from the desktop.
- On the Tools menu, click Options.
- Click the Addressing tab.
- In the box labeled Show This Address Book First, select Personal Address Book.
- Look for the box labeled When Sending Items Check Names Against the Following Address Books in the Order Listed Below; make sure the Personal Address Book is first.
- Click Apply or OK.
- On the Tools menu, click the Services tab.
- Click The Microsoft Network Online Service.
- Click Properties, then Address Book.
- Make sure the box labeled Connect to MSN to Check Names is not selected.
- Click OK twice.
- Compose your message and use the addresses from your Personal Address Book.
- Select Send.
- Select Deliver Now from Tools when all messages are ready to be transferred.

You must add the e-mail address of recipient in your Personal Address Book prior to sending the mail.

Can I Access and Read Mail Offline?

Absolutely, thanks to Microsoft Exchange, which comes as part of Windows 95. Open Exchange, and select Deliver Now. You will be prompted for a password and Exchange will sign on. "Exchange" your mail, and then close the connection. In order for Exchange to open and close the connection for you, make sure that you have completed the following instructions:

- From the Tools Menu, select Services.
- In the box on the right, highlight The Microsoft Network Online Service.
- Double-click Properties.
- Select the tab for Transport.
- Check the following boxes:

  - `Download Mail When E-mail Starts up from MSN`
  - `Transferring Mail from Remote Mail`

How Can I Avoid Junk Mail?

In this case, junk mail counts against the clock and you pay to receive it—unless you know a trick. Rather than start MSN from the desktop icon, do the following:

- Open your inbox from the desktop.
- Select Tools, Remote Mail.
- Select Tools, Update Headers.

This establishes your connection to MSN and shows what mail is sitting in your box. At this point, you can select to transfer or delete mail. This saves online time and helps keep your monthly bill to a minimum.

After seeing what is in your mailbox, you can select the MSN icon from the desktop and MSN will load.

Following the instructions in the prior question, make sure your Transport tab has the following checked: Disconnect After Updating Headers from Remote Mail. This will further save online time.

How Do I Know If I Have Mail Waiting When I Sign On?

When you sign on, you are notified if you have mail waiting. Unfortunately, you are not notified of mail that arrives during your online session. It's a good idea to check for mail again before you sign off. I want all of my e-mail as soon as it arrives—don't you?

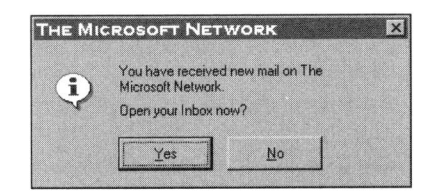

Can I Permanently Save My E-mail?

Usually, when you read your MSN mail, it is moved from MSN to your computer's hard drive, where it remains until you delete it. A friend of mine, who would appreciate remaining nameless, just realized that her husband could read all of our correspondence since it was saved on her hard drive. If he read it, he probably learned a bit more about their marriage. Ahem . . . excuse me!

Can I Check on the Status of Mail That I've Sent?

If you cc (carbon copy) yourself on a piece of mail, you will know if it was sent correctly through the server. You should get an error notice when mail has not been addressed correctly, but depending on the volume and destination, it may take 24 hours to get the error message back.

How Do I Know If My Boss Got the Mail I Sent?

When you are composing the mail, select Properties from the File menu. Depending on your preference, make sure you check the box labeled Delivery Receipt or Read Receipt. When your boss receives the mail (or reads the mail), a message notifying you will be automatically generated. Delivery receipts are not available on mail sent beyond The Microsoft Network.

How Do I Locate Members from Other Countries?

Do the following:

- Open Microsoft Exchange.
- On the Tools menu, click to select the Address Book.
- In the Show Names From The box, select Microsoft Network.
- On the Tools menu, click Find.
- In the Country box, select the name of the country you want.
- Click OK.

I had great fun looking up MSN member lists from Bermuda, Saudi Arabia, and Vatican City, but I didn't find any friends in those locations. As soon as I send them e-mail, they'll be my friends, right?

What Do I Do When I Have a Mail Problem?

When I have a mail problem, as opposed to a male problem, I first look for a solution in the Member Assistance area. When you have the same kind of problem, select Member Assistance from the MSN Central screen. Your next selection will be the Member-to-Member BBS (GO TO ussupport). First check for a similar problem and a solution to it. If you don't find one, add a message with your problem. Then check back a few hours later to see if you have received a response.

If this doesn't work for you, send a message to **Postmaster@MSN.com** and describe the problem you are encountering. Of course, this won't help if you can't send outbound mail. In that case, you should call MSN's Customer Service.

To find the MSN Customer Service phone number to use in your location, check the Help menu and select Member Support Numbers. You'll find phone numbers for MSN support worldwide.

Forums, Bulletin Boards, File Libraries, and Chats

What Is a Forum?

We've come a long way since ancient Rome. You won't find imposing marble structures that have survived centuries on MSN, but like the original forums, you will find the forums on MSN to be gathering places. Within forums you will find bulletin boards (also known as BBS or message boards), download libraries, electronic mail, chat rooms, viewable files (not downloadable), electronic forms, Internet access (e-mail and newsgroups), and shortcuts.

What Is a BBS?

On MSN, "BBS" is used somewhat interchangeably with "message boards." Both are found within forums. The term "BBS" comes from Bulletin Board Systems. Commercial systems such as The Microsoft Network are much larger than BBSs in the traditional sense. For the last decade or so BBSs have generally been smaller communication systems targeted to specific areas of interest such as computer user groups, science fiction clubs, and community activities—to name just three.

What Is a Kiosk?

According to the dictionary it is a freestanding outdoor structure, such as a newsstand or a bandstand. So, how does that pertain to MSN? In the forums of MSN, you'll find out that kiosks are the announcement areas. From the kiosk, you'll learn about forum policies, who the manager is, how to contact the manager, and the news of upcoming events.

What Happens to the Messages I Post?

For efficiency, your messages are first sent to several servers before they are available for reading on the boards. There may be a delay of seconds, or, rarely, minutes, depending on the volume of activity on The Microsoft Network. You'll see your message the next time you enter the forum.

Who Can Delete My Messages?

Your messages can be deleted by forum managers if you fail to adhere to the membership agreement. You were required to review and agree to the agreement when you first signed on to The Microsoft Network. As with any online service, there are standards for decency and fairness that will be guarded by the forum managers and MSN. Criticism of a software package is not something that would get your message deleted. A similar message filled with unacceptable language will likely result in your message being removed from view.

I Can't Find a Message I Posted. Was It Deleted?

Your message may not have pertained to the topic at hand. Irrelevant postings may be moved by forum managers, and you may or may not be advised that your message has been moved.

Also, the message boards are updated each time you visit, so you will not see the same messages you saw on a prior visit. New messages appear in boldface type, and once you have read them, the type reverts to "normal." When I read through a message board, I generally pick and choose the messages I want to read based on the noted subject. When I am done, I select Mark All Conversations as Read from the Tools menu. That way, the next time I will only see new messages and conversations.

When you return to the forum, you may think I have deceived you, as a few messages will appear in normal type indicating that you have read them. When you delve into each message thread, you will find boldfaced—new—responses to the original query. Choose Expand All Conversations from the View menu for a clearer view.

Where in the Forum Can I Find the GO Word?

Prior to entering the forum, use your right mouse button to highlight the icon. Next, select Properties to see the GO Word.

If you are already in the forum, go to the File menu and select Properties. In either case, you will see the GO Word listed among the properties. Wouldn't it be nice if the GO Word was included in the forum's graphical layout?

XYZ Is My Favorite Forum . . . Sometimes the Chat Button Is Missing. What's Going on?

Like all forum managers, the manager in XYZ has the ability to easily change the screens/titles seen by you and all other MSN members. Some forum managers have elected to put up the chat button only when a moderated chat is scheduled. In those cases, when you find no button, no chat is currently scheduled.

Can I Save All the Text from an Online Session?

How about another yes-and-no answer? Are Chips Ahoy a good substitute for homemade oatmeal raisin cookies? Someone I know thinks so.

You can save text from chat sessions, but there's no handy way to save all of the messages from a message board.

As you are participating in a chat, you can save the content from the session. This is a particularly handy—and fun—feature to use if you are attending a chat session with famous people such as popular entertainers or writers, or even unpopular politicians.

To save a record of a chat, go to the File menu and select Save History. To preserve all formatting in the chat history, save the file as Rich Text Format (.rtf). To automatically save a record of a chat before you leave it, click the Tools menu, click Options, and make sure to check Save Chat History Before Clearing or Exiting.

Since there's no built-in system for recording the content of the message boards on MSN, you can always save pertinent messages and documents on your hard drive.

How Do I Know Who Is in a Forum or Chat Room?

There's no active list of who is in a forum, but whenever you are in a chat room, you will see a list of all participants on the right side your screen. If you click on any participant's name, you will then see his or her profile.

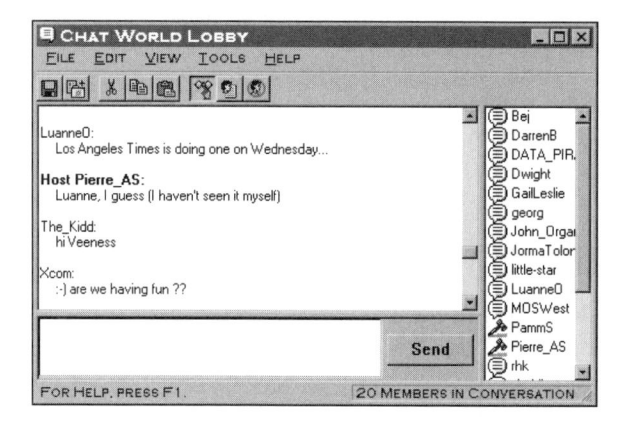

When I am in a chat room, I'm constantly checking profiles. Some members have very creative IDs. Since the Member Directory is so handy, I use it to see how they describe themselves in the directory.

To find out a bit more your fellow members in the chat room, slide your mouse over to the box on the right and double-click on each interesting name. Who knows—that guy named RoadSign just might be my friend from Alaska!

Can I Read the Message Boards Offline?

This handy, time-saving and money-saving feature is not available on MSN. We can hope that it is added in future releases, but your best bet is to keep an eye on the message boards and files in the Member Assistance area. Some innovative user is likely to develop a program to allow you to grab messages quickly for offline reading. It never hurts to ask!

Can I Write E-mail from within a Forum?

There is a tricky way to do this. From the Compose menu, select Reply by Email, just as if you were replying to the message on the BBS (message board). Then change the To: name and you can send your message anywhere you'd like. With the proper address, it can even be an Internet message.

Can I Have Two Forums Open at the Same Time?

With multitasking, you can have two forums open at the same time, but I'm not sure why you'd want to. MSN makes it easy to return to the last forum with a simple click. Generally, the last areas you were in can be minimized to the status bar at the bottom of the screen. Because MSN's pricing system can bill you for the time spent in a forum, this design prevents you from being billed for being in two forums at once. That's a relief!

The best reason to have two forums open at the same time is if you are downloading in one forum and reading message boards in another.

How Do I Start a Download?

When you're in a file library, you'll select from a number of files on a scrollbox. Double-click on the attached file's icon. You will be presented with some basic information on the file's contents. Once you review that information, select the radio button indicating Download File. The status bar will let you know how much time is remaining in your download. If you wish to sign off at the end of the download, go to the File menu and select Transfer and Disconnect. You can do this after the transfer has begun.

You can even continue to look around other forums after this point, but if you have selected Transfer and Disconnect, you will be logged off the system at the end of the file transfer.

Can I Download Files at the End of My Online Session?

Well, yes and no. The answer lies in your work habits. You can make the most efficient use of your online time by downloading at the end of your online session. Downloads start as soon as you make your selection; you may wish to select the option to Transfer and Disconnect so that you can walk away from your computer.

It is possible for you to continue reading message boards and participate in chat areas while downloading. You can even jump to another forum and downloading will continue in the background, albeit a bit slower. That's multitasking for you folks who like and appreciate the technical terms.

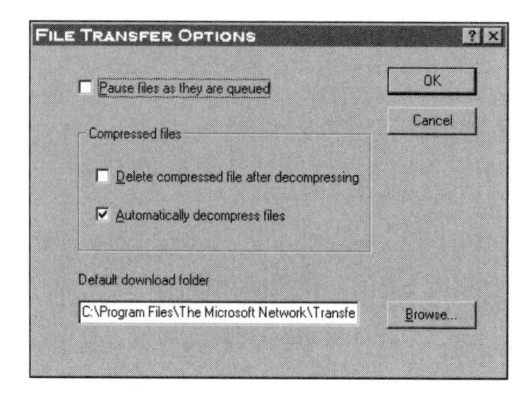

Multitasking makes it possible for you to have multiple activities running. You can start a download and continue reading message boards in the same forum or continue your activities in another area of MSN. You can even jump between forums selecting additional files for downloading.

I have been working on a 486 DX2-66, with 16 MB of RAM, and I make my online connections at 28.8. While multitasking may truly be operating, I am not impressed with the speed of the ongoing tasks.

It is possible to progressively jump from forum to forum, marking files for download, selecting pause after each selection. In effect you are chaining the files in a sequential download. Unfortunately, you can't save them all for one final download to start at the end of the session.

Generally, I think you will be most happy if you select downloads judiciously. If you visit only a single forum during a session, you show great restraint, and I could stand a lesson or two from you! If you plan on downloading files from a single forum—or the last forum you attend in a session—you can select, download and sign off all at the same time. This way you don't have to sit and wait for the download to finish.

File downloads start immediately upon selection, so be sure you are ready to be delayed in your activities.

Oh Where, Oh Where, Do My Files Go?

When you select a file to be retrieved, your PC will ask you to verify the destination. A default destination will appear, but you can change the destination to suit the organization of your files. I know I like to keep travel files in a folder designated for travel, rather than in the folder designated for sports.

To change the file transfer default folder while you are in a BBS, do the following:

- Click Tools.
- Select File Transfer Status.
- Click the Tools menu.
- Select Options.
- In the Default Download Folder box, type the path to the folder where you want to store files from this BBS.

How Do I Open Archived Files?

The Microsoft Network has the built-in capability to open most current archived formats upon delivery to your PC. Almost all files on MSN are .ZIP files. You can select for MSN to automatically unzip the file upon delivery. If you need another program to uncompress the files, the Properties sheet will advise you.

Will MSN Compress Files for Me?

File compression speeds the transmission of files, saving you online time and money. It also increases the transmission efficiency for the online systems, such as MSN, because it allows more files to be transferred at peak use periods.

If the file you are downloading was compressed, File Transfer Status detects this and automatically uncompresses it if the option named Automatically Decompress Files is checked in the File Transfer Options dialog box. To check this, select the Tools menu and then Options when File Transfer Status appears on your screen.

What Are GIFs, PICTs, JPEGs, and What Do I Do with Them?

GIFs, PICTs, and JPEGs are all formats for storing graphic images. You'll hear several pronunciations for these funny names, but thankfully, when we read and write them online, it doesn't matter how you pronounce them.

When you download one of these files, you'll need to make sure you have the right viewer on hand. All of the images that I've found online were readable by MSN's software. In the event that an image is not viewable through MSN, the file instructions will guide you to the best viewer for the image. There are viewers that can read some or all formats. If you don't have the requisite viewer, you will most likely find one in the same file library.

How Do I Listen to Sounds/Waves on MSN?

The Media Player found in Windows 95 is the perfect tool for playing the most popular multimedia files including CD audio, MIDI files, WAV files, and AVI video files. Media Player simplifies your online life, as it allows you to simply select and play. If you run across a multimedia file that requires something other than Media Player, you'll generally find directions to the appropriate tool in the same file library.

Is There Shareware That Will Help Me Make the Most of My Time on MSN?

Innovative MSN users will soon be developing tools for getting *more* out of their favorite online service. MSN Support, in the Member Assistance area (GO TO ussupport), will always be the first place to ask fellow users about these programs. I anticipate that we'll soon find tools to assist in writing e-mail, and counting and tracking online charges, as well as gizmos for storing, retrieving, and using GO Words.

The Shareware Libraries (GO TO shareware) is another top-notch place to check for tools.

Are There Any Printing Tips from MSN?

You probably won't want to use your dot-matrix printer to print a copy of a detailed Web page. Beyond that, it is hard to generalize because of the large number of printers out there. I'm working with a Postscript laser printer, and if there is a print option under the File menu, a good replica comes out of my printer.

Internet

Am I Charged for Internet Access?

Internet access is charged just like any other basic service on MSN. Depending on which subscription program you selected, your Internet time is calculated as part of your online time. Given the pricing plan options, you are charged from $2.00 to $2.50 per hour for time spent on MSN or on the Internet.

Is My Internet Access Restricted in Any Way?

From the launch of MSN, members in the United States have had full Internet access. The Web browser is available via download or with Microsoft Plus! from your computer software retailer. International users will gain full Internet access with future enhancements.

Once you have requested and been assigned the token for adult content, you will be able to proceed without restriction. This same token allows for access to the adult content on MSN as well as Usenet Newsgroups that have been identified as having adult content. If you let your children use your account, they will have the same access you do. Does that concern you?

How Do I Know If I Am Still in MSN or If I Have Jumped to an Internet Site?

MSN has been designed to make it so easy for you to navigate that you may not always know w*here* you are. To reach the Web sites, you'll have to activate your Web browser. The **http://** address line at the top of the screen—and the flying windows logo with the clouds—are the best indications you've left the electronic borders of MSN. If you are reading newsgroups, you'll generally find their icons in the same folders as other MSN bulletin boards. You'll find references to mailing lists on bulletin boards along with information on how to subscribe to them.

If not today, you will soon find that your electronic movement from MSN to the Internet is seamless. MSN has made it possible for Web page owners to buy an icon (hot link) on MSN, which transports users straight to their sites. Just think, you might see a McDonalds icon, and when you click on it, you are transported to McDonalds' (server) in Oakbrook, Illinois. In this hypothetical case, McDonalds' is not an ICP on MSN; they are an advertiser who has purchased an icon or billboard to attract your attention.

What Are Usenet Newsgroups?

Usenet Newsgroups are international message boards. There are thousands from which to choose. Some garner only a few messages each day, whereas others gather hundreds. Dozens of newsgroups are added each week. I find that reading five newsgroups a day is about all I can handle, because of the volume newsgroups generate.

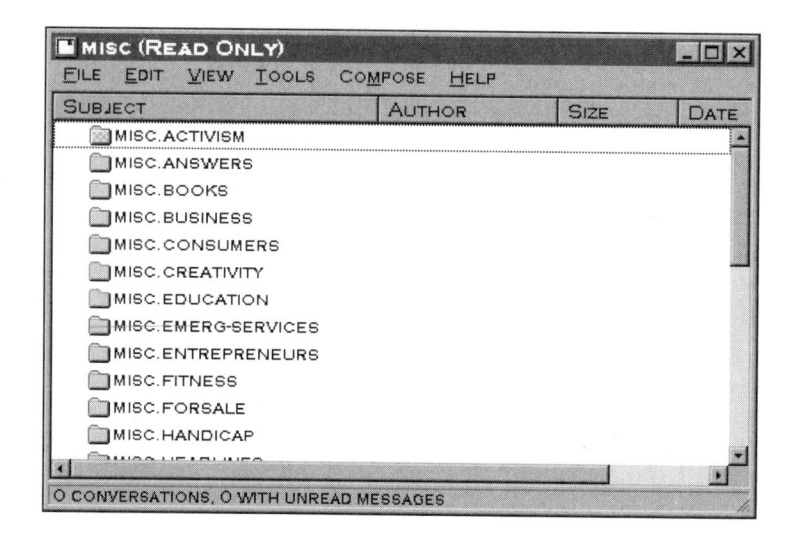

You'll also know you are reading newsgroups by their names. Most of the 12,000 newsgroups have names with the following classifications.

Classification	Description	Example
comp	Computer science and information on hardware and software systems	comp.os.ms-windows
misc	Groups with themes not easily classified under other headings	misc.kids
news	Groups associated the Usenet news network	news.groups, news.answers
rec	Groups oriented toward the arts, hobbies, and recreational activities	rec.crafts.winemaking
sci	Discussions marked by special and practical knowledge, relating to research or applications in established sciences	sci.space.science

What Is the World Wide Web?

It's been a long time since Alexander Graham Bell developed the first two-way electronic communications system. Since then, phone lines and satellites have created an electronic web around the world. The lines that link computer networks and all of the computers connected to those lines make up the Internet.

The World Wide Web is a subset of the Internet and is a system for organizing, linking, and providing point-and-click access among Internet-related files, resources, and services.

Hypertext links are embedded within documents, and they provide cross-references to other documents, actions, links, or menus. Microsoft's Internet Explorer makes the World Wide Web fun to use. Hot-linked (actionable text) is presented in colors. Simply click on the colored words and you will be transported to another related or referenced site for additional information.

How Do I Get to the World Wide Web?

You'll need to have Microsoft's Internet Browser, which is available with Microsoft Plus! or through a download from MSN (GO TO MSN105).

What Is Html?

Hamburger, tomato, mayo, and lettuce at Burger King—it's a bit messy on the computer keyboard. Oh, you know I'm kidding! Html is the abbreviation for Hyper Text Markup Language—the dominant format for creating World Wide Web pages. You only need to know this if you are creating your own pages or if you want to understand every reference you see to html.

What Does It Mean to FTP a File?

Oh . . . to bring humor in at this point, but I'd better not. Used alternatively as a noun and a verb, File Transfer Protocol (FTP), defines the communications standards used to upload and download files to and from an FTP server.

With FTP, you can log in to an account on a remote computer in order to send or receive files. As you read newsgroups, you'll often see references to files that you can FTP to your computer. In some instances you will not be able to grab the noted file without an account on the host system. Often you will be directed to an anonymous FTP site that allows open access to its archives.

To access FTP on MSN, use Start, select Run, type **FTP**, and click OK.

What Is a Listserv or Mailing List?

A listserv or mailing list is a message board that comes to you in your e-mail box. You subscribe to a list; messages sent by participants are broadcast to all members. I was inundated by 70 to 80 pieces of mail a day, so I requested a digest, which was compacted into a single, albeit long, e-mail message.

I recently participated in a mailing list on Knitting. No laughing! The participants included women and men from around the world who share tips on techniques, knitting shops, and yarn sources. They also had a terrific thread on knitting in business meetings. Those in academia encountered the fewest hindrances when they attempted to put wasted meeting time to good use.

How Do I Find Good Internet Sites?

Throughout MSN, you'll find references to stellar Internet sites. Most often you'll find the URLs for World Wide Web pages. With MSN's Internet browser, you'll be able to make the quick transition to those sites.

Not only will you find pointers, but you'll be able to generate your own hotlist of sites to return to. A hotlist can be thought of as your Favorite Places list for the Internet.

To begin your list of favorite places, let's take a five-star tour of The Microsoft Network by turning the page.

PART 3

A Five Star Tour of The Microsoft Network

Is it too late to start at the very beginning? Why is Julie Andrews invading my brain? "Let's start at the very beginning . . . it's a very good place to start . . . when we read we begin with A-B-C, when we sing we begin with do-re-mi . . ." Oh, to be a Von Trapp with a tour of the Alps.

OK, so we're halfway through the book and it's time to talk about what you'll find on MSN. It *is* about time, right? On MSN we begin with *categories.* From the MSN Central screen, head to the Categories to find the abundance of content on MSN.

You could spend hundreds of hours prowling through the categories, but is *that* what you really want to do? It's probably better that *I* spend the time prowling, so you can jump to MSN's hottest sites using the tips that follow.

MSN is adding forums and folders faster than I can type this section. What you will tour in these pages is a solid representation of the content available at press time.

I've delved deep into the layers of MSN and will take you through them in alphabetical category order. In some cases, only the top-level category is worthy of attention, while, in other cases, selected forums will be highlighted.

You'll even find topics that are cross-referenced in two or more areas. Medicine is an example. It can be found under Professions in the Business & Finance category, and it can also be found under the Health & Fitness category. For the purposes of this Five Star Tour, I've located it under Health & Fitness.

At the end of each description, I'll include the GO Word and indicate if you'll need the Internet browser. GO Words are space sensitive but not case sensitive.

In a few instances, there is no GO Word for the specific category, area, or forum. In those cases, I'll provide the closest GO Word accompanied by directions detailing the next two to three steps to the destination.

You may encounter charges or fees for some features, forums, or downloads. I'd love to make note of them for you, but at press time, some costs were projected and others were certainly in flux. As time goes on, we can expect to encounter more "paid" forums because Microsoft's pricing system makes that an incentive for the forum content providers.

When you do encounter charges, each is announced before it is incurred. Just pay attention as you flip through the forums of MSN, and you will not have gray hairs when you get your bill.

Arts & Entertainment

Dozens of entertaining features for the quietly recreational are home based in Arts & Entertainment. Architecture, the Reading and Writing Forums, Comics, Movies, Music, Newspapers, Magazines, TV, Radio, and the Theatre form the beginnings of your electronic arts travels.

Go to
Entertainment

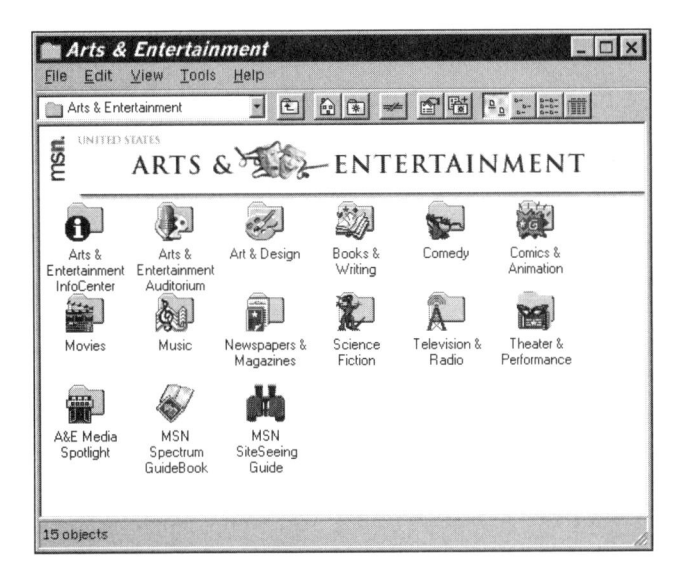

Jazz Central Station

Jazz Central Station on The Microsoft Network provides the global jazz community with the most informative and creative network, linking all aspects of jazz including history, festivals, tour schedules, exclusive chats, and classic photos. Create your own smokey lounge in Jazz Central Station.

Go to
Jazz Central Station

Go To
Showbiz

For the full use of the features, make the Internet connection.

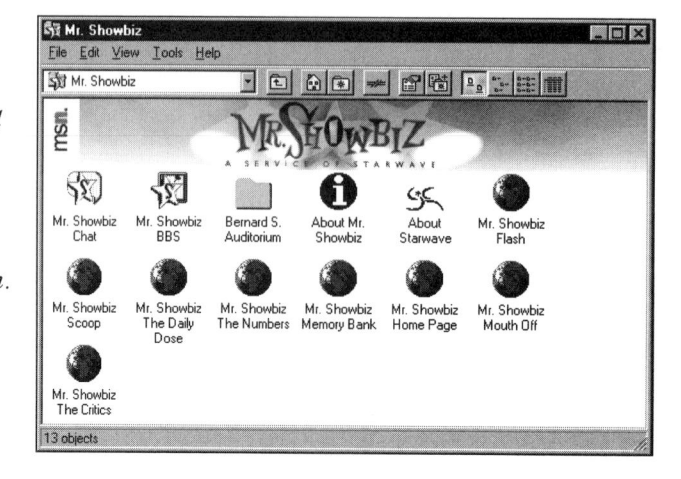

Mr. Showbiz

Let Mr. Showbiz entertain you with interviews with your favorite celebrities and sound bites from your favorite bands. On other days, you may just want to stop by for a humor break. The Mr. Showbiz service includes up-to-the-minute entertainment news, celebrity profiles, movie reviews, TV ratings, and just plain entertainment fun.

Court TV

For me, it started with the Broderick case in San Diego. For others, it may have been the William Kennedy Smith trial in Palm Beach—and for the latecomers, it was most certainly the Orenthal James Simpson trial in Los Angeles. Court TV has been there guiding us through the proceedings and the delays. For the bird's-eye view and inside scoop on today's legal proceedings, visit Court TV on MSN. You can find Brentwood on the map now, right?

Go to
TV

Select the Court TV Law Center.

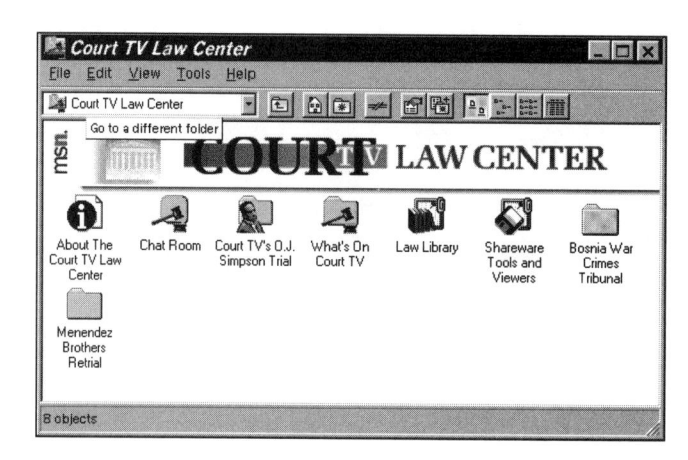

Go To
TVHost

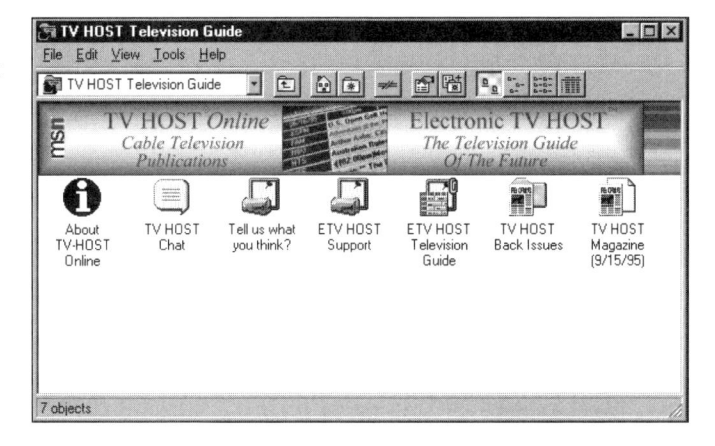

TV Host

In my other life—when I am not working on a book—I am a couch potato. I just love September and each year's new TV season—and now I've discovered TV Host Online. The TV Host Forum on MSN contains an online version of the famous cable television magazine. Here it is called TV Host Magazine - Online Edition. With it, you can scan, plan, and create you personal television guide—customized to your home area.

Cinemania Connection

Derived from Microsoft's movie database, Cinemania Connection is online . . . with exclusive reviews of new movies by nationally known critics, the latest movie

Go to
Cinemania

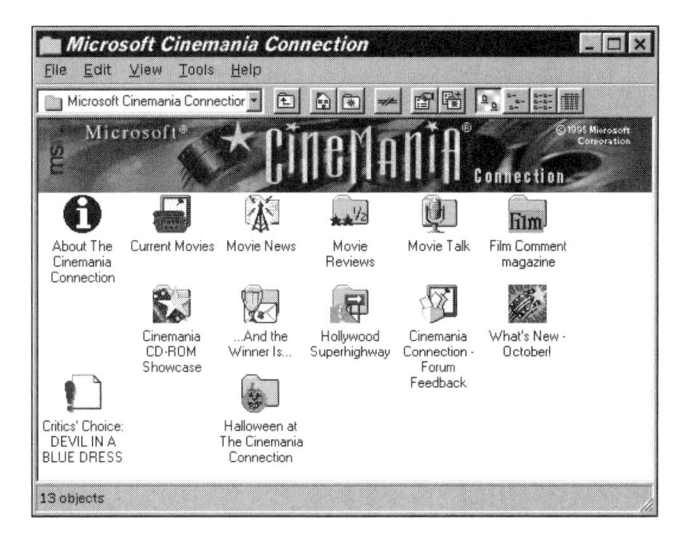

reviews, and biographies of the people involved in making the movies of yesterday and today. Each weekend's box office results are announced here. And there's the hottest in video news and the special guest series, where you can chat with actors directors, writers, producers, and filmmakers. You'll have great fun with "And the Winner Is...," featuring winners lists from the Oscars, Cannes Film Festival, L.A. Critics Association, N.Y. Film Critics, the National Society of Film Critics, and the Independent Spirit Awards.

Music Central Connection

Music Central is your one-stop interactive music source. This area is the online component to the Microsoft Music Central CD-ROM. You'll find the latest music news and reviews, along with concert and tour information and lists of the top selling titles in the top 25 U.S. markets.

Go to
musiccentral

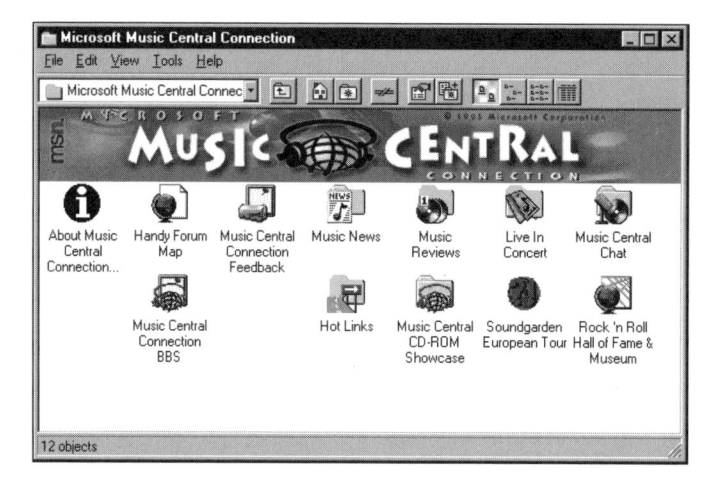

Music Central Newsstand

At the Music Central Newsstand, view music news, concerts and recording reviews, articles, and club and show listings featured in seven weekly newspapers from the United States and Canada: *Austin Chronicle, Chicago Reader, Seattle Rocket, Toronto Now, New York Village Voice, Los Angeles LA Weekly,* and the *San Francisco Bay Guardian.*

For the full use of the features, make the Internet connection.

Go to
musiccentral

- *Select Music News.*
- *Select Music Central Newsstand.*

Village Voice

The *Village Voice* is the nation's largest alternative weekly. On MSN, this renowned publisher has set up the New York City Music Update. In this area you'll find the Essential Guides to New York and Los Angeles, as well as the Village Voice Feature Archive and Reviews. As an added bonus, this area includes a link to the Voice Web Site.

Go to
MusicCentral

- *Select Music News.*
- *Select Music Central Newsstand.*
- *Select New York Village Voice.*

For the full use of the features, make the Internet connection.

Business & Finance

The metropolitan business center on MSN is located in the Business & Finance category, of course. It's here that you can perfect your job search techniques, maximize your nest egg, and conduct research on the competition.

Go to
Business

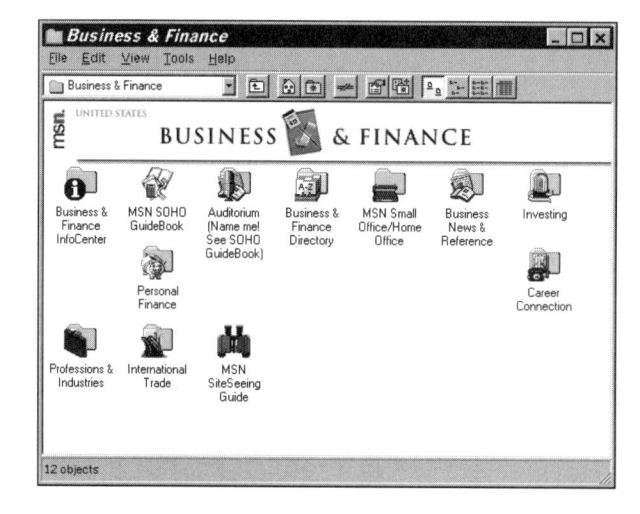

Mainstream Career Center

There's no just treading water midstream with the Mainstream Career Center. This area features career skills assessment, career events, resume building, interviewing

Go to
CareerConnect

- *Select Career Opportunities.*
- *Select Mainstream Career Center.*

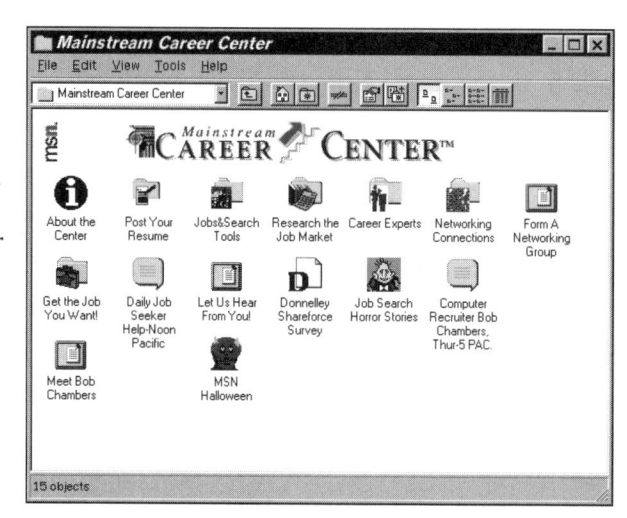

skills, job search assistance, networking contacts, research directories, and job postings. You can build your career search on job openings, industry and company information, self discovery, resume help, new ideas, personality growth, career direction, educational information, and much more.

Winning Resumes

Tired of flippin' burgers? If you're thinking about a new job, stop by the WinWay Career Forum and take a look at the resume samples. There are five resumes and two prepared letters to inspire your best resume and letter writing. You may find information that will help you with the right "look" that will attract the decision makers to your skills.

Go to
Resume Samples

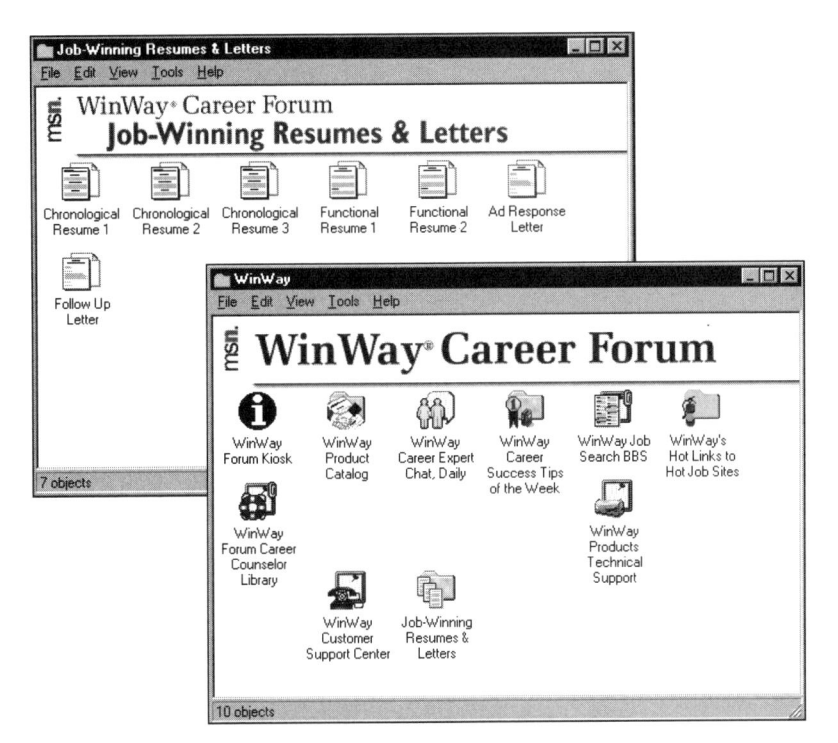

Small Office Home Office

One of MSN's strongest areas is the Small Office Home Office (SOHO) area. Since Microsoft's products are so well entrenched in the SOHO arena, Microsoft has pulled together the best resources for this area. Small business publications, research, services, computing and networking are featured along with *Venture*

Go to
SOHO

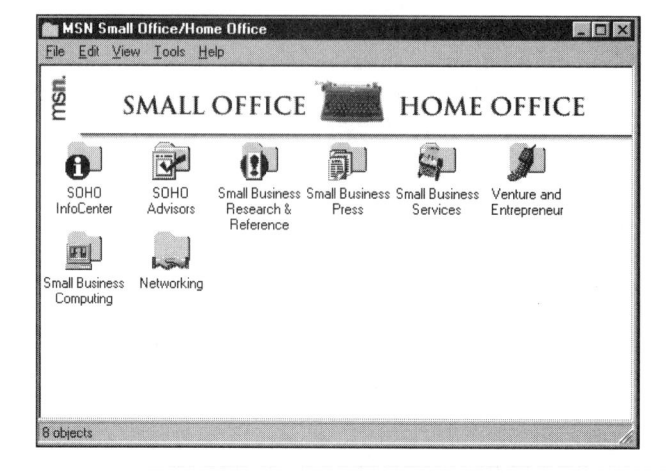

and *Entrepreneur* magazines. American Management Association, Dun & Bradstreet Information Services, Equifax, and the Small Business Administration are bonuses within the SOHO area, along with *Home Office Computing* magazine and *Accounting Today*.

Ubiquitous FedEx

The FedEx area on The Microsoft Network has been compiled based upon Federal Express' 20-year foundation of top-notch customer service. The current Service Guide in MSN makes for easy user interaction. The rate charts, detailed service availability areas, and pop-up windows display everything you need to know to guarantee shipping success. Links to the FedEx Web site are incorporated. There

Go to
Fed Ex

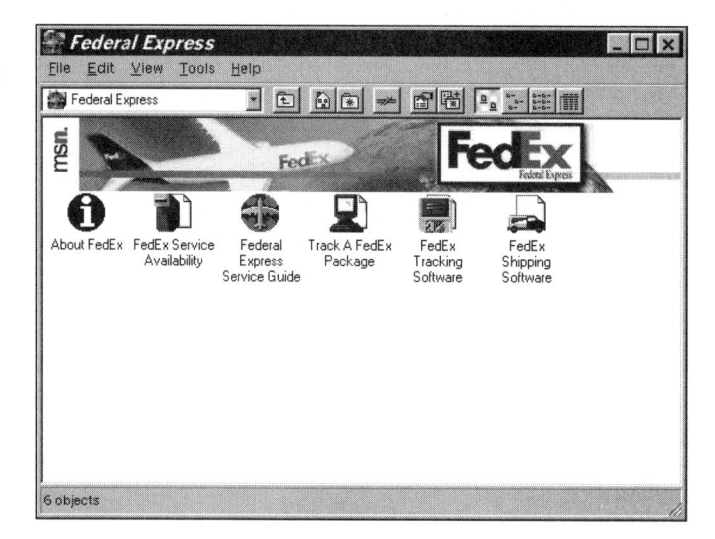

you'll gain instant access to FedEx shipping and tracking services—and you can request free tracking software for Macintosh or Windows.

I recently used the tracking service to verify a shipment to my editor. He really had received printouts of the screens in the centerfold section. But that didn't help once the package was lost in the jungle of his office. I think the next invention needs to be an electronic beeper, embedded in the package, that sends out a signal. It should beep until the designated recipient calls the sender to confirm receipt.

For the full use of the features, make the Internet connection.

Big, Basic Brown

Vroom. . . . That early afternoon rumble means that "my" UPS truck is coming down the street. If you prefer to ship with basic brown, our pals at UPS have not been left in the dust on the electronic superhighway. Now, there's no better UPS delivery man than Gary Hawk in Maryland. I just had to work Gary into one of these books. From the UPS site on MSN, you can e-mail to customer service, track a package, and access the UPS Web Site. It's only missing one thing—profiles of the finest drivers . . . starting with Gary.

For the full use of the features, make the Internet connection.

Go to
UPS

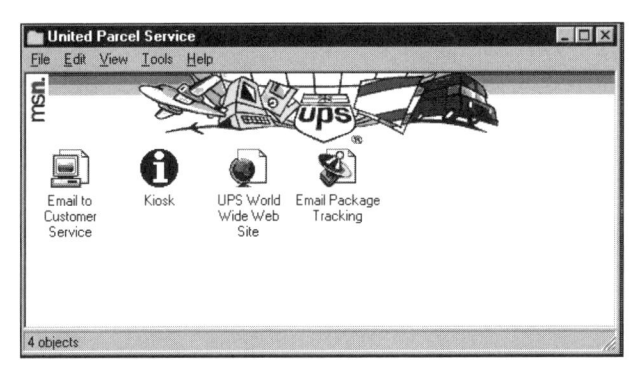

Hoover's Business Resources

Not too long ago, I was treated poorly in the "nature" store. I think you know the chain of stores, featuring science, nature, and the environment. I decided it was time to write to the president of that company—and I found all the information I needed in Hoovers. The good news is that I received a $25 gift certificate when the president responded.

Hoover's Business Resources on MSN is a service of The Reference Press. Over one million people access Hoover's online each month and explore their growing

Go to
Hoovers

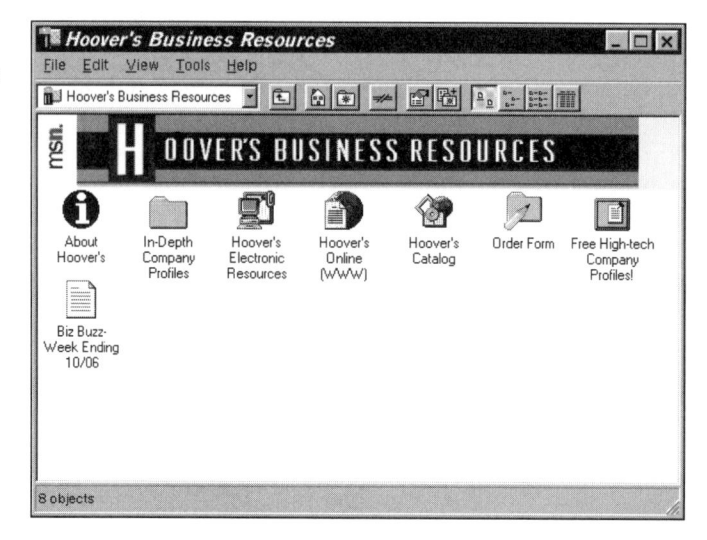

storehouse of company information. Within this area you'll have a chance to discover free company profiles in designated markets, in-depth company profiles (for 10¢ each), Hoover's Web site with 8,500 companies, and the week's top 10 business news stories.

For the full use of the features, make the Internet connection.

Decision Point

For many of us, the decision that it's time to start investing is fraught with confusion. Decision Point can help us to make the "what," "where," and "when"

Go to
DP

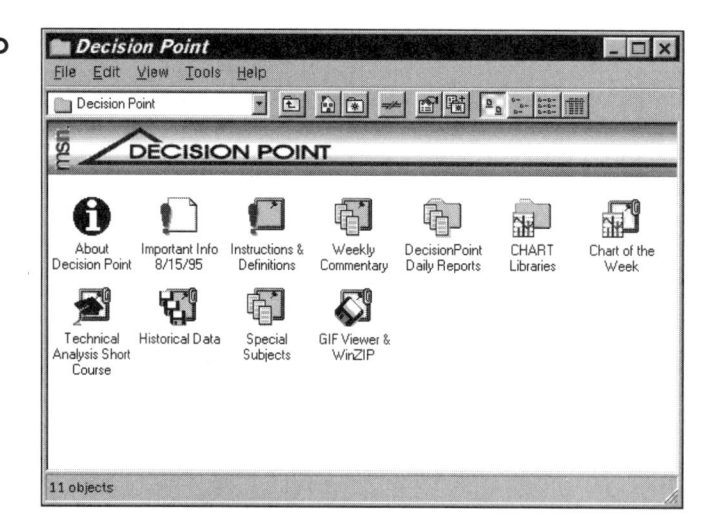

decisions. The Decision Point area is devoted to the technical analysis of stocks, mutual funds, and the stock market. You can use this area to learn, refine, and profitably utilize technical analysis skills. You can take advantage of the weekly commentary, daily market signals, eight daily reports covering 152 stocks and 160 mutual funds, chart and historical data libraries, and a special subjects reading area. There's no reason to start from scratch in your investment analysis, when you can turn to Decision Point for expert analysis.

Fidelity Online Investor Center

Save for a nest egg, a house, a college education, or your golden years. Fidelity Online Investor Center features new funds, products, and services as well as reprints of recent articles from Fidelity publications. The Mutual Fund Library contains information on fund objectives, and you can request fund materials to be sent to you by mail. The Workplace Saving area—in my opinion, the most important tool—helps you maximize your investment in your retirement savings plan. The Investment and Retirement Planning area includes educational materials, investment planners, and worksheets to help you create a personal portfolio or plan for a child's college costs, and even your own retirement. If you recommend this book to a few more friends, I might be able to establish an IRA here.

Note: Schwab Investors will find Schwab Online at GO TO Schwab.

Go to
Investing

- *Select Market & Securities Research.*
- *Select Fidelity Online Investor Center.*

Computers & Software

As you might expect from Microsoft, you'll find a great deal of depth in the content of Computers & Software. I didn't count the levels, but I know you'll be amazed. As MSN becomes a greater force in the computing universe, this area will continue to grow and perhaps become the dominant computer resource among online services. Don't be concerned if you are not a computer techie—we can all take advantage of the resources available here. There's a full range of software and hardware companies, and we'll just be taking a quick peek at what's currently available.

Go to
Computing

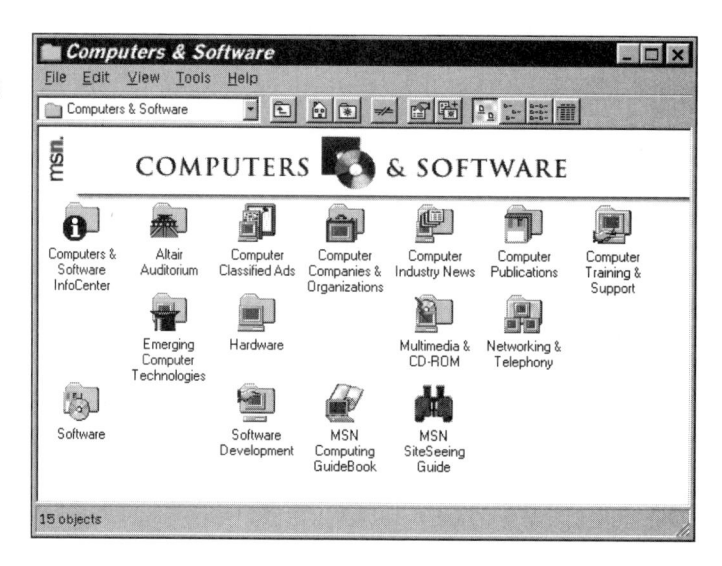

Software Companies

We're just out of the starting gate and already there are 38 software companies online with MSN. Counted among these leaders are Broderbund, Activision, Adobe, Corel, Novell, and Symantec. Turn to these providers for problem fixes, software updates, demos, and technical expertise.

FYI *Computer periodicals are a bit hidden in two folders within the Computers & Software area. GO TO CompPublishers or ComputePubs.*

Go to
Software

Newsbytes

Newsbytes is a daily, international, online newswire, providing independent computer and telecommunications news to an estimated 4.5 million readers worldwide on major online networks, magazines, newspapers, and newsletters.

Like other major wire services, Newsbytes accepts no advertising. Reports are compiled by professional, staff journalists who adhere to the highest editorial standards. Editorial content is based solely on its news value. Choose from daily summaries or the complete daily files.

Go to
Newsbytes

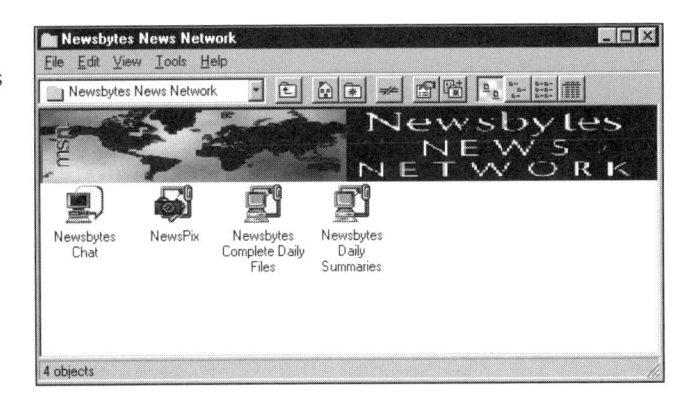

Go to
PCWC

PC World Communications

PC World Communications Online incorporates the best of the award-winning content of *PC World*, *Multimedia World*, and the IDG Newsletter group as well as PC World's Small Office Home Office Online and Windows 95 Online electronic publications. Selected articles from current issues are yours to review. Stop by often to see what's been added.

For the full use of the features, make the Internet connection.

NewMedia

If it's about multimedia, you can count on NewMedia to cover it for computer and multimedia pros. *NewMedia* magazine is the premier publication for managers, developers, and implementers of NewMedia products and services. At this site,

Go to
NewMedia

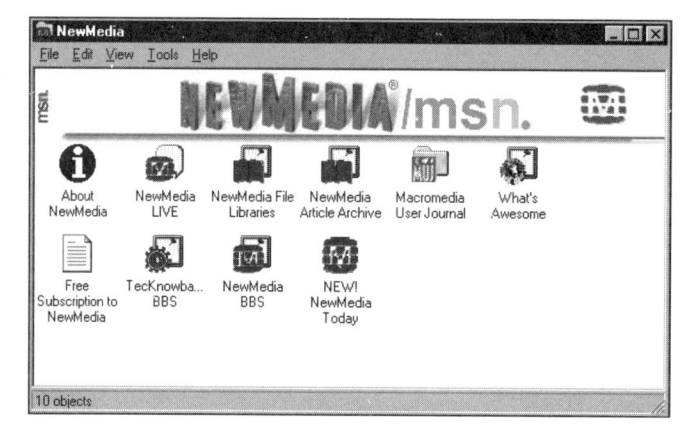

you'll find plenty of information from the print magazines plus stories written specifically for the online audience of MSN. Add file libraries, article archive, multimedia files, and the BBS for interacting with editors and fellow NewMedia readers, and you'll be all set. The article archive includes stories since January 1995. With the browser, you can even request a free subscription to *NewMedia* magazine.

ZD Net Magazines

It seems like Ziff Davis has been a leader in computer magazines since before computers. With the ZD Net Magazines Rack, you'll have access to *PC Magazine*, *Windows Sources*, *PC Week*, *PC Computing*, *Computer Shopper*, *Computer Life*, *Family PC*, *Computer Gaming World*, and *Interactive Week*, as well as the Cobb's PC Productivity Center. You'll find highlights from current issues, plus customer utilities and chats with computer industry luminaries.

For the full use of the features, make the Internet connection.

Go to
ZDNetMags

GO TO ZDNet and take a look at the loot in its software libraries.

MIDI & Electronic Music Forum

I can't tell you the first thing about producing music electronically, but I'm fascinated by the music samples and sound bites available in this forum. You could almost have a quiz game trying to decide if the song names matched the mood of the names . . . *Eye of the Beholder, Pan in Space, The Bad Blues, Solitudes of Silence,* and *You Don't Know About Love.*

Multimedia & CD-ROM

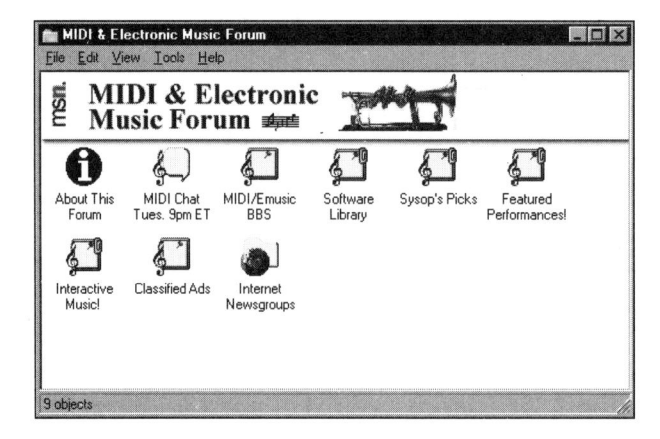

The Multimedia & CD-ROM Forum covers all aspects of multimedia applications and peripherals, including video, sound, and, of course, multimedia presentations. It is in the process of building a world-class multimedia library with shareware, graphics, sounds, and information files. This place could use a fun, colorful banner to pull it together.

Go to
Multimedia

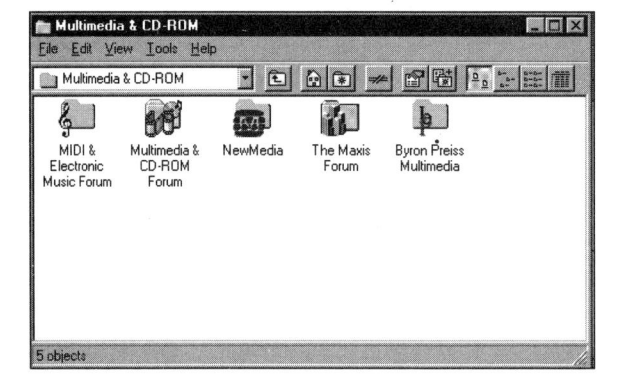

Computer Games Forum

Given how often they see me sitting at the computer in the window, my neighbors must think I'm spending time with computer games. I'm not a gamer. You will find discussion of the latest and greatest games here, but you won't find me in the chat rooms. The Computer Games File Library is the place to share the game winning strategy and tip files—and you'll find shareware and freeware game files there, too.

Go to
CompGames

Desktop Publishing Forum

In another life, I created newsletters. I wish that MSN's DTP Forum had been running then. I could have saved a few dozen headaches. This forum is dedicated to the discussion and sharing of ideas pertaining to all aspects of desktop publishing, from print media to multimedia. The highlights include the Internet links (why go seeking them when they're all right here?) and the DTP File Libraries. The file libraries include a gold mine of shareware and freeware fonts, noncopyrighted artwork, useful utilities, patches and updates for commercial programs, and demos.

For the full use of the features, make the Internet connection.

Go to
DTP

Maxis

The makers of the famed SimCity have created an exciting forum on MSN. You'll find downloadable demos, updaters, and free games courtesy of Maxis in the Cool

Go to
Maxis

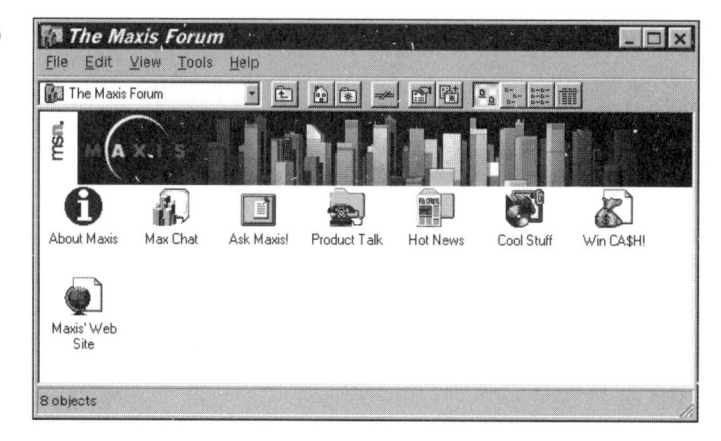

Stuff area, where you'll keep coming back for more. Maxis puts the power of exploration, learning, and creativity in the hands and minds of it's customers—online, too. You can even win big cash prizes ($250) for your expertise with Maxis products.

Shareware

I don't know why they call it shareware—I think it should be called treasureware. The Shareware Forum is the place to find shareware files, chat about shareware, and meet with others interested in shareware. In one of the subforums, the ASP Forum where you can download shareware files from the Association of Shareware Professionals (GO TO ASP). Another subforum is the ESC Forum—the Educational Software Cooperative (GO TO ESC). That's where you'll find a variety of educational shareware titles.

Go to
ShareWareForum

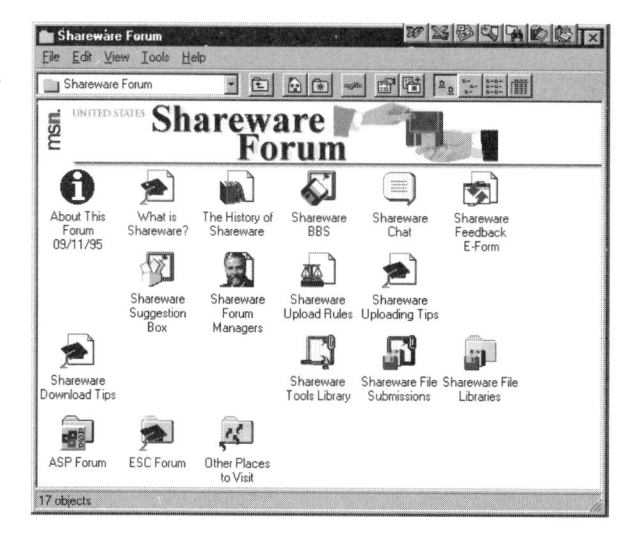

Go to
mskb

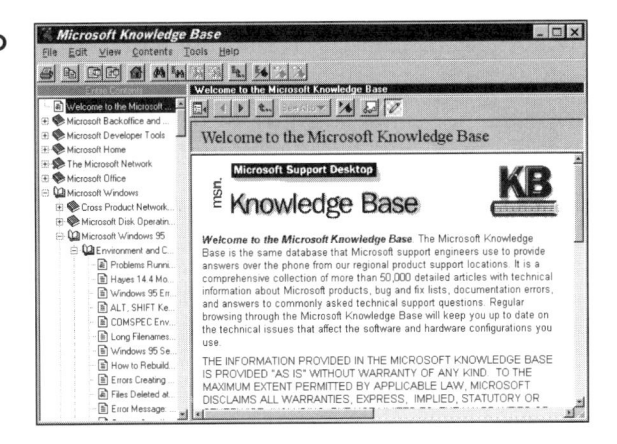

Microsoft Knowledge Base

Microsoft Knowledge Base is the same database that Microsoft support engineers use to provide customer service. It's a comprehensive collection of more than 50,000 detailed articles with technical information about Microsoft products, bugs and fixes, documentation errors, and answers to commonly asked questions. With easy online access this is the first place to go whenever you run into a glitch with a Microsoft product. Try not to bother yourself with the fact that you are paying Microsoft for online time while searching for clues to a Microsoft product.

Microsoft Windows 95

The Windows 95 area is your online place to learn the most about Windows 95 and how to pick off any little burrs that might be sticking to your electronic ankles. One of the must-sees is the Tip-'O-The-Day in the main area of the forum. Another is the Software Compatibility List, the first place to check before you try your current applications with Windows 95. Behind the Free Software icon, you'll find the Power Toys and the Windows 95 Resource Kit Utilities and Help File.

Go to
Windows

GO TO OS for forums on computer operating systems software including DOS, Windows 95, Macintosh, OS/2, and Windows NT.

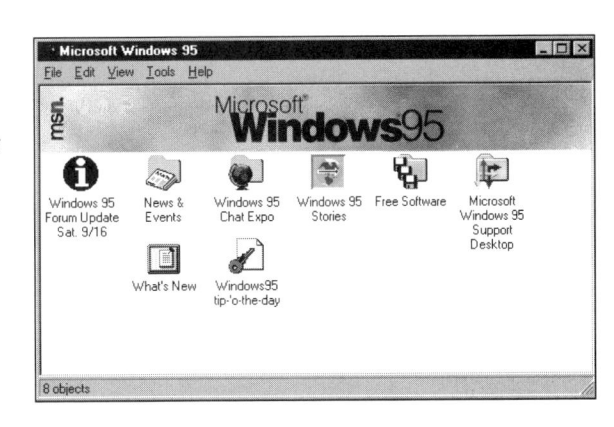

Go to
Komando

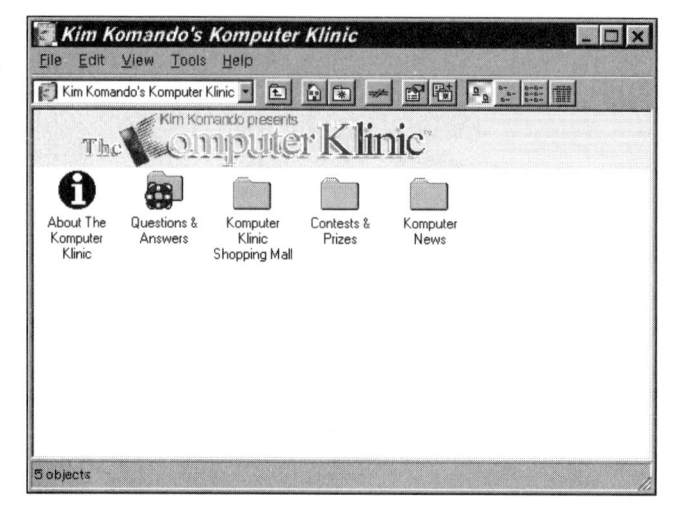

Komputer Klinic

Kim Komando hosts the Komputer Klinic, which is conveniently located on your computer. The Komputer Klinic Mall is the easy way to save time and money by taking advantage of high-quality products. Plus, you'll find a great selection of computer books there, too! If this area is anything like her place on America Online, you'll have a blast with the contests.

Online Service Providers

Does anyone need a humor break—or perhaps a primal scream? When I saw this folder marked "Online Service Providers," I just had to take a look inside. What online services would possibly have a forum or link to MSN? Would you believe none other than The Microsoft Network?

Go to
Online Providers

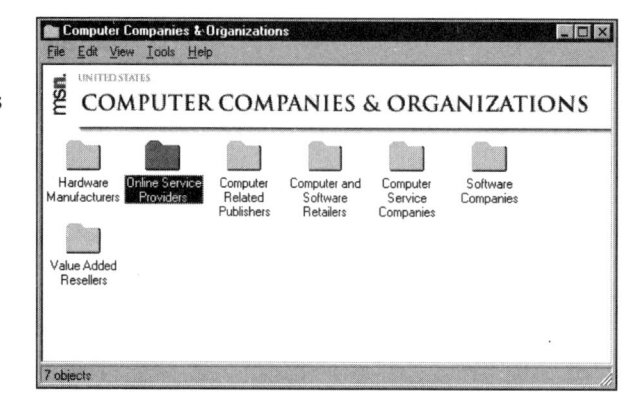

Education & Reference

Ringed by laurel leaves, the echelons of education are arrayed for quick reference. From the basics of the primary grades to the lofty heights of universities, Microsoft has put together a veritable library of information just mouse-clicks away.

Go to
Education

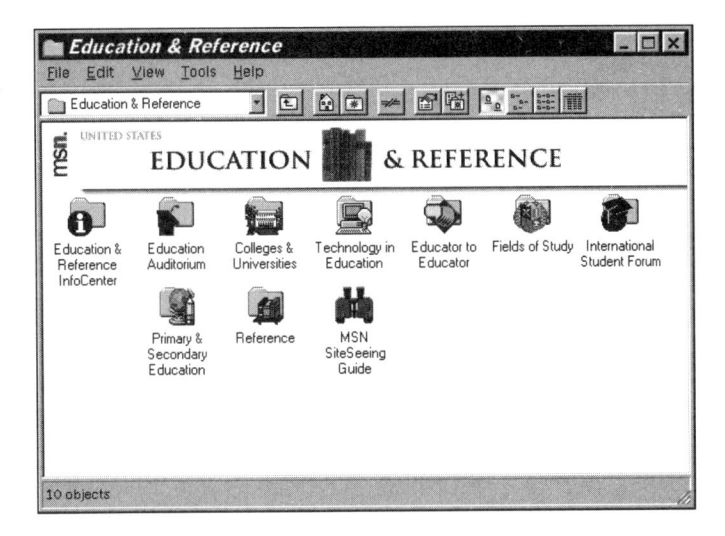

Encarta Encyclopedia

By now you've most certainly heard of Microsoft Encarta, the dominant encyclopedia on CD. The Intro Edition, available as an online download, includes a limited

Go to
EncartaForum

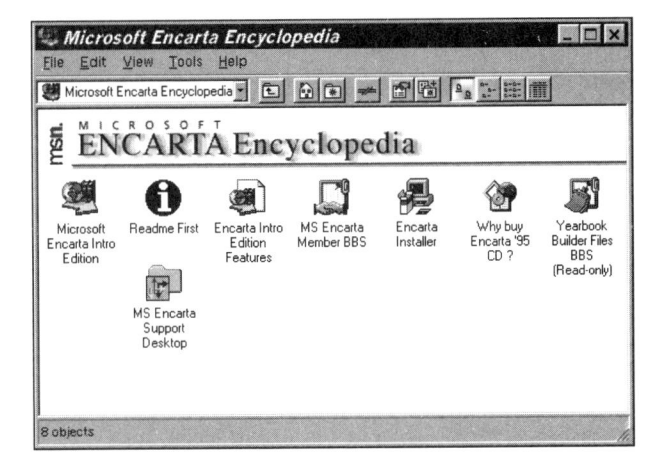

selection of content from the CD ROM version. The Intro Edition includes the complete text of Encarta '95 along with 5,000 photos and 360 maps. The Find tool makes it easy to locate articles. Following a 10-minute download, the Encarta Intro Edition will take 1 MB of space on your hard disk. Once installed, users can directly access Encarta Intro Edition from the Microsoft Home Zone. Just as with Bookshelf, you can only use the Encarta Intro Edition when you are connected to MSN. It's up to you decide if this is such a good deal that you want to sign on each time and use your minute-by-minute charges.

Bookshelf Forum

MSN includes a special edition of Microsoft Bookshelf. The Microsoft Bookshelf Intro Edition was designed with novices in mind. To use Bookshelf, you'll have to download the file from MSN before you can begin. Just as with Encarta, you can only use Bookshelf Intro Edition when you are connected to MSN. The Bookshelf Intro Edition is accessible through The Microsoft Network in an area called the Home Zone.

Go to
MSBooks

The Princeton Review

The Princeton Review online is devoted to everything you need to know about getting into college, graduate, and professional school. Admission and financial aid information, software for practice tests, message boards, chat areas, and Princeton Review locations are the features in this online education center. There's no guarantee of an Ivy League education, but the Princeton Review may provide the jump start your teen needs.

Go to
Princeton
Review

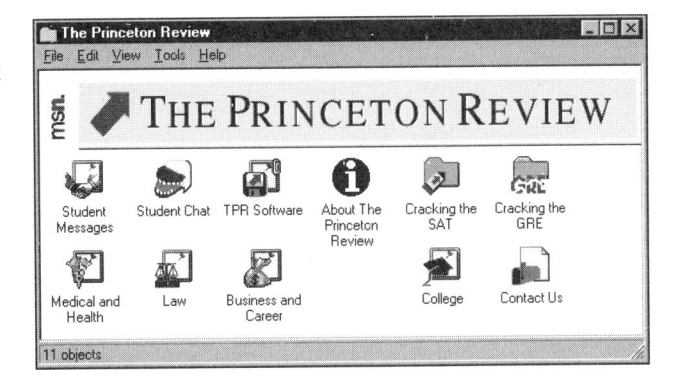

Kaplan Online

For another test prep, try the nation's #1 leader. The Kaplan site features a subscription-based seminar series led by admissions experts, live conferences on test preparation, downloadable test preparation software, practice tests, and instruction. Downloadable search software helps students identify schools that match their own personal criteria. Hmmm . . . I wonder if Kaplan and the Princeton Review have BBS folders for comparing their services?

Go to
Kaplan

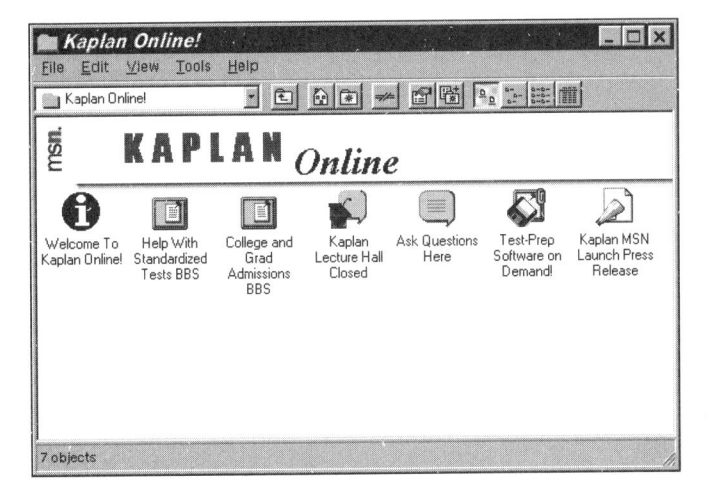

Health & Fitness

Health & Fitness is the starting point for Exercise and Physical Fitness, Health Care Professionals, Human Sexuality BBS, Mental Wellness and Counseling, Nutrition,

Go to
Health

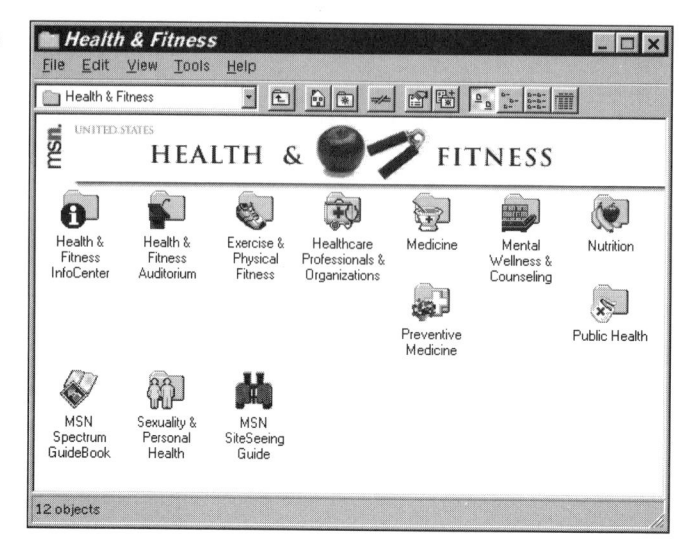

Public Health, Preventive Medicine, and the DisAbilities Forum. Of course, the real highlights here are the links to the Internet, with the folder entitled Health & Fitness Internet picks.

For the full use of the features, make the Internet connection.

Medicine Forum

Closing clinics, affordable insurance, quality care, and HMOs are all buzzwords in today's world of medicine. The Medicine area contains forums that deal with modern medicine including such specialties as oncology and pediatrics and alternative medicine such as acupuncture, as well as issues such as abortion, preventive medicine, medical equipment, and technologies. From this area you

Go to
Medicine

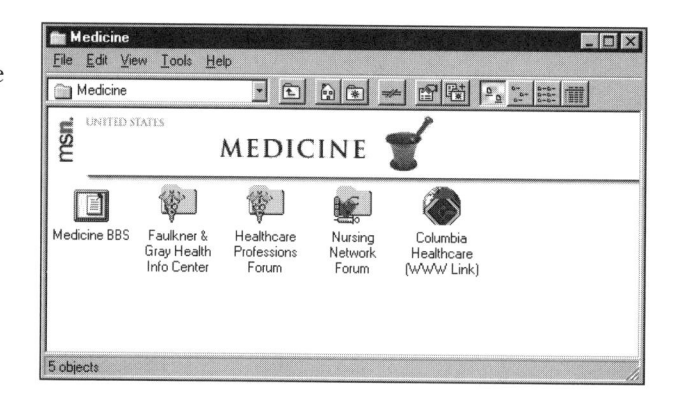

can access the sci.med, alt.med., and bit.med newsgroups. The Nursing Forum, Healthcare Professions Forum, and the Columbia Healthcare WWW link are the main features found here.

For the full use of the features, make the Internet connection.

Home & Family

In *The Three Little Pigs*, we learned that it's best to live in a brick house when the wolves are at the door. With the resources available in MSN's Home & Family, you'll be able to reinforce your home and family with metaphorical bricks. In this shelter, you'll find information on all the home-based topics: parenting, home improvement, working women, work-at-home Dads, youth sports, and children's room design, as well as forums devoted to teens and kids.

For the full use of the features, make the Internet connection.

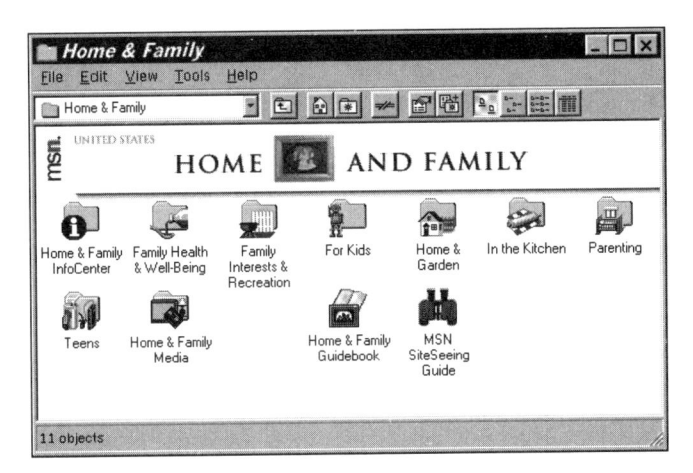

Go to
Home

Theme Parks!

When was the last time you were on an E-ticket ride? Do you know the restrictions for pregnant women and small children? Theme Parks from around the world are covered in this exciting forum. From Disney World to Sea World to Six Flags, you'll find friends with tips and ideas for making the most of your days at the parks. In the files you'll find information on the parks' hours and special events, as well as lots of fun photos to download.

For the full use of the features, make the Internet connection.

Go to
Theme Parks

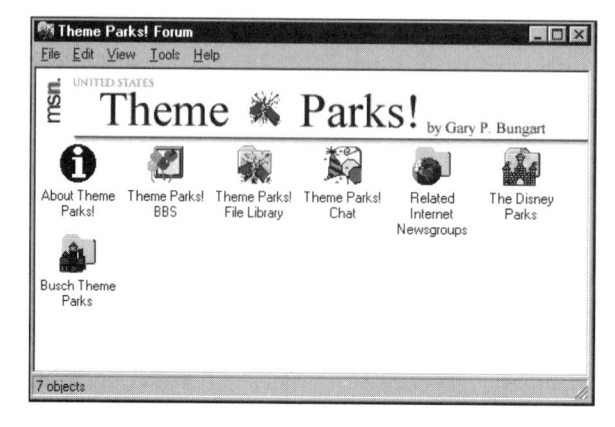

Best Friends AnimalNet

If your best friend is something other than human, it may be time to check out the pet forum on MSN. I flushed my goldfish when I was nine. These days my computer is my best friend. The Best Friends AnimalNet is the online home for animal lovers. It features news, education, and entertainment relating to animals and information on the Best Friends Animal Sanctuary. The AnimalNet Newsstand provides *Best Friends* and *Natural Pet* magazines to all comers.

Go to
animalnet

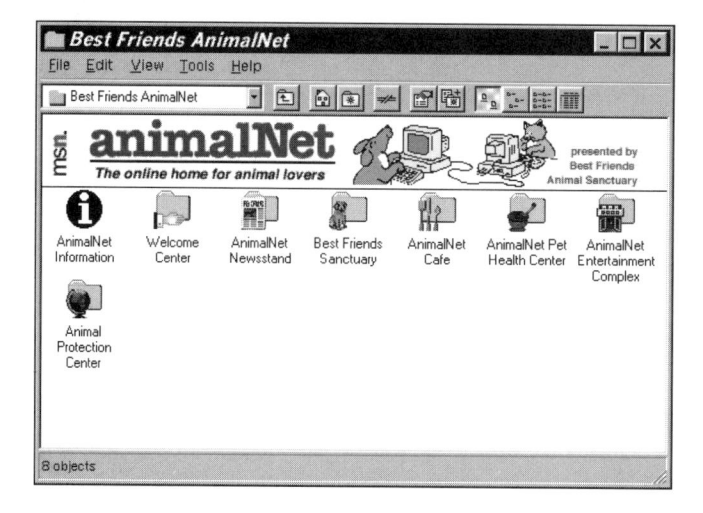

Photography

I started with a Brownie and now have an almost-idiot-proof-if-you-remove-the-lens-cap camera. To spruce up my skills, I need to spend more time in MSN's

Go to
Photo

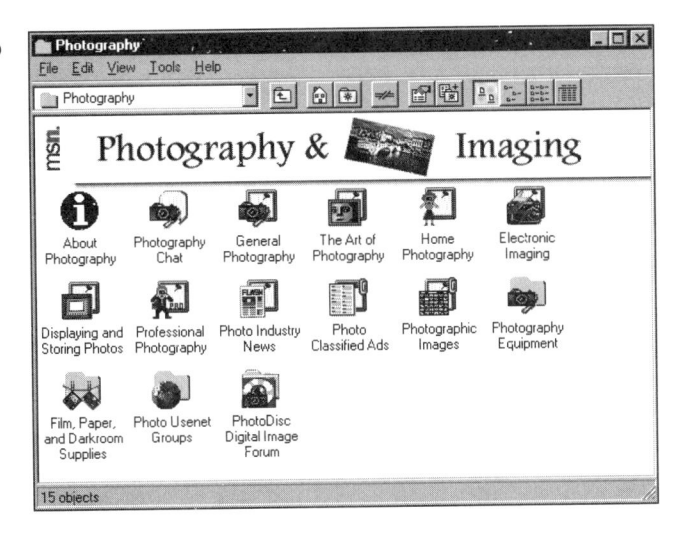

Photography Forum, where the world of photography is ready to be explored. This is the central place to learn all about the equipment, techniques, and enjoyment of capturing images. One hidden gem in the Photographic Images area is the folder of downloadable pics of celebrities. In the PhotoDisc Digital Image Forum, you can choose from hundreds of medium-resolution 24-bit images for less than the cost of a single traditional stock photograph. You can also purchase images for use in your projects at a very reasonable fee—$9.95 to $14.95—downloaded as attachments. With luck you'll find a few free teaser images as well. Plus, you'll even find discussions of film, processing, and darkroom supplies.

For the full use of the features, make the Internet connection.

Splash Kids

Splash is the best place for online kids. They can kick back in the Clubhouse for stories, comics, interviews, puzzles, contests, and more. Games and art programs are ready for fun and learning. I love the fascinating Fun Factory, which includes links to some of the best kid-friendly places on the Internet. Tic-Tac-Toe, Pegs, 9-Puzzle, and Minesweep are some of the best places around. I only wish the Mr. Potato Head link had worked. Maybe it will when you get there.

For the full use of the features, make the Internet connection.

Go to
Splash

KidStar Online

KidStar Online is an exciting place where kids can learn, have fun, showcase artwork, talk to other kids, and win prizes. It's a super hangout for kids, where they can share stories of their activities and pets and enter cool kid contests for prizes. The KidStar Kitchen features kid-friendly recipes—more than milk and cookies—for after-school snacks. Kids' tastes have come a long way from my favorite after-school snack of salami and milk, along with reruns of *Hazel* and *Flipper*.

For the full use of the features, make the Internet connection.

Go to
KidStar

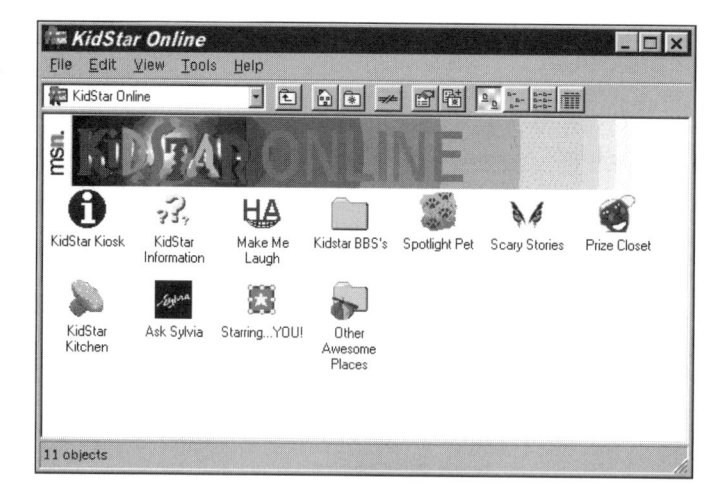

Go to
Ingenius

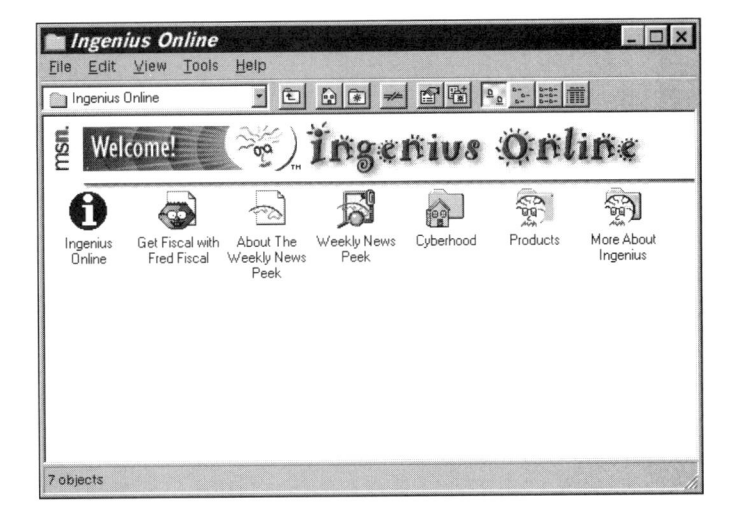

Ingenius Online

Ingenius Online might as well be called News for Kids. The weekly news peek from What on Earth gives a quick summary of the week's top international news stories for young people. Along with the six story summaries, the junior set gets links to MSN spots and other Web sites, sound bites from the top newsmakers, and contributions from kids.

Gardening Delights

There are yellow tomatoes in my garden. Should I eat them? Perhaps I should check first with the Gardening Forum. You won't catch me with manure under my

Go to
Garden

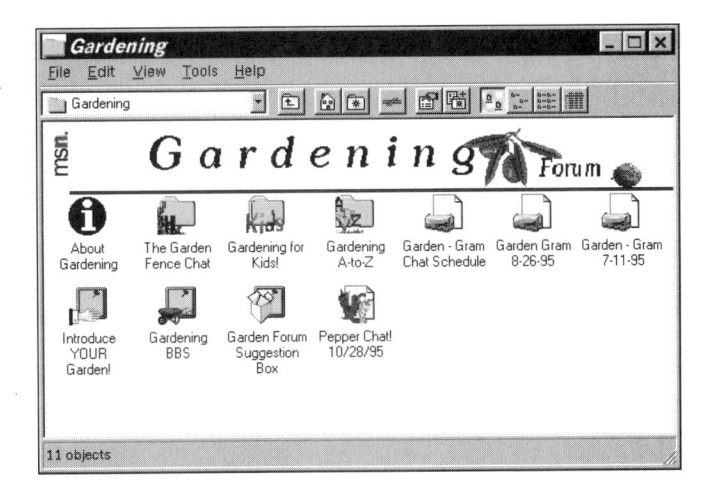

fingernails, but these are the folks who know how to help Mary Mary Quite Contrary get her garden to grow. Gardening from A to Z covers the alphabetic range of gardening topics from asters to zinnias.

In the Kitchen

There's ample evidence of male dominance in this kitchen, as the first two icons cover the Ale & Lager Beerbrewing Forum and the Wine, Beer, Spirits, and Cigars Forum. In my humble opinion, the best part is What's Cooking Online, where I discovered a collection of Fast & Easy recipes that helped out on days I worked far too long on this book. Links to Internet food resources can be found here, too.

For the full use of the features, make the Internet connection.

Go to
InTheKitchen

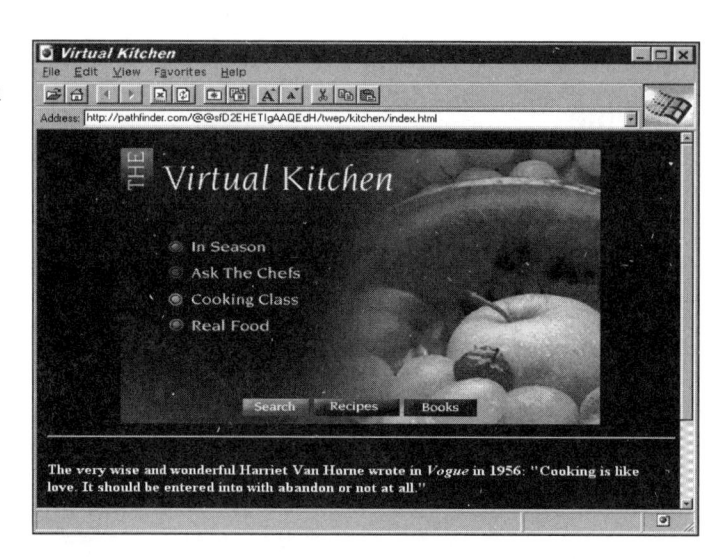

Pathfinder's Kitchen

Pathfinder's Virtual Kitchen brings forth a luscious bounty to our screens. Now if only we could magically bring the seasonal food treasures to the table. Jane Jetson could. The primary topics include In Season, Ask the Chefs, Cooking Class, Real Food, Recipes, and Books. There's even a very useful search tool. OK, so it is a promo for Time Warner's book sales. Let's see . . . I don't have to leave my house, I have access to fabulous recipes and gorgeous, changing food photos. Where else will you find such inspiring recipes as Asparagus with Sun-Dried Tomato Vinaigrette and Fettucine Florentine. Have I made my case?

For the full use of the features, make the Internet connection.

Go to
News

- *Select Time Warner's Pathfinder.*
- *Select Virtual Kitchen.*

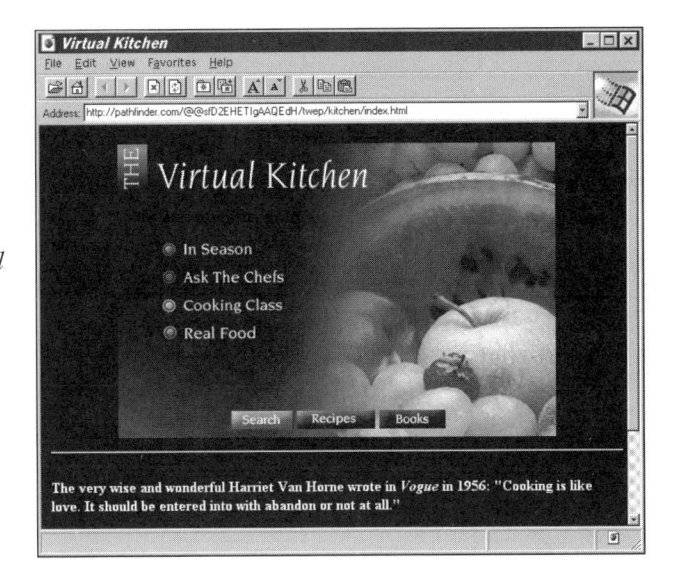

Parenting

There's no place like home and no substitute for the love and attention of one's parents. Oooooh, I sound like famed radio talk show host "Dr. Laura." Concerns of work at home, Dads, and working mothers share the spotlight along with Children First and the Family Planet. This area keeps growing—with Adoption, Parenting in the 90s, and the Pregnancy, Labor, and Nursing Forum.

For the full use of the features, make the Internet connection.

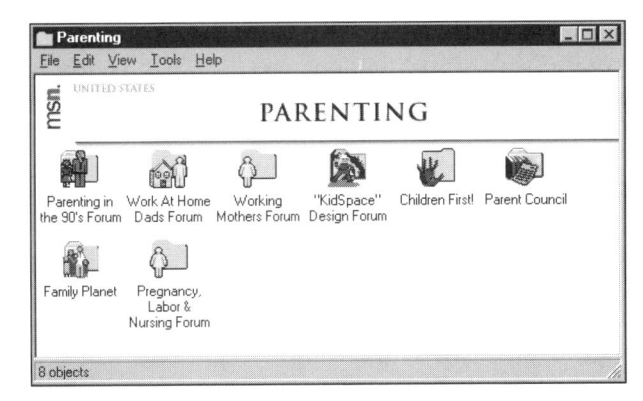

Go to
Parents

Children First

Children First is presented by the National PTA in partnership with leading educational associations and health agencies. Parents turn to Children First to gain current

Go to
Children

information on programs, guidance, and publications. With the knowledge gained here, parents can find encouragement to work with their school on their community's children's issues. There's even an interesting, and perhaps challenging, quiz for parents on HIV/AIDS transmission. Test yourself, test your kids. You'll also find links to parents and kids Internet sites.

For the full use of the features, make the Internet connection.

Lanier Travel Guides

Lanier Travel Guides has set up the Family Travel Forum on MSN to help you plan those fun "are we there yet?" trips. You'll find libraries including national parks, adventure travel, theme parks, family resorts, condo vacations, all-suite hotels, and lodging around the world, along with favorites like Hawaii and Disney World.

Go to
FamilyInterests

- *Select Lanier Travel Guides.*

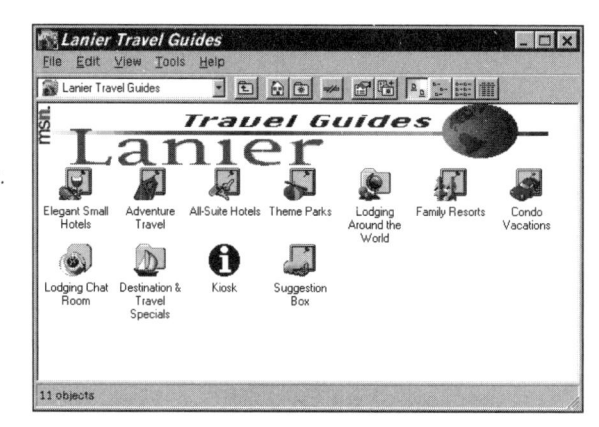

Interests, Leisure & Hobbies

All work and no play makes Jack a dull boy? What about Bill Gates? Featured in this section is the best of play and relaxation—not work! Car tinkerers, model train engineers, creative crafters, coin collectors, and tenacious travelers will find their claim to fame (and reason to relax) in Interests, Leisure & Hobbies.

For the full use of the features, make the Internet connection.

Go to
interests

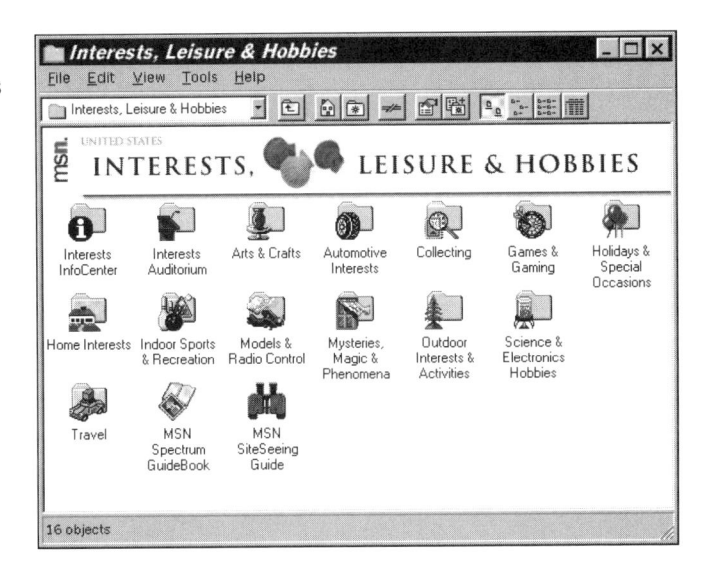

Arts & Crafts

Crafty fingers? You'll be at home in the Arts & Crafts area with forums on textiles, photography, woodworking, pottery, sculpture, painting, and other crafts. The Arts & Crafts BBS has discussion areas for kids' crafts, beads, rubber-stamping, holiday crafts, papermaking, and whatever you can think of! Crafters Marketplace is the place for Barbie collectors, jewelry makers, bear collectors, and the online quilt guild. Stitch incorporates quilting, sewing, and needle arts along with links to Internet sites and newsgroups. The complete realm of shoptalk for woodworkers can be found in the WoodWorking Forum. If it pertains to crafting, it's stuck in here with a hot glue gun.

For the full use of the features, make the Internet connection.

Go to
Craft

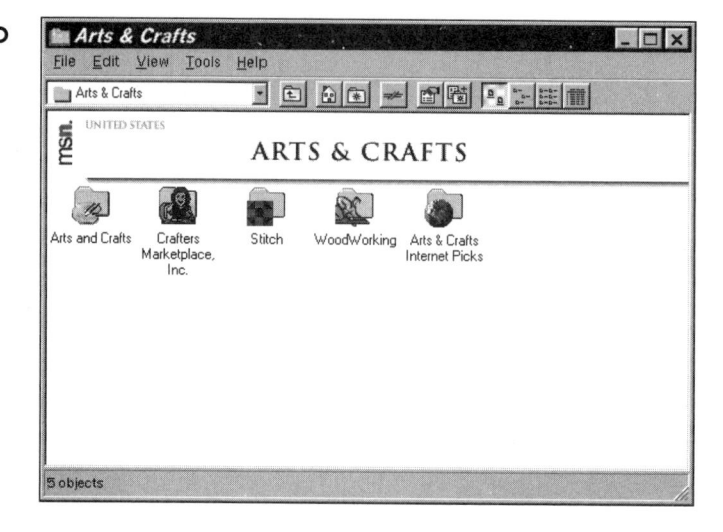

[Arts & Crafts window screenshot showing: Arts and Crafts, Crafters Marketplace, Inc., Stitch, WoodWorking, Arts & Crafts Internet Picks]

Automotive Forum

I have very high expectations of my car . . . I want it to have good gas mileage, no repairs, and a 10-year life. Perhaps, with the help of the Automotive Forum Maintenance Tips BBS, I can make that happen with my next car. The Automotive forum is your source for online auto guidance and information in the selection, repair, and maintenance of your speedwagon.

The Showroom File Area is a super highlight featuring tutorials on how to buy a car, compare leases, and save money. I think you'll find the Auto Loan Calculator to be a very useful freebie.

Go to
AutoForum

You'll find the Motorcycling Forum with GO TO Motorcycle.

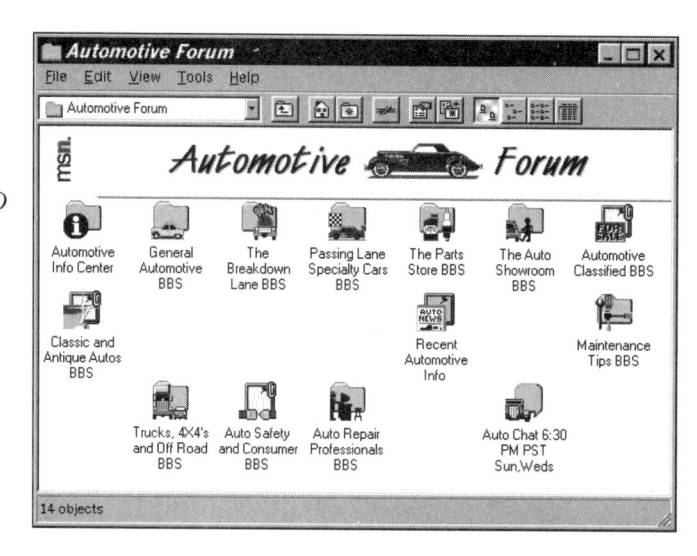

[Automotive Forum window screenshot showing 14 objects: Automotive Info Center, General Automotive BBS, The Breakdown Lane BBS, Passing Lane Specialty Cars BBS, The Parts Store BBS, The Auto Showroom BBS, Automotive Classified BBS, Classic and Antique Autos BBS, Recent Automotive Info, Maintenance Tips BBS, Trucks, 4X4's and Off Road BBS, Auto Safety and Consumer BBS, Auto Repair Professionals BBS, Auto Chat 6:30 PM PST Sun,Weds]

Go to
Collecting

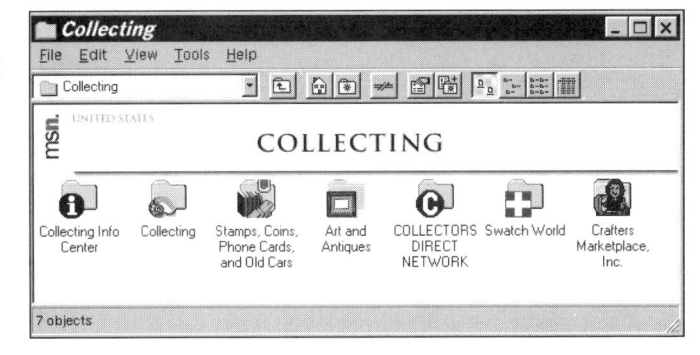

Collecting

The collecting area contains forums on the complete realm of collecting: artwork, antiques, memorabilia, trading cards, stamps, coins, rocks, comic books, and more. Perhaps the most unique of the collecting forums is Swatch World (GO TO Swatch), the site for Swatch watch collectors. Collector's Direct Network's Political Memorabilia (GO TO Political) should be a fun place to assess the past!

For the full use of the features, make the Internet connection.

Games

Shall we play mind games together? In the Games Forum, it's possible to talk about or participate in all types of games. The realm includes video games, role playing,

Go to
GamesForum

computer games, gambling chess, collectible card games, and a quiz area to further test your skills. This developing forum has already expanded with a horse racing forum, a virtual airline, and a role-playing game forum. Virtual Trek appeals to Star Trekkers of all life forms.

For the full use of the features, make the Internet connection.

Creative E-Mail

Turn your e-mail into a greeting card! You can have the most creative MSN mail with the ready images available from American Greetings. In the Personal Cardshop you can create a card online, and with E-mail Signature Art you can download exciting creative designs to spruce up your e-mail. The items can be purchased once (for about 50¢ to 75¢) and used over and over again.

Go to
Gift

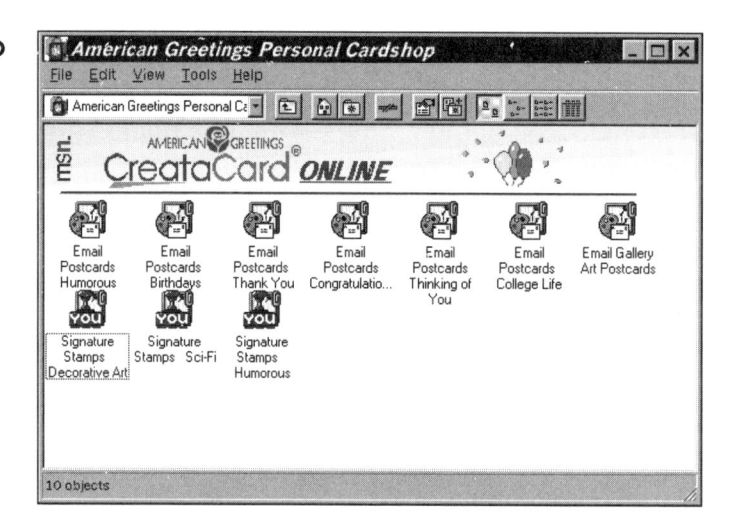

Gourmet GiftNet

Fine foods, gourmet gifts, and culinary accessories from around the world are ready for your selection in the Gourmet GiftNet. For birthdays, holidays, Christmas, or any time, you can shop from your desktop. Gourmet coffee gift sets and tantalizing chocolate creations will be delivered for you. You'll find a most impressive selection in this gift headquarters.

Go to
GourmetGift

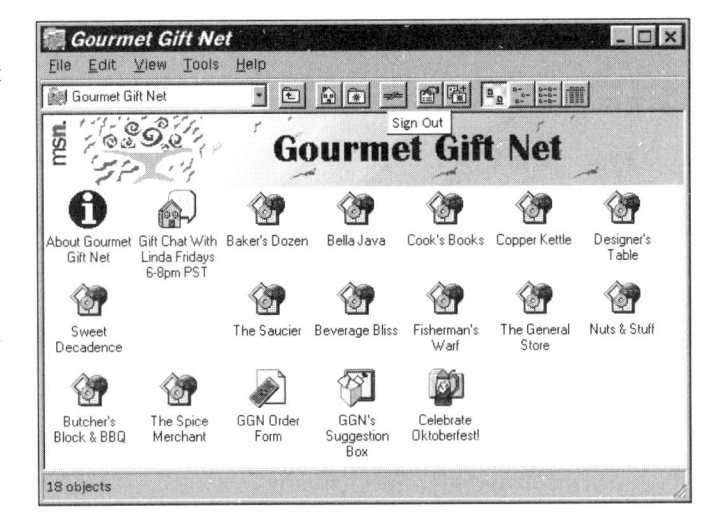

Magic and Illusions

Faster than you can pull a rabbit from a hat, you'll be entranced at the Magic and Illusions Forum. As you would guess, this forum promotes the art and enjoyment of magic. Highlights include the Magic School and special interest message boards for aspiring magicians. This place has my vote for the most innovative forum topic.

Go to
Magic

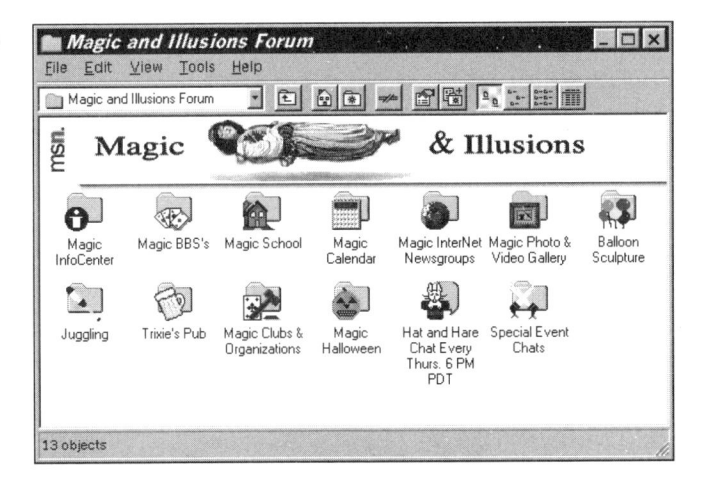

Go to
Astrology

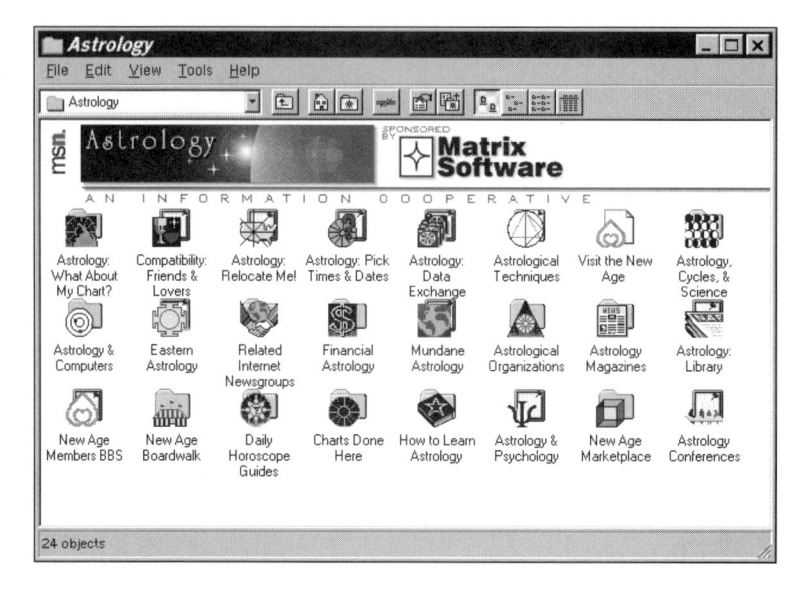

Astrology

Bring a new perspective to your daily life with MSN's Astrology Forum. Take a peek at your daily horoscope and, for real fun, have your chart done. There's a link to Internet newsgroups to help you expand your horizons. I'm particularly curious about my financial future, so I took a look at the Financial Astrology area. This could be a very good year.

For the full use of the features, make the Internet connection.

Alien Encounters

Explore your fantasies with alien beings, UFOs, and strange encounters in the Alien Encounters and UFOs Forum. With your fellow searchers you can explore aliens in antiquity, historic UFO events, and even view photos from an alien autopsy. (See the screen on the next page.)

Travel

Start here to travel to worldwide destinations, national treasures, and regional attractions. Of course, my favorite is Theme Parks!, which is home to Disney, Busch, Six Flags, and other theme parks (GO TO Theme Parks). In the Travel Forum, you can take part in travel chatter (and message boards) for U.S. and Worldwide destinations. Because of my travels to various UK destinations, I always start by checking the boards for Bermuda, England, Scotland, and Australia. I'm outta here—where's my passport?

Go to
Alien

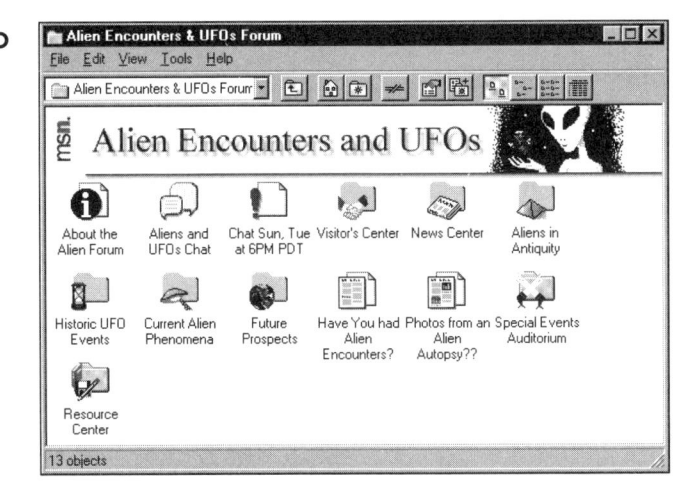

Go to
Travel

News & Weather

Generally, you can find up-to-the-minute news in News & Weather, but you have to know where to look. Occasionally, you'll find yesterday's news in MSN News.

Go to
News

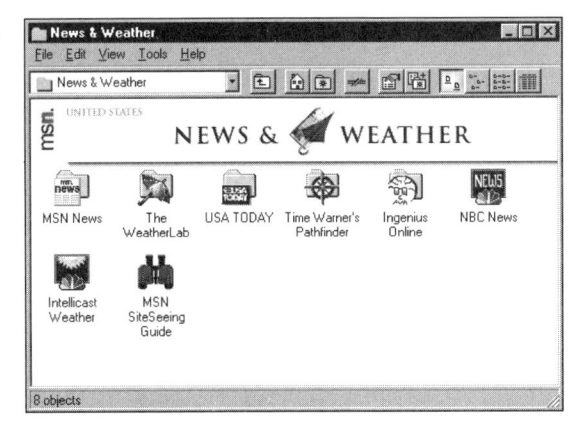

Other times it is up to the minute. I guess you could say it's a little irregular and needs to consume prunes on a daily basis.

Luckily, you can turn to real news organizations, including USA Today, NBC News, and Time Warner's Pathfinder, for the latest news. Until MSN News comes up to speed, count on the professional news organizations for their newsgathering and reporting expertise.

MSN News

This is one way to get the news on MSN, but it's not my favorite way. Why not? First, it takes awhile for this page to build. Second, you can't print from this page or its links. Third, can anybody tell me what day it is? How do I know if it is really today's news?

For the full use of the features, make the Internet connection.

Note: For easy-to-read, printable news, check MSN's This Just In (GO TO thisjustin). You'll quickly know if it is current and up to date.

Go to
readerMSNnews

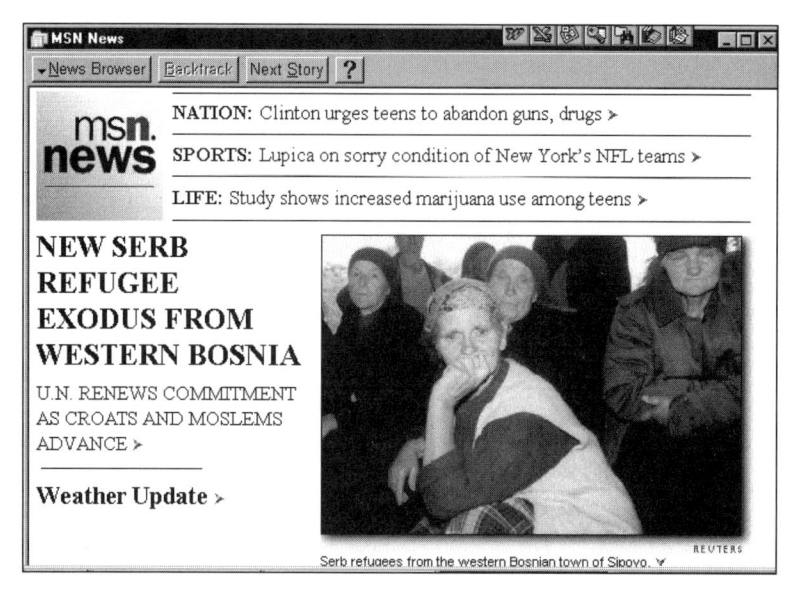

The WeatherLab

If you know where you are, you can get the weather details from The WeatherLab. Timely weather forecasts for over 600 U.S. and international cities are featured

Go to
TheWeatherLab

along with detailed weather maps for all continents. Plus, you'll have the chance to see satellite and radar images. The coverage is rounded out with articles, features, news, and reports. Hurricane evaders and tornado chasers will find an online home here. Weather safety articles serve as the basis of the features. The dreamy Cloudscapes folder is reserved for digital cloud snapshots and animations along with the content provider's SmartRadar product.

> **FYI** *Another good source for weather news is NBC News Intellicast (GO TO weathercast).*

USA TODAY

On your electronic doorstep you'll find the electronic version of *USA Today* on MSN. USA TODAY Online is a complete, regularly updated news and information service, including deep sports information and up-to-the-minute scores, colorful graphics, worldwide weather, and the features you love from the printed edition. You'll recognize the features: Front Page, Sports, Life, Weather, Snapshot, Money, Feedback, and the Crossword Puzzle. For access, you must have the browser and Internet connection.

For the full use of the features, make the Internet connection.

Go to
news

- *Select the USA Today icon.*

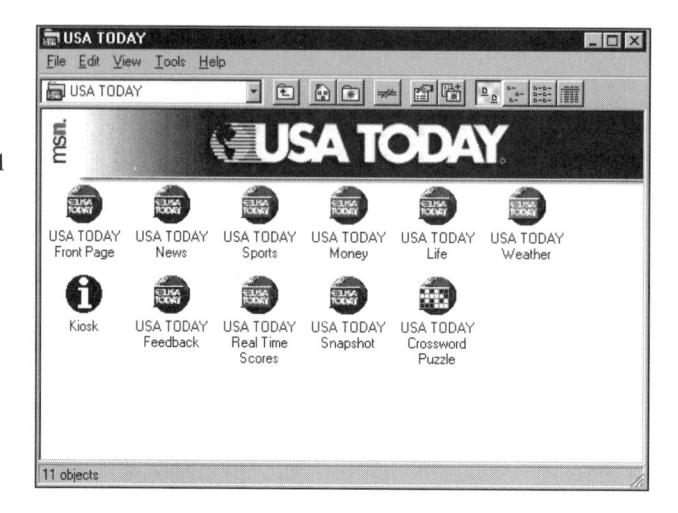

NBC Supernet

At NBC News on Supernet you'll find one of the best online sources for news and information. The Supernet connection brings the latest headlines and the stories behind them. Die-hard fans of NBC News can further their affiliation with information on favorite news programs and personalities. A shortcut to the AP News Summary can be found here, too.

Go to
NBCnews

People & Communities

Shared communities of men and women, cultures, and religions come together for sharing, advice, and support under the banner of People & Communities. Friends of Europe, History & Archaeology, Women's Wire, and the Mind Garden are representative of the communities found in this area.

Go to
Community

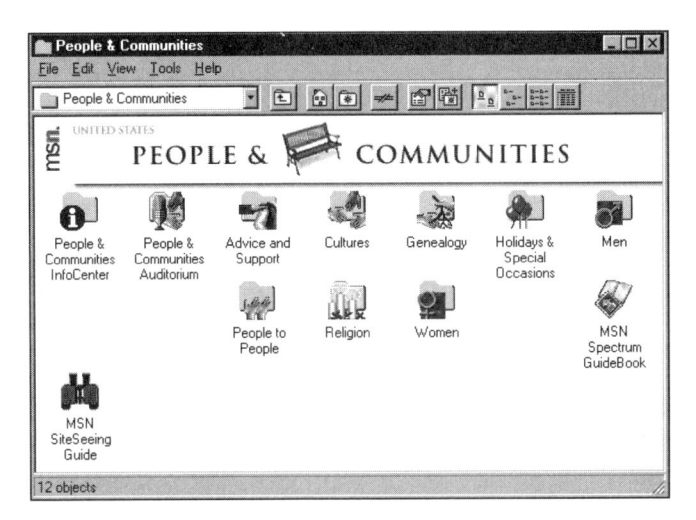

Genealogy

Ancestral investigations start here. Root seekers have found their counterparts online as they search for knowledge of their forebearers. Genealogy areas can be

Go to
Genealogy

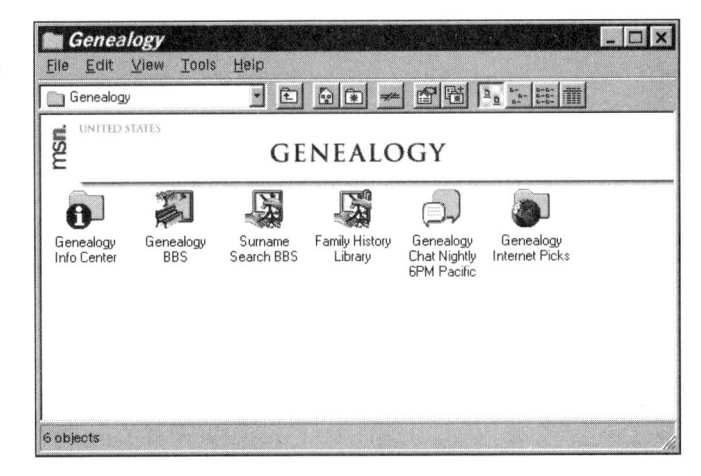

found on all of the online services—members have found each other to be great resources in the quest for their family trees. Members share tips in the chats and on the BBS—and many treasure the files found in the genealogy library, particularly in the lineage library.

For the full use of the features, make the Internet connection.

People to People

The People to People area contains forums for particular focus groups: gays and lesbians, New Age followers, disabled individuals, and generational groups. It's the place for communities to form, and I recommend that you check this area in the future to see if it has expanded. As time goes on, many MSN users will find their special communities here.

Go to
People

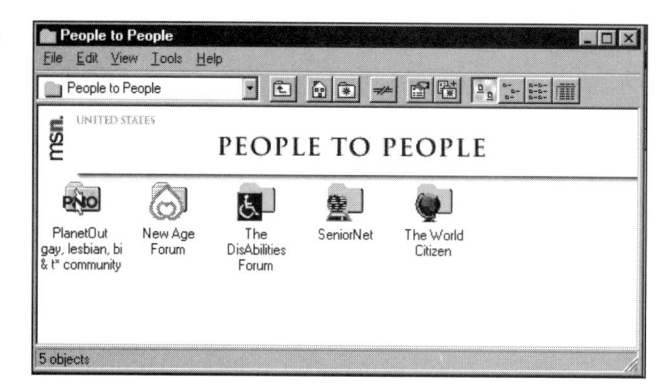

New Age Forum

The first New Ager I knew was named Barbara, and she was my supervisor's wife. I found her enlightening because her perspective of the world was so different from mine. I don't think she and I have the same definition for the word *stress*. If you're more like Barbara than me, this may be your favorite site on MSN. For those seeking or enjoying holistic alternatives and a natural lifestyle, a large community has gathered at the New Age forum. Focusing on whole communities, spirits, food, and the whole person, this may just be the best new start to a full life. Investigating the details of retreats, spas, massages, natural healing, and healthy foods makes me feel guilty about sitting here in my rocking chair, drinking my Coke. Maybe, you'll even find Barbara here.

Go to
New Age

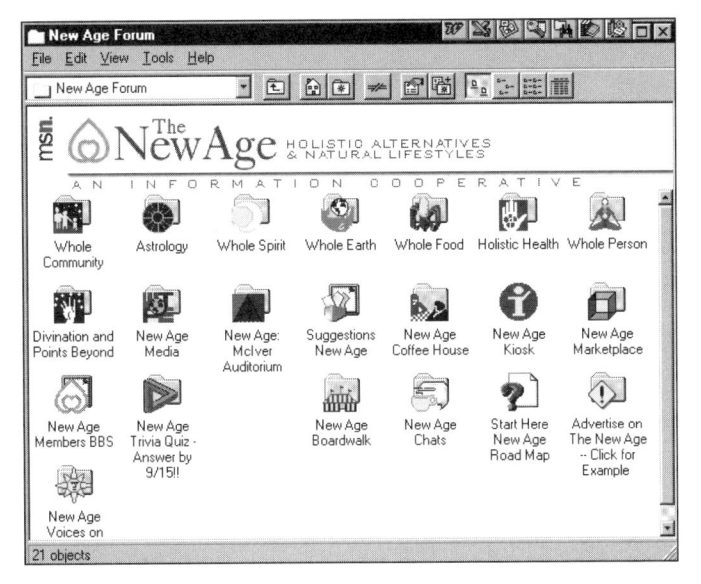

DisAbilities Forum

In the DisAbilities Forum, members can discuss any aspect of disability. The forum focuses on equal access, empowerment, and enlightenment. Employment rights, resources, insurance issues, legal issues, romance, and reunions indicate the range of topics shared by the dynamic members. Computer and noncomputer access technology helps members to stay active. If former Miss America Heather Whitestone is online, you might find her sharing her wealth of knowledge and poise in the DisAbilities Forum.

Go to
Disabilities

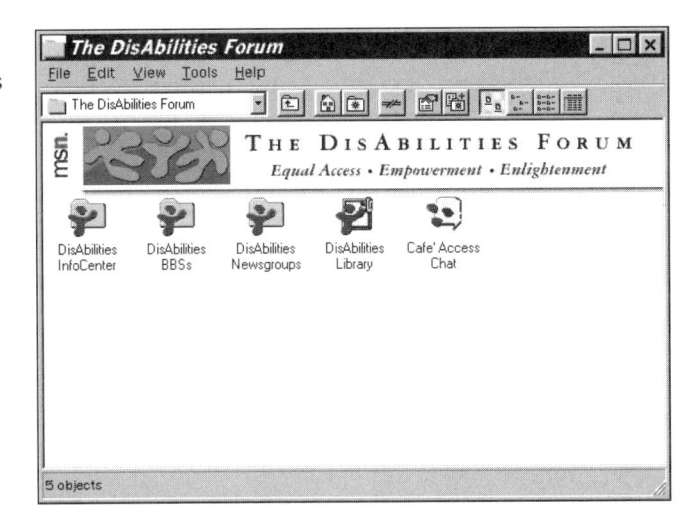

Go to
SeniorNet

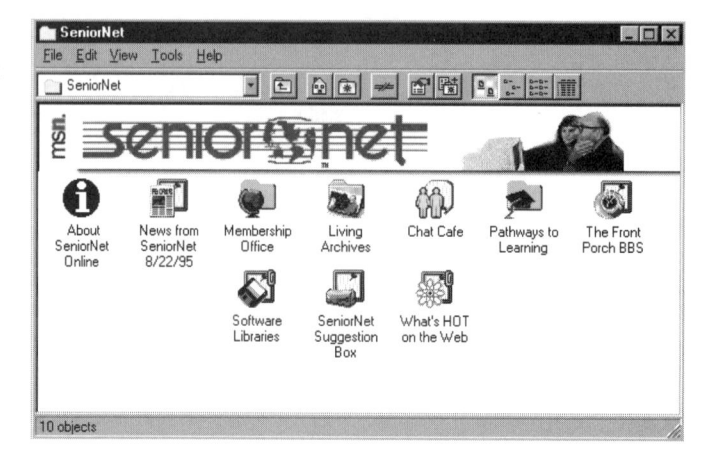

SeniorNet

You just might not believe the vitality and action to be found in SeniorNet Online. It is the home base for computer-using seniors. SeniorNet also has a forum on America Online, so they know how to create dynamic forums of interest to this lively audience. In the Living Archives, SeniorNet members share their perspectives of World War II, the Golden Age of Entertainment, the Evolution of Technology, and Traditions in Cooking. SeniorNet's software libraries contain numerous folders with files and programs for Education & Learning, Family and the Home, Recipes, Utilities, Graphics, Health, Recreation & Sports, and Travel.

For the full use of the features, make the Internet connection.

Inspiration from the Mind Garden

For a daily inspirational quote, go to the Mind Garden Forum. (See the screen on the next page.) With each day's quote, you'll have a fresh perspective and a change to your vision. It's the first step in personal growth.

"Tomorrow's world will belong to those who bring it the greatest hope."

Friends of Europe Forum

The many cultures of Europe come together under this area of MSN. The forum will host guest speakers from all over Europe, and each country has it's own forum. This is a cultural forum, and it also provides a great way to discover customs, the arts, politics, and places to go before you start for your destination.

For the full use of the features, make the Internet connection.

Go to
Inspiration

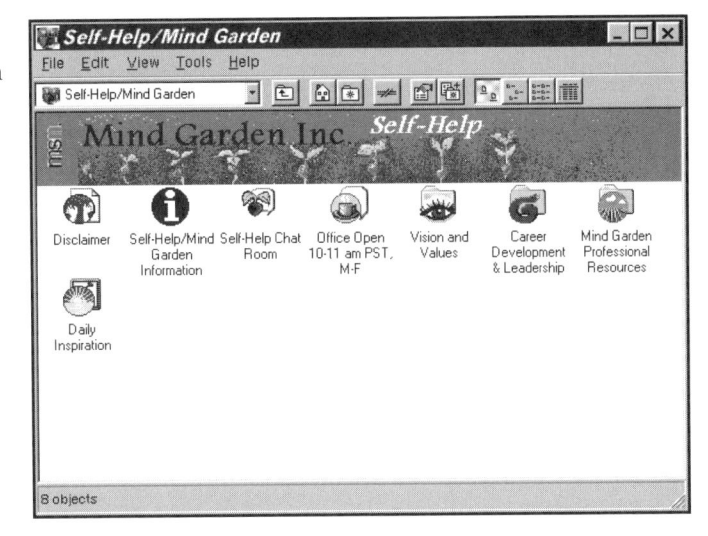

Go to
Europe

History & Archaeology

Expand your mind with the study of history and archaeology. In this area you'll find a chronological record of significant events, study of the past, and study of the people and events of the past. Parents and students should make this area one of their top priorities for discovery. If you know what's here before you receive the assignment, you'll be leaps ahead in your studies. This area is packed richly with information that arrives in folder after folder. Where are we on the timeline of humankind?

Go to
History

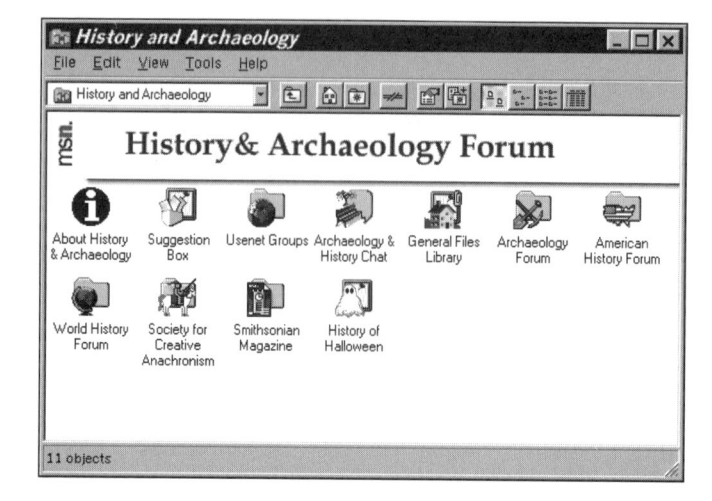

Women's Wire

Women's Wire is an interactive publisher providing women-focused online content, including articles, resource lists, book excerpts, and expert columns. Women's Wire seeks to make a difference in the lives of women around the world through MSN. Three of the main departments include Health & Fitness, Career & Finance, and Fashion & Shopping. Other great features include the online physician and the StyleWatch. There's even a link to the Women's Wire Web Site.

For the full use of the features, make the Internet connection.

Go to
WWire

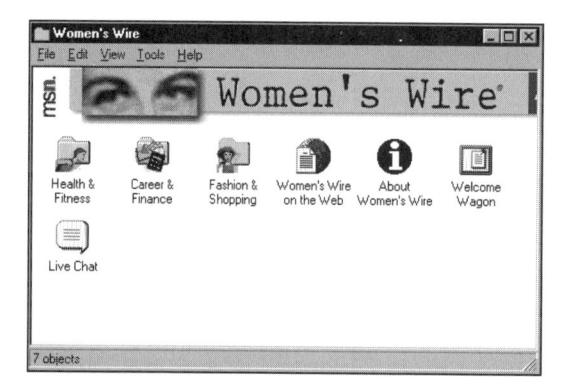

Public Affairs

Bob Packwood has nothing to do with Public Affairs—other than the fact that both are concerned with government. Consumer services, the Armed Forces Forum, politics, public health, the media—and more—call Public Affairs their home address.

Go to
Public

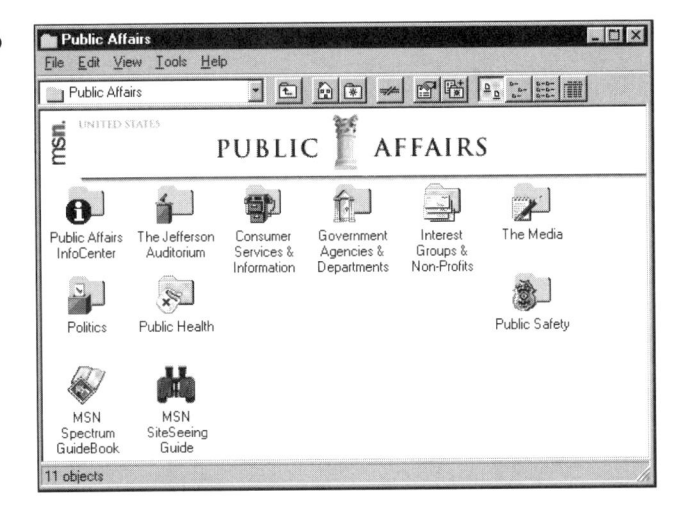

Armed Forces Forum

The armed forces areas on other online services are pretty popular, so I'm hoping that this one will soon be catching up to the content and activity level that's found elsewhere. As you would expect, the Armed Forces Forum features information and resources for members of the Armed Forces and their families, as well as the organizations and businesses that provide support. The forum includes the armed forces of the world, but thus far it primarily covers the concerns of U.S. armed forces.

Go to
AFF

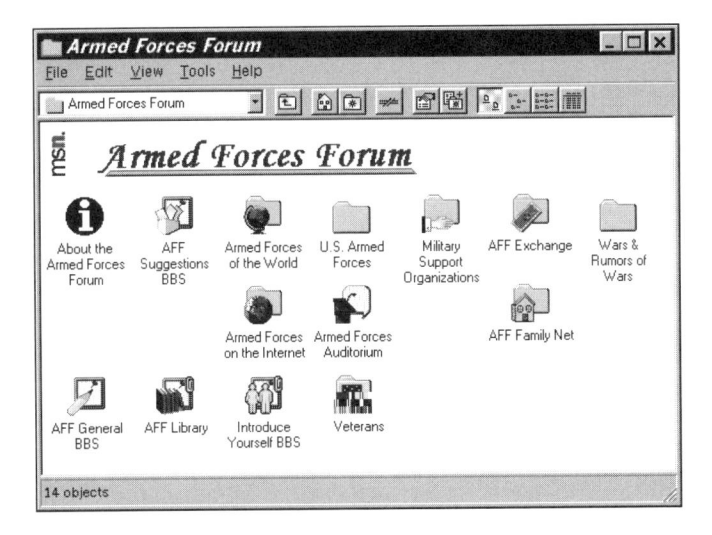

NET Political Network

NET Political NewsTalk Network broadcasts 'round the clock to listeners across the country. Through the NET Forum, MSN members can share their thoughts on the principles of free enterprise, traditional family values, personal property rights, and limited givernment. This is where you'll encounter political "hot quotes," review Paul Weyrich commentaries, have the opportunity to engage in chats with congressmen, senators and insiders, and take on the provocative political topics of the day. The campaign trail is clearly marked in this political network.

Go to
Nettown

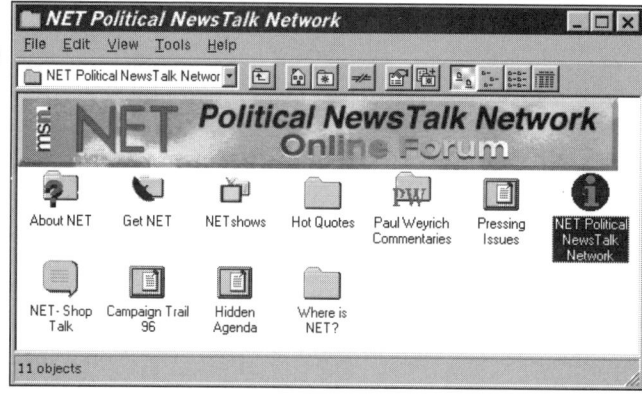

GoverNet

Interact with the political machine in GoverNet. The home base for political information and debate, GoverNet covers the political spectrum. Monitor the Congressional Report Card, and keep an eye on legislation through Voter Alert. As the campaign progresses, you'll be able to follow your favorite candidate's daily moves on the campaign trail. Political junkies love this place. Students of the art of politics will turn to GoverNet for the text of historical speeches.

Go to
GoverNet

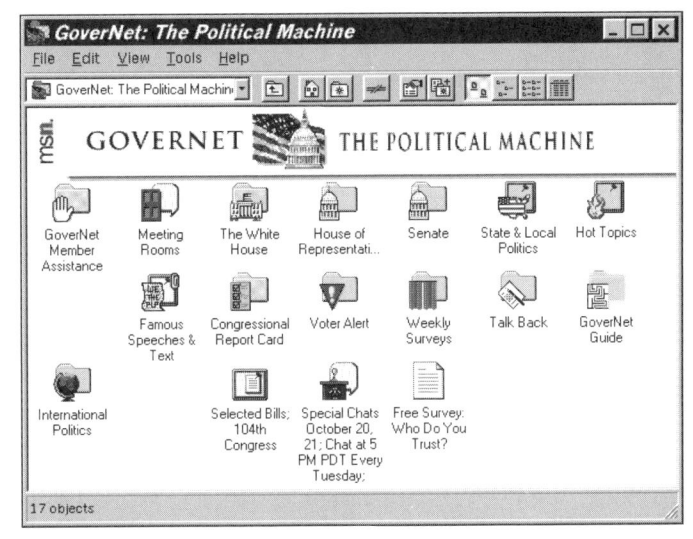

Science & Technology

Science & Technology is the place for the technically abled. Count me out! You'll undoubtedly know if you belong here in the range of forums including Biology & Life Sciences, Chemistry & Biochemistry, Communications Technology, Computers & Electronics, Geology & Geography, Engineering, Environment, The Futurist, Industry & Infrastructure, Medicine, Math & Physics, Transportation, Astronomy & Space, and ScienceFair.

Go to
Science

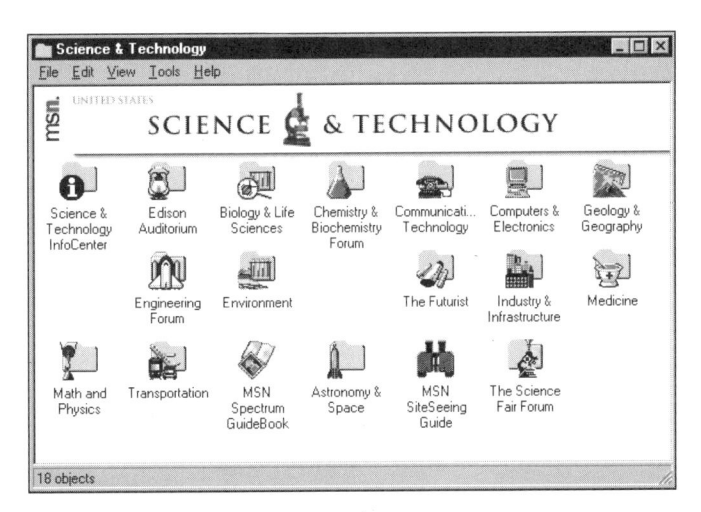

Go to
Space

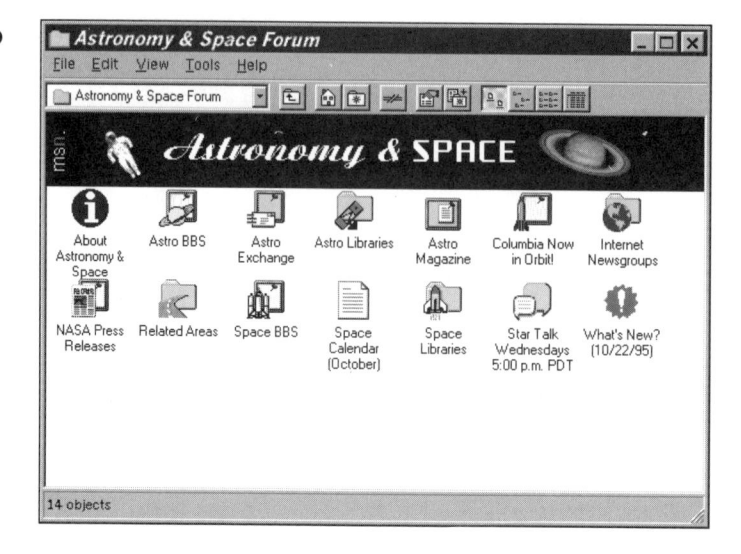

Astronomy & Space

There's nothing like a summer night and a clear view of the stars. Just lie back and contemplate how inconsequential we are in the mysterious big picture. Man continues to be fascinated with the mysteries of the solar system, and the rapid-fire discussion on astronomy and the exploration of space of the Astronomy & Space Forum is matched to amateur astronomers and space enthusiasts and their quest. Valuable gems can be found in the Space Library, which contains files and enthralling photographs detailing the highlights of manned and unmanned missions. NASA press releases are added as issued.

ScienceFair

Will an ant farm win the blue ribbon at the science fair? This area of MSN is devoted to the science fair generation. Backyard projects and science fair productions are included, and it's a great place for parents who are homeschooling older children. Students and others will appreciate investigations. This is the place to stop for resources, experiments, tips, and challenges from others who love science. Do you need to review the scientific method? You can count on a review session here. The Planet Savers BBS includes tips and experiments for a better, cleaner earth.

Go to
ScienceFair

Smithsonian and Air & Space

The nation's science and history leader, Smithsonian, provides forums and magazines that explore the frontiers of science and the marvels of the natural world. Through Smithsonian you'll take a fresh look at the arts, history, and the environment. Air & Space/Smithsonian covers the stratospheric range of air and space topics of the past, present, and future. Through both you'll encounter columns and feature article summaries from the printed magazines, as well as forums for communicating with editors and authors.

Go to
Smithsonian

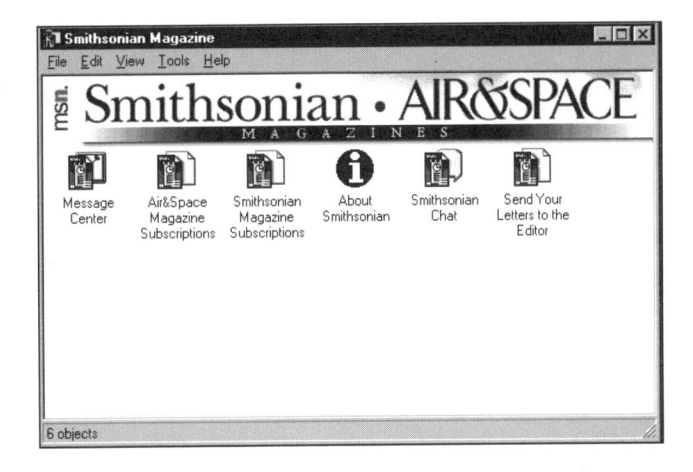

Special Events

MSN's Special Events area is filled with coverage of top-notch events such as the America's Cup (didn't we lose? Is it still called that?), the British Grand Prix, Runner's World Prefontaine Classic, and the Edinburgh Festival. The Special Events Chat Archive is the place to check for transcripts of chats with such notable guests as Wolfgang Puck. We can count on this area for more excitement as MSN hits full stride.

Go to
Events

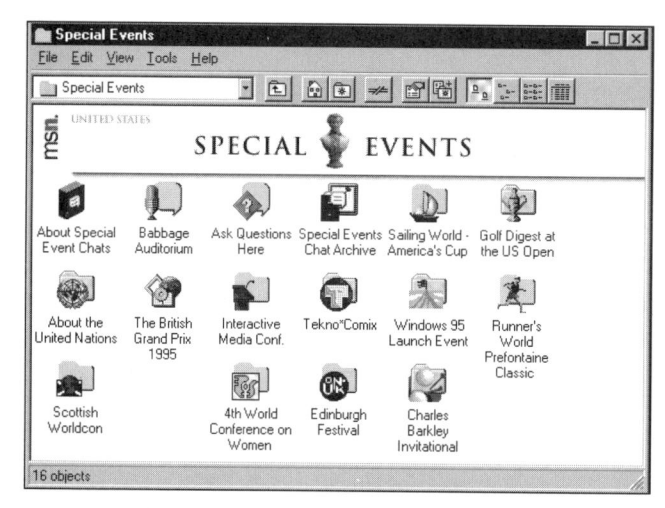

Sports & Recreation

All types of sports—professional, amateur, and recreational—are located in the Sports & Recreation area. If it's not here right now, this area will soon include daily results, standings, statistics, fantasy sports, and more great sporting stuff.

For the full use of the features, make the Internet connection.

ShaqWorld Online

If you're a fan of the Shaq, you must know about ShaqWorld Online on MSN. Packed with entertainment and sports, it covers basketball with a vengeance. Scores, stats, graphics, and insights abound. Beyond the court, ShaqWorld will feature the best in music, film, and television as well as The Shaq Paq, a fan club for the younger set. While this screen indicates that it's coming soon, the real thing will be on your screen by the time this book is in your hands.

Go to
Sports

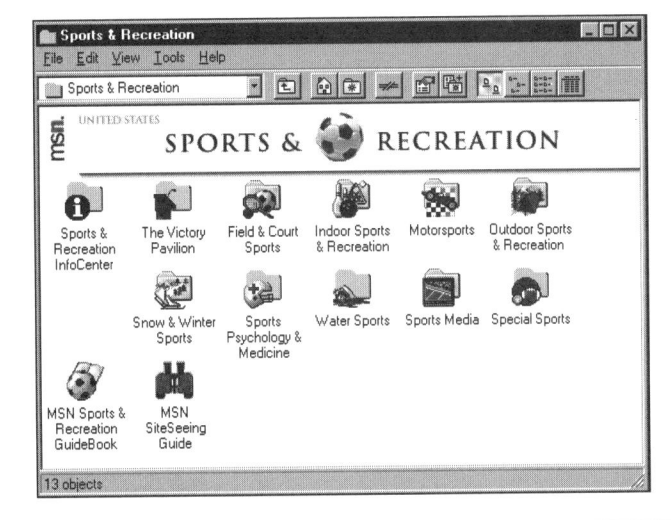

Go to
FieldSports

- Select ShaqWorld Online.

Online Games, Inc.

There's just something about males and fantasies. They even have to create them for sports! My guess is that most of the chromosomal lineup here will be of the same gender. Join in and play the eight different Fantasy Sports Games on MSN. Bring your best game and playing skills including strategies for lineup, negotiating for trades, and sports knowledge for drafting players. Fantasy games for football, baseball, basketball, and hockey are included in the lineup.

Go to
Sportsgames

You'll also find Fantasy Sports, Inc. at GO TO Fantasy_sports.

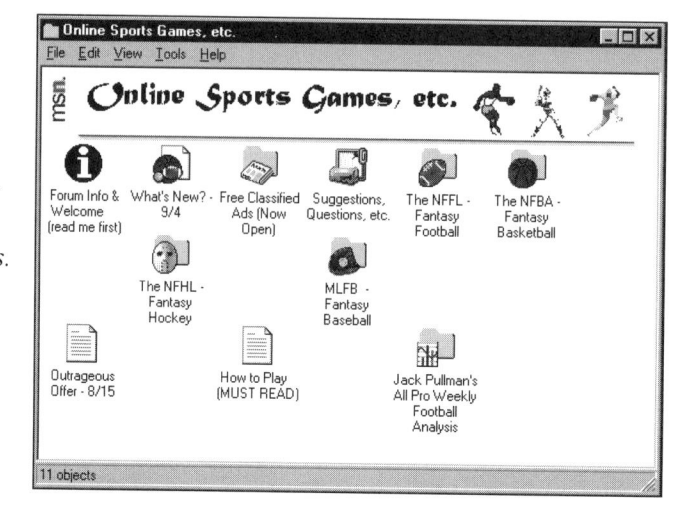

Martial Arts Network

I've always wanted to have strategy and control for my temper tantrums. Perhaps I need to vent through the martial arts. In the Martial Arts Network, you can gather together with your friends from all over the world in your quest for more knowledge on Tai Kwon Do, Karate, Hapkido, Aikido, and Judo. You'll find lots more powerful stuff including the electronic editions of *Black Belt Magazine, Karate/Kung Fu Illustrated,* and *Martial Arts Training Magazine.* Masters, grand masters, school owners, movie stars, and tournament champions gather in the forum to share their expertise.

Go to
MAN

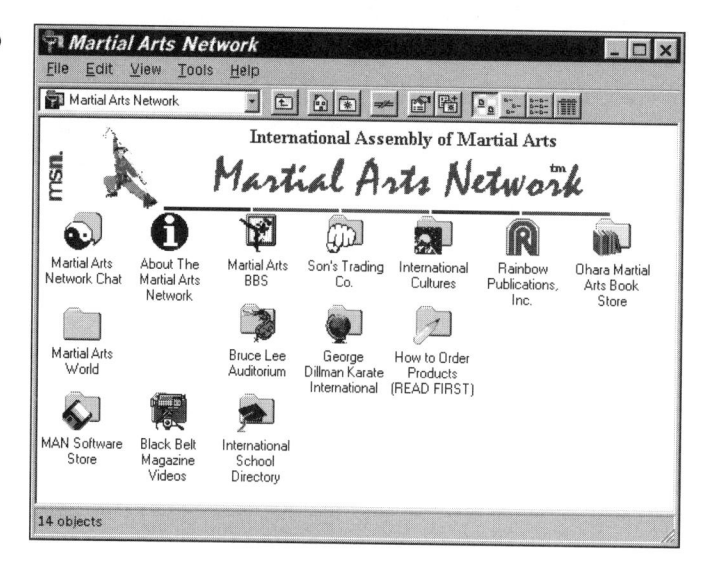

Scuba Online

I should have checked this site before my last trip to Hawaii. Never mind that Microsoft was still in its pre-Windows era when I last saw the sands of Waikiki. Still, though, I could have used some better instructions before I attempted to drown through a snorkel tube. True fans of water sports—scuba divers, snorkelers, and people who love the water—will appreciate (more than I) the articles from MSN Scuba, the online interactive magazine. The main topics cover equipment, travel, tech diving, and training.

Go to
Scuba! On-line

I think they could have come up with something easier to remember!

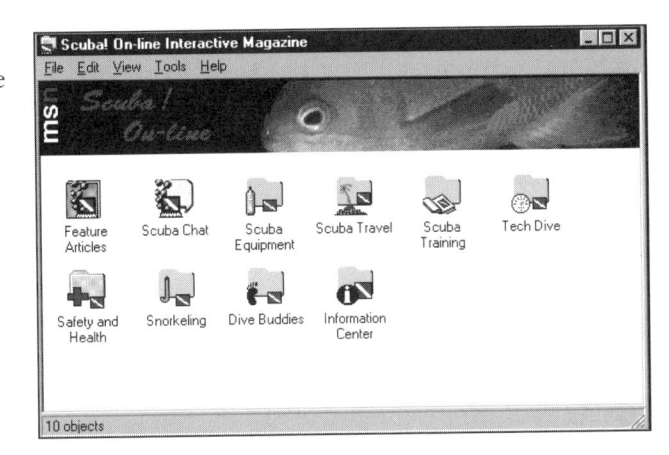

Sports Media

In one location, you can track the progress of your favorite teams. Up-to-date statistics and information on sporting events have been gathered in one online stadium: MSN's Sports Media area. ESPN, USA Today, NBC Sports, and Sports Illustrated are the leading providers in this area.

For the full use of the features, make the Internet connection.

ESPN SportsZone

With ESPN SportsZone you can wake up to the latest sports news, scores, and statistics. Every morning a brief news summary will arrive in your e-mail box—for free. The SportsZone takes you into the huddle, the press box, and the locker room for the inside scoop. Join in and interact with sports personalities and columnists. With a link to the ESPN Studios Web Page, you stay on top of the televised sports events.

Go to
SportsMedia

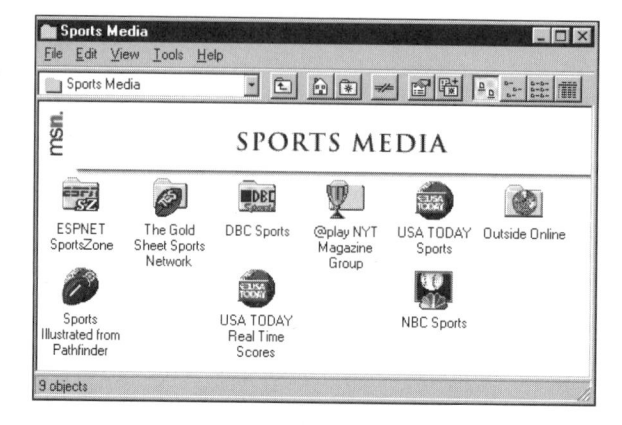

Go to
SportsMedia

- Select SportsZone.

@Play

@Play is the MSN forum for The New York Times Magazine Group, which encompasses *Golf Digest, Golf World, Cruising World, Snow Country, Tennis Magazine, Cruising World,* and *Sailing World.* Each of four principal areas concentrates on a sporting activity and related lifestyle. Online readers can count on @Play for expert instruction, knowledgeable equipment reviews, and informed opinion.

Internet Center

In the section entitled "You, Too, Can Be an Internet Dynamo," I've covered the full realm of the Internet Center. Since I'm covering every area in the categories, I

Go to
atplay

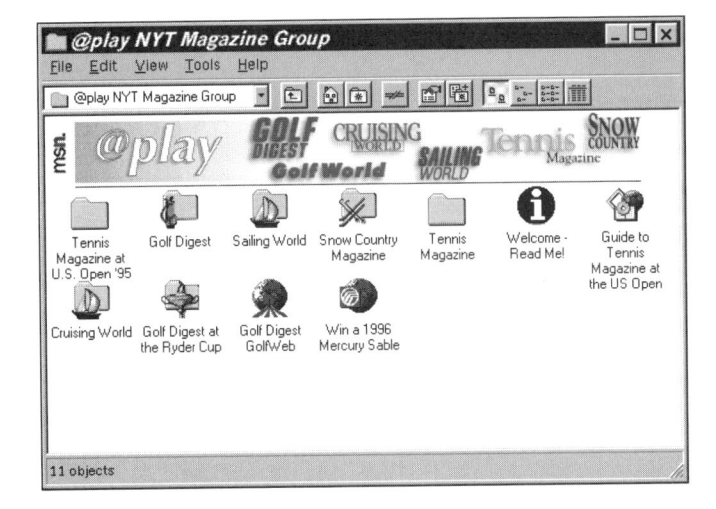

Go to
Internet

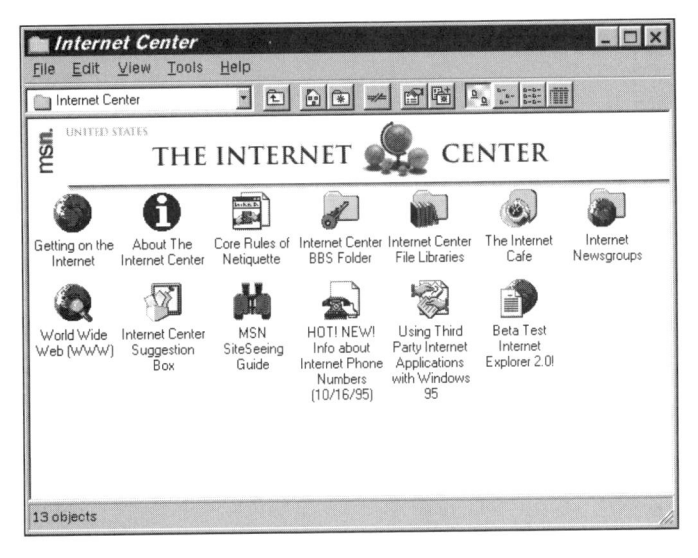

couldn't leave out this most important area. It focuses primarily on the Web and Newsgroups—the two most popular Internet features.

MSN Passport

Like an explorer, I've found the International Terminal on MSN. The Passport area is the central gathering point for international content. Each international branch of MSN is conducted in its own language. If you like to experiment, you can select the

Go to
Passport

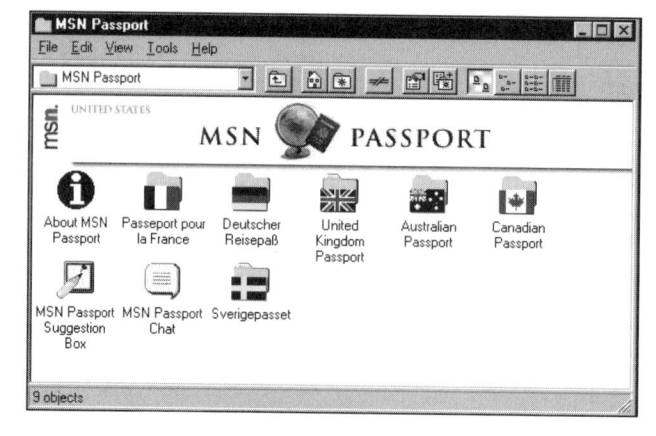

content designated for other languages. You are completely welcome to browse through the content of other countries, but please remember that they are not committed to supporting languages other than their own.

Chat World

It's really hard for me to get excited about chat rooms—they're just not my favorite places. You might encounter the same people every day or you might not. They may even be talking about cleaning their toenails. I can't even tell you what you'll

Go to
ChatWorld

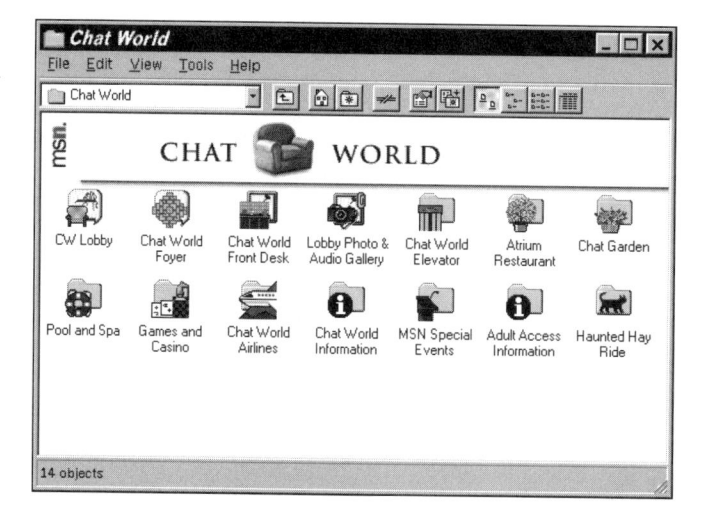

find there—it's different every day. But, if you're lonely or have nothing better to do, give it a try—you never know who you'll meet or what you might encounter. You might even make a lifelong friend.

Before you enter, keep in mind that the Lobby is monitored 24 hours a day. All other rooms, accommodating from 2 to 25, are not monitored.

> *I do want to raise a little red flag here for parents. Mom and Dad—please be aware that Johnnie's new friends may not be as nice as they seem. Betty may not really be a woman and Robbie may not be a seven-year-old boy. There is a segment of online users who enjoy creating new personalities online. I think it is in your family's best interest to keep an eye on time spent in chat rooms.*

PART 4

You, Too, Can Be an Internet Dynamo

Have you mastered the Internet? Of course you haven't. Who has? But what about the little things? Do you know how to drop all those Internet terms into your conversations to make yourself sound knowledgeable? It can be downright embarrassing when you're not sure if you're using the correct terms. In fact, *I* still stumble—ask my editor.

In this primer, I'll guide you through the Internet terms that are required knowledge for survival in cyberspace (there's your first term). By the time you're done reading this section, you'll not only know how to use the terms, you'll also know what they mean—not to mention that you'll know a lot more about using the Internet, too.

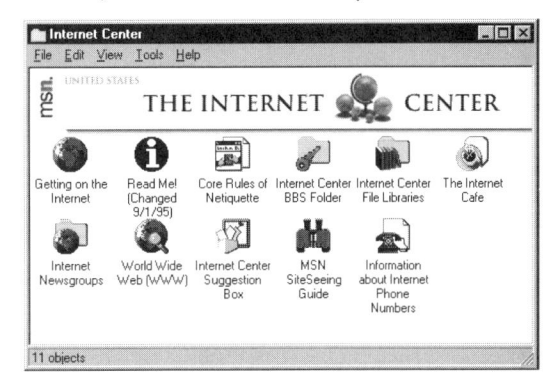

What's the Difference between MSN and the Internet?

MSN is the online service provided by Microsoft. MSN has its own proprietary content—features and forums organized and controlled by MSN. But MSN also serves as a gateway to the Internet. In other words, MSN is not technically part of the Internet, but it does provide a convenient way for you to get to the Internet.

What we now call the Internet was originally devised under an umbrella organization called ARPA in 1969. ARPA was the Advanced Research Projects Agency, a U.S. governmental agency that linked universities, the military, and defense contractors. The computer network that ARPA formed was called, sensibly enough, ARPANET. The major purpose for the network was to provide a way to keep computers talking to each other in the event of a nuclear attack (supposedly by the Soviets).

The idea was simple: Design a set of communications rules, or protocols, that could be commonly used by different computers as a way to talk to each other. This set of protocols has come to be known as TCP/IP. Trust me, you don't want to know much more about it than that. Essentially, TCP/IP is just a common language that all computers on the Internet use to exchange information like files and other data.

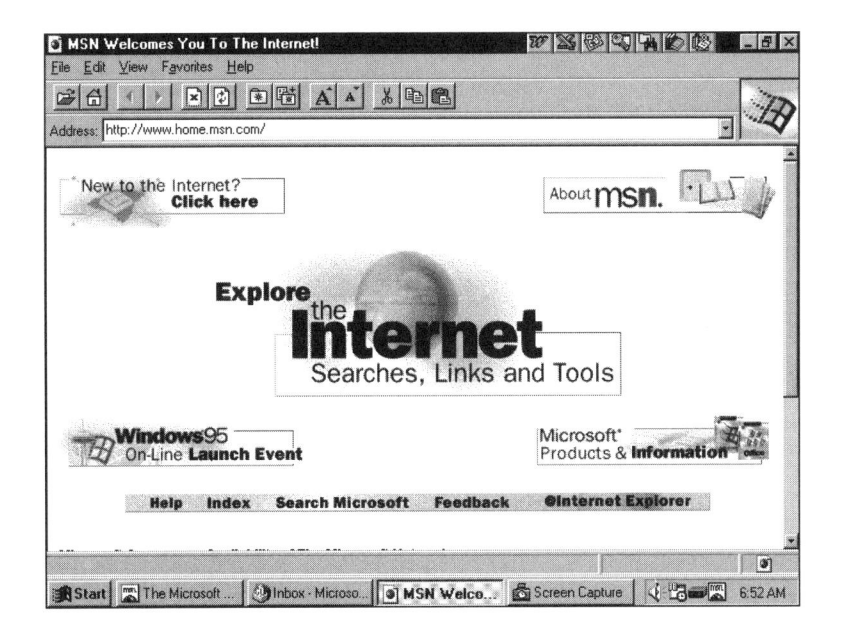

ARPA is long-since gone, but the networking system it created—the Internet—survives today and in fact is more popular than ever. Universities, the military, and several other government contractors still serve as the "backbone" of the Internet. (The term "backbone" refers to very fast connections made between very fast computers, so that the time required to send and receive information from your humble ol' PC to another computer is kept to a minimum.)

Today, the term "Internet" refers just about all computers connected to networks—because most online services (including MSN) provide access to the Internet.

The other main way of connecting to the Internet is through an Internet Service Provider (ISP), which is a company that basically provides you with a link to the Internet backbone. Connecting a home computer to the Internet via an ISP isn't always easy to do, although it's gotten a lot easier in recent months. But if you connect to the Internet via an online service like MSN, you can let the service do all of the technical dirty work. When you use MSN to connect to the Internet, it's literally just a matter of pointing and clicking. You don't need a lot of special TCP/IP and other communications software to get on the Net.

As an online service, The Microsoft Network provides content in addition to an Internet connection. There are hundreds of forums on MSN. These forums are the basis for the community of MSN. Online services provide content in addition to what you will get with a standard Internet service provider. Such features include areas run by software and hardware companies, health organizations, non-profit groups, and entertainment companies. The point to keep in mind is that Microsoft controls all of the forums and other content that make up MSN. But as soon as you venture out into the Internet, you're accessing content that Microsoft has no control over—except in certain cases where MSN restricts access to some Internet sites (to protect minors, usually).

You may read or hear of individuals connecting to the Internet for less than you pay for you monthly MSN bill. Again, thse individuals have contracted with Internet Service Providers. ISPs merely provide Internet access—without the benefit or organized forums and the community that MSN provides. For most families, an Internet connection through an online service is the best bet to ensure that parents retain control over information, access, and support.

What in the World Is the World Wide Web?

At this point, I need to explain the difference between the Internet and the World Wide Web (or just "the Web" for short). When the Internet was first created, users exchanged information by sending text back and forth. And that's the way the Internet worked for more than 20 years. In fact, until recently, Internet computers couldn't view graphics, sound, or other multimedia information directly online. Sure, you could download a specially encoded graphic to your computer from another computer linked to the Internet. But you couldn't directly view the graphic online. You first had to store the graphic file on your computer, and then use one or more special programs to decode and display the graphic. What a pain!

Most of this fol-der-ol was solved thanks to an enterprising young man named Mark Andreessen, who in the late 1980s worked for a governmental agency called the National Center for Supercomputing Applications (NCSA). Mark developed a way to look at graphics online—a real breakthrough, since the Internet up until then was kind of boring to look at and very difficult for most people to use.

Mark developed a special tool that could read files that contained special Hyper Text Markup Language (HTML) codes. His tool eventually led to the formation of the World Wide Web, which simply refers to sites and files (stored on the Internet) that are encoded in HTML format.

You don't need to know anything about HTML to use the Internet and the World Wide Web. I just bring it up because the most entertaining and visually appealing places on the Internet are "Web sites," or computers that store HTML-encoded documents. But in order for you to look at HTML documents, you need a tool like the one Mark Andreessen created. The tool you need is called a *Web browser*. Basically, a browser converts HTML code into graphics, text, and other multimedia content so that you can view it all directly online.

One other feature about HTML documents that's worth noting: *Hypertext*. Web pages usually contain words that appear in underline. These words are called hypertext *links*, because all you need to do is click on them, and your browser will take you to a location that the link points to. By using hypertext links at Web sites, you can literally jump from one part of the world to another in a matter of seconds.

If you're still fuzzy on the difference between the Internet and the Web, don't worry. I'll have more to say about this distinction later in the chapter. For now, I just want to give you enough primer information to get you started in cyberspace.

Making the Connection

Now I need to explain that there are really two parts to your MSN software. The first part is the main application you had the option to include when you first installed Windows 95 on your system. The second application is Microsoft Explorer—Microsoft's browser that give you access to Web sites around the world. You can download the browser from MSN (GO TO MSN105). You will pay for downloading time based on the speed of your modem connection. For an additional fee, you can drive to your local computer retailer to purchase Microsoft Plus!, which includes Microsoft Explorer as well as creative add-ons for Windows 95.

Still with me? This may get confusing. There are two applications, two access numbers and two types of connections that you can make to enter MSN: MSN itself and MSN's Web browser. Depending on your access needs, you will generally chose one of two phone numbers for your connection, and when you sign on, you can start from the MSN icon or from the Internet icon on your desktop.

Each time you sign on to MSN, you can choose to sign on to *just* MSN (using one phone number) or MSN Plus Internet (another phone number).

Keep in mind that MSN/Internet access is provided over a different network than standard MSN service. I'm in the major market of Los Angeles. We have several access lines for those seeking a straight MSN connection. There are fewer access lines for MSN/Internet access. It's quite likely that in your community or region, you will have "free" phone access to MSN, but you'll incur a charge for a connection to MSN/Internet.

As you explore MSN, you will soon discover that many forums offer direct links—or shortcuts—to the Internet. Internet and Web sites are seamlessly linked to MSN—if you have the browser and an Internet connection. Without the browser, you'll still have access to Internet e-mail and Usenet newsgroups.

You'll probably want to be judicious and frugal in selecting your online connection, because you want the most online time for the least cost, right? If cost is no obstacle, or if your MSN/Internet connection is free, always connect with the MSN/Internet connection.

If your budget has greater constraints, it may be necessary to stay primarily with the MSN connection except for times when you really need full Internet access. Eventually, you may find that the additional information from the MSN/Internet connection is worth every penny of incremental phone charges, courtesy of the phone company. To encourage MSN to add phone numbers in your area, feel free to send lots of e-mail to the chief powers at MSN, requesting additional phone lines to save you and your neighbors money.

For the purposes of this section, I'm assuming that you've installed Microsoft's browser, and that you are connecting to MSN using a phone access line designated as MSN/Internet. Otherwise, why are we here?

> **FYI**
>
> *The Internet Explorer (add-on) allows users to browse the World Wide Web, FTP, and Gopher sites.*
>
> *Windows 95 includes FTP and Telnet Clients. That means you can use FTP and Telnet even without using the browser.*
>
> *For other Internet functions—including Gopher, WAIS, and Finger—you'll need to use third-party programs.*

Internet Encounters

As you speed across the Internet, you'll encounter e-mail, mailing lists, FTP, Gopher, Telnet, Finger, Usenet newsgroups, and Web "pages."

- **E-mail** is pretty easy to understand and master. As long as you've typed the address correctly, or correctly placed it in the address book, your message will get to where it's supposed to go.
- **Mailing lists** can be thought of as e-mail forums for specific topics. For instance, I subscribe to one called the knitlist; it's just like having a bulletin board arrive in my mailbox periodically.
- I like to think of **Usenet newsgroups** as international message boards. You may like the Travel Forum (GO TO Travel) on MSN. If so, you might want to take your "travels" onto the Internet by going to the alt.travel newsgroup.
- With **FTP**, you can access other computers, grab files, and download them to yours. For many FTP sites, you can also upload files of your own so that others can use them.
- For our non-technical purposes, think of **Gopher** as similar to FTP in that it allows you to reach other sites to grab files. It typically provides text-based information.
- With **Telnet,** you can access other computers and direct them to meet your needs. You can even maneuver through other systems to look up the information you need. Telnet's text-based interface provides interactive services on the Internet.
- The **Finger** command can find out information about other users and computers.
- The **World Wide Web** has made almost as much news lately as O.J. Simpson. As I hinted at earlier, the Web is a collection of graphic files, photos, video clips, sounds, and hypertext documents. These days, it seems as though everyone who's online is creating Web pages. I don't have my own "home page" yet, but my publisher does. (A home page is just the starting location at a particular Web site. I don't know who decided to call Web documents "pages," but it's a term that doesn't make a lot of sense, since a "page" can be as long or as short as the author wants. Anyway, you might as well get used to seeing and hearing the term.) You'll also find thousands upon thousands of pages that have been created by businesses, governmental organizations, universities, and private groups. Geez. Everybody wants to get into the act.

As I get further along in this section, I'll show you how the same site can be accessed three ways—with FTP, Gopher, and Web access. Of course, the site has to be established for each type of connection.

From MSN's home page on the web, you can access InfoSeek, Lycos, and Yahoo in one central location. These three sources provide some of the best web search tools available. Since MSN provides them in one location, you can use Lycos if the InfoSeek server is busy, or use Yahoo if both the InfoSeek and Lycos servers are busy, or.... Well, you get the idea.

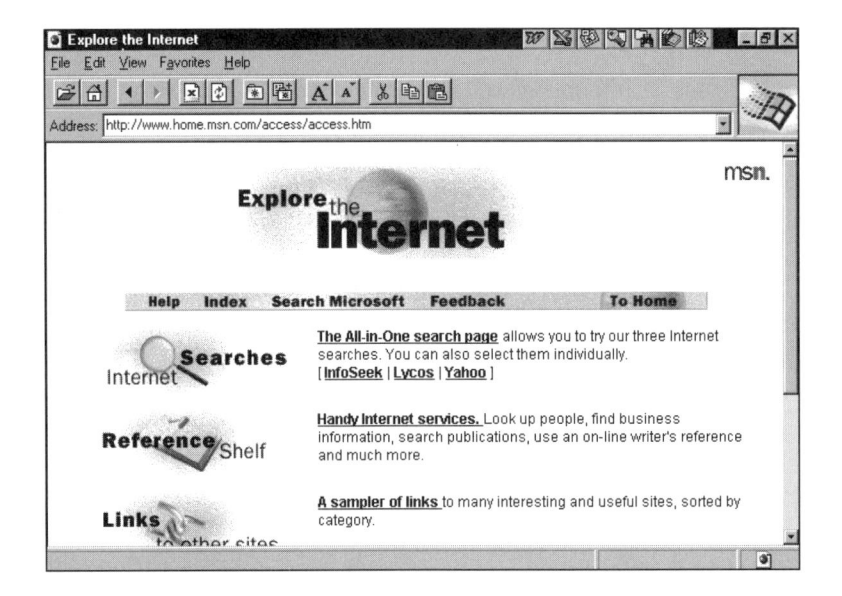

> **World Wide Web, FTP, Gopher, and Telnet**
> *You have access to all of these functions through the Internet Explorer and through Internet shortcuts.*
>
> *To conduct your search, right-click on the MSN icon on the status bar in the lower right corner of your screen. Select Find and make sure "Of type" says All Services (MSN and Internet).*

What Are the Boundaries of MSN? The Internet?

At this writing, the boundaries of MSN depend more on your connection type than anything else. In many ways, MSN is a service without boundaries. When you select a feature, such as *USA Today*, it appears as a forum presented by a third party—an independent content provider (ICP). In reality, there is a contractual arrangement between MSN and *USA Today* in order to link MSN users to this site.

You, Too, Can Be an Internet Dynamo

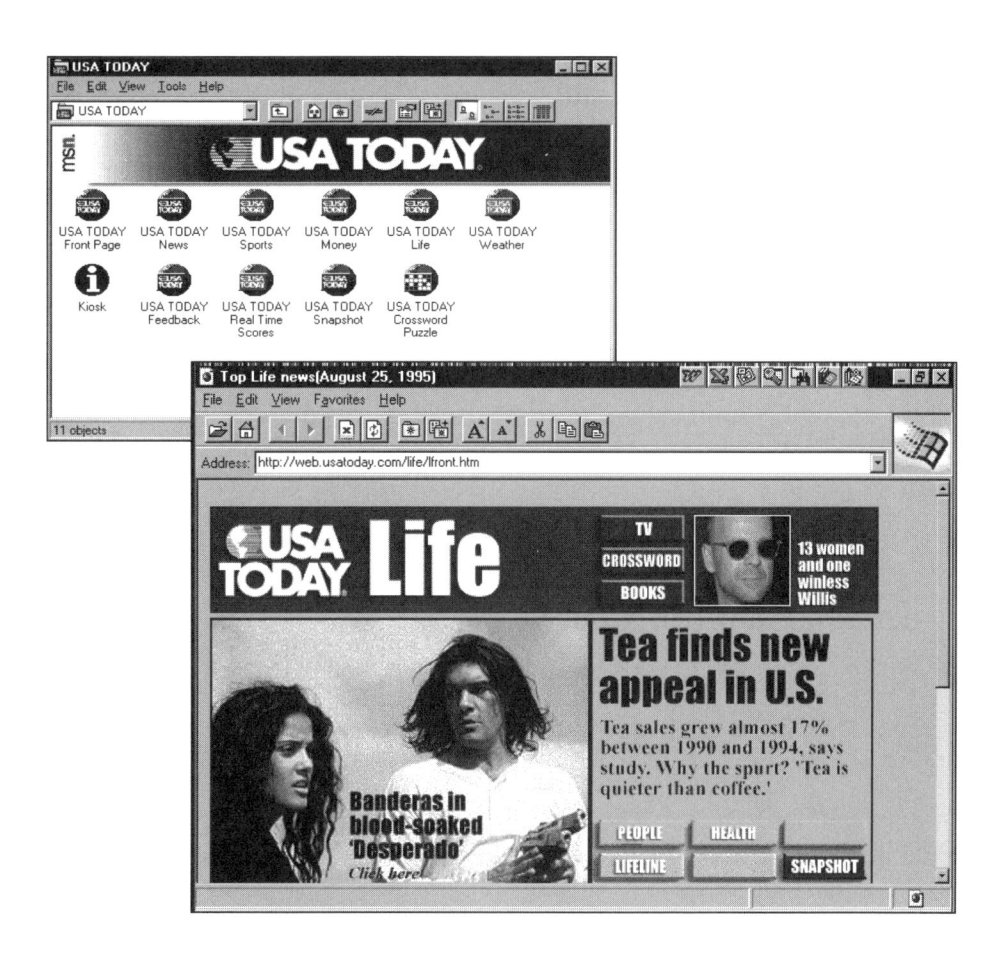

When you attempt to delve into *USA Today*, you must have the Internet browser installed and you must have connected with the MSN/Internet connection because *USA Today* is maintained as a World Wide Web site. That way, when you select *USA Today*, you'll be able to delve into each section, which arrives on your screen as a World Wide Web page.

Without the browser and Internet connection, you won't get past the *USA Today* icon screen.

With the magic of MSN, a variety of forums and services are forged together under one galvanized roof. What appear as forums designed and managed by content providers can be truly MSN sponsored, independent forums (residing on MSN's servers), independent forums residing elsewhere (hence the browser), or advertised links. Yep, it's true, companies can contract with MSN and pay an advertising fee for a link that carries you to their non-MSN service. The electrons scurry forth like ants in search of water, ignoring doors, walls and windows because, as I've mentioned, online boundaries are pretty fuzzy, and at times, seemingly non-existent.

When Do You Need the Browser?

Here's a table designed to help you determine which Internet features require MSN's Web browser.

Internet Feature	MSN Standard	Internet Explorer (Browser)	Win 95 Includes Clients
e-mail	X		
Usenet Newsgroups	X		
World Wide Web		X	
Gopher		X	
FTP		X	X
Telnet			X

Must I Use Microsoft's Browser?

According to Microsoft, you can use the Web browser of your choice. According to other users, other browsers might not run flawlessly. For the purposes of this book, I am assuming that you are using Microsoft's browser, Microsoft Explorer. That wasn't too hard to figure out, was it?

There's one other fine reason to use Microsoft's browser—if you find yourself having problems and needing customer support, you'll only have to go to one site for help.

Why Do I Need Internet E-mail?

With your MSN account, you can send e-mail to your friends around the globe. Internet e-mail is the first, most familiar, and most used form of communication over the Internet.

In fact, e-mail is my lifeline. Some people need a phone. Not me. But I go into withdrawal without a computer. I use Internet e-mail every day. I have friends on three online services, which doesn't really complicate my life, because I can send mail from MSN to just about anywhere. Many of my relatives have Internet addresses at home or at work. We convinced our neighbors in Maryland (back when I actually lived in Maryland) to sign up for an online service. Then we were able to regularly send missives cross-country. I also use Internet e-mail to stay in touch with former co-workers, and I exchange manuscript files with my editor, publisher, and copy editor via e-mail. When my family and I moved to California, we kept our closest friends and relatives up to date on our itinerary—and when we settled, I sent our new address and phone number via e-mail. E-mail is simply *the* easiest way to communicate with friends, family, and business associates. Have I convinced you yet?

Mailing Lists

Better than the daily visit from your mail carrier is the frequent communication you can have when you subscribe to a mailing list, which is also known as a listserver (or just "listserv"). I like to think of mailing lists as a bulletin board or newsgroup that arrives in my electronic mailbox.

Mailing list topics are just about unlimited. Crafters, car customizers, and criminologists can all subscribe to discussion groups that focus on these specific interests. When someone sends e-mail to the list, the message is redistributed via e-mail to all subscribers.

Most mailing lists are open to anyone interested in the topic. Some lists have membership restrictions, while others have message content restrictions. A third version is called a "moderated" list. Only those messages that have been approved by a moderator pass through to your mailbox.

How Do I Subscribe to a List?

In your travels, you may encounter manually maintained lists and automated lists. To join a manually maintained list, you should contact the administrator at

    listname-request@host.domain

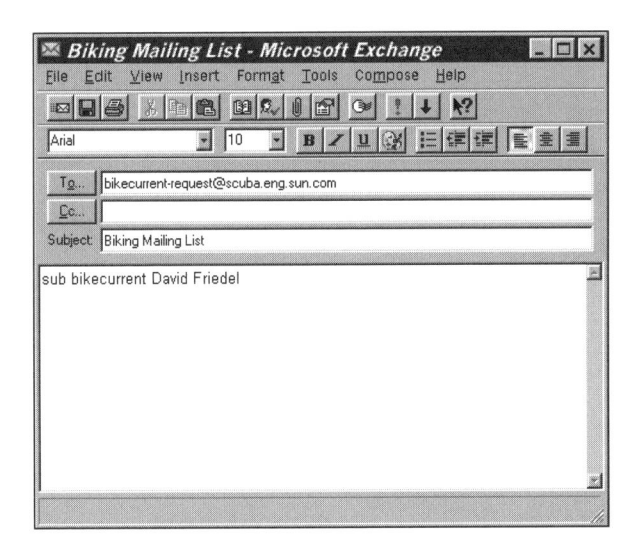

An automated list is maintained by a program called a mail server. It handles subscriptions and mail distribution. To subscribe to an automated list, send the command

```
SUB listname yourfirstname yourlastname
```

to the designated mail server.

Mail servers do not generally read what's in the subject line. But I enter the topics here so that I can easily find a message in my "Sent" mailbox in the event I need a record of when I sent the request.

For further information on a list's available commands, you can send a message to the mailserver's address—with the single word **help** in the message area.

Hint: The help command will bring back information on how to receive each day's mail in a digest form. Unless you are really desperate for each piece of mail, the digest version will save you time, money, and your sanity.

How Do I Find Interesting Mailing Lists?

If you participate in newsgroups, that may be the first place to find pertinent mailing lists. On the Internet, there are a number of other sources for mailing lists. As an example, here are three easy-to-use sources for mailing lists.

Usenet newsgroups: news.lists and news.answers

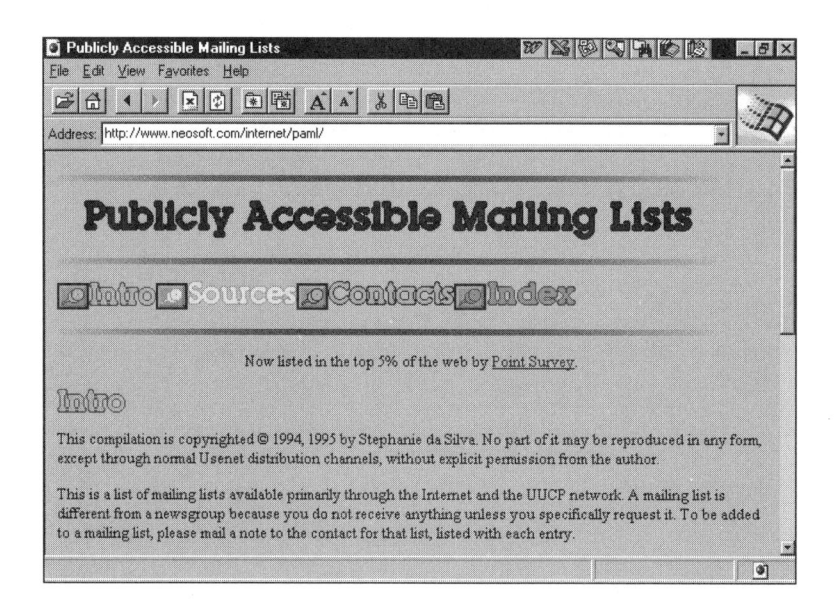

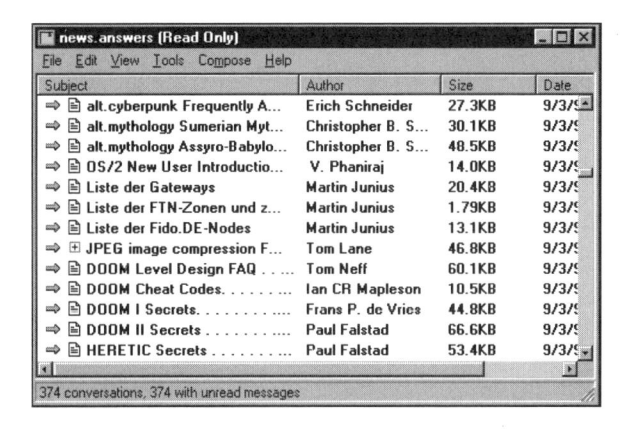

Via e-mail: mail-server@rtfm.mit.edu with send usenet/news.answers/mail/mailing-lists/* in the body. For a gigantic list with hundreds of pages and 5,000 lists, send a message to listserv@bitnic.bitnet with LIST GLOBAL in the body of the message.

The Publicly Accessible Mailing Lists Web Page is very easy to use and is probably your best bet for finding other bicyclists, knitters or whatever hobby strikes your fancy.

World Wide Web:
http://www.neosoft.com/internet/paml/

What's a Newsgroup?

Usenet newsgroups can be thought of as international message boards. If you're already familiar with the BBSes or Message Boards on MSN, you'll soon find the newsgroups to be the next great interpersonal exchange. Usenet newsgroups have been created on thousands of topics. Some people call them Usenets, but most call them newsgroups. Few bother to say the complete term.

You'll recognize newsgroups by their distinctive domain names, which include alt, misc, comp, news, rec, sci, soc, and talk. The traffic volume on newsgroups can be quite heavy. It's not unusual for a newsgroup to get 100 to 200 messages in a 24-hour period. Each group has its own personality. It's considered good etiquette to read a newsgroup for a few days before posting anything to it. Regulars find it frustrating to be asked the same questions over and over again by newbies. If you are going to post, the best first question to ask is whether the group has an FAQ—a document of frequently asked questions about the mission or topic of the group. Many groups post the news of their FAQs weekly, so the rule of thumb should be to read a group for a week before posting.

The best feature of newsgroups is that you can share your knowledge and experiences with a much wider group of people than you might find on MSN. There are groups for parents, kids, crafters, car buffs, scholars, and students of life. I've been fascinated by groups pertaining to parenting, kids' health, and pregnancy because I find doctors' offices and insurance companies to be a bit intimidating. The other members of the newsgroups have shared their stories of diagnoses and treatments in ways that have led me to be a better medical consumer.

I've also checked the newsgroups to find solutions to my computer problems, locate unusual craft materials, and to help others when I have answers to their queries.

You can search for newsgroups in the Internet Center (GO TO Newsgroups) or use the Find Function. The example below shows how to use Find to locate newsgroups pertaining to kids.

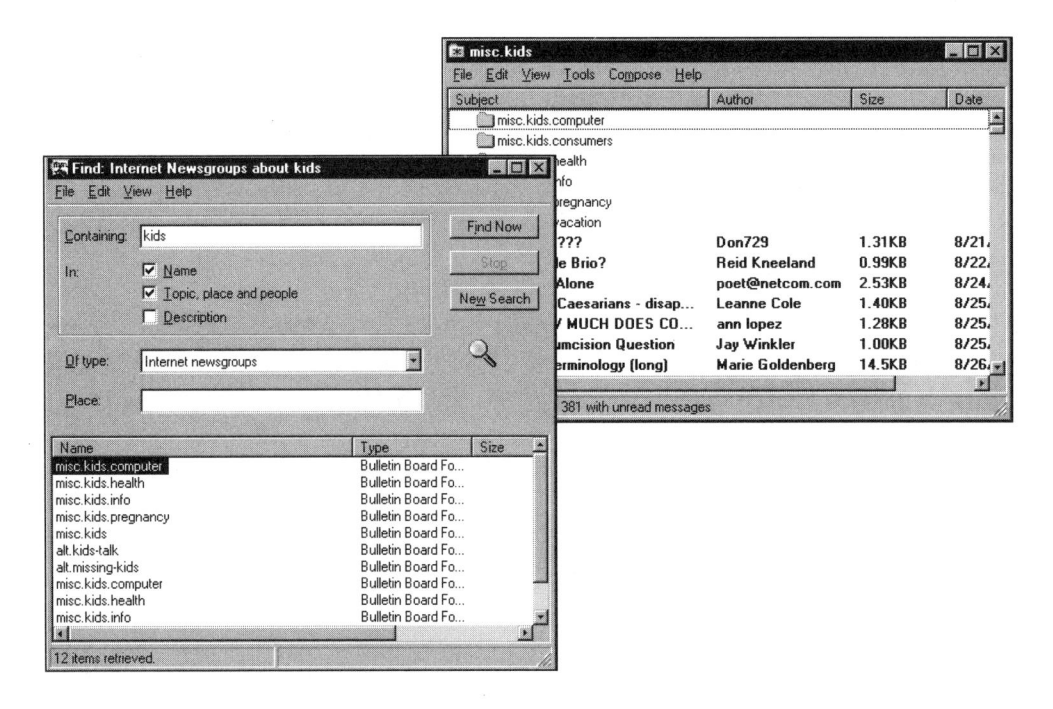

Newsgroups are brought in as MSN content, so you don't need the Internet browser to read or participate in newsgroups. Not all newsgroups are visible to MSN members, though. To gain access to the "restricted" newsgroups, you'll need to run the Full Access EForm found at GO TO Newsgroups. Each newsgroup can be added to your Favorite Places.

> **FYI** *If you know the name of the newsgroup you want to read, you can use the browser to bring it to the forefront for you. In the browser's address line, type news: followed by the name of the newsgroup.*

For example

```
news:misc.kids
```

brings the misc.kids newsgroup to the front of your screen. I should point out that, unlike other URLs, you don't need to add two slashes after the protocol. In fact, if you add the slashes, you'll get an error message. So the address **news:misc.kids** is correct, but **news://misc.kids** will send MSN off an a wild kid chase.

> *When posting information that others might find offensive, you'll need to use ROT13 encoding. In the Compose Message window, select the Tools Menu, and then click ROT13 Encode/Decode. You can also use this same function to decode encoded messages.*

Tantalizing Telnet

With Telnet, you can download files, play games against other people, read and write messages, link to other computers, and much more. Telnet allows you to access Internet sites or accounts remotely. You can also reach catalogs or databases not available via FTP or Gopher. Telnet differs from FTP in that FTP only allows you to browse directories and download files. Telnet allows you to access other computers and control them as if they were on your desk.

You can use the Add/Remove Programs function of Windows 95 to add the TCP/IP stack if you haven't already done so. Then, run the FTP client or Telnet client.

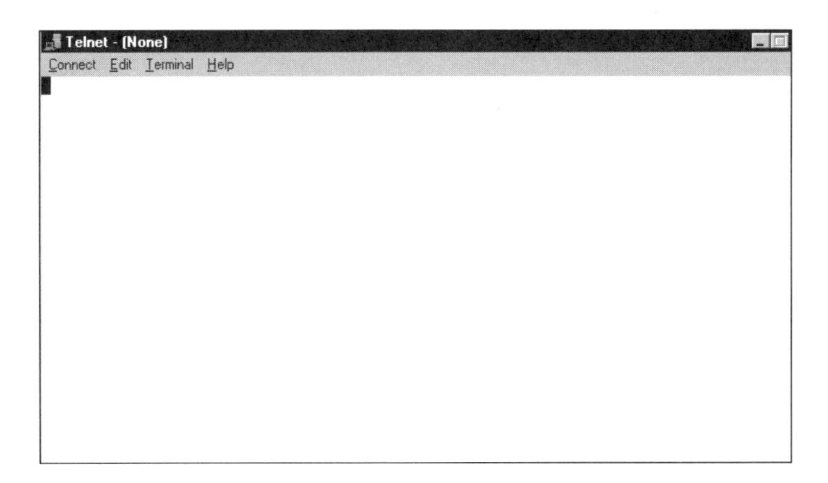

- From the Start Menu, click Run and then type **Telnet.**
- In Telnet click the Connect menu and then Remote System.
- In the Connect dialog box, type the host name of the Telnet site.
- *For example, try:* ***Fedworld.gov***
- In the Term Type box, select a terminal mode.
- In the Port box, select a port. (The default is Telnet.)
- To start the Telnet session, click the Connect button.
- To capture data to a file, type: **terminal/start logging**
- Then use your MSN member ID and designate a password for entry.
- Online Help offers more information about using Telnet.

The Three Caballeros

Why do Disney songs run through my head? I must be regressing in my less-than-young age. That aside, as I continue through this section, I'm going to use a few more screen shots to illustrate what's available on the Internet. Some sites have been set up with multiple types of access in mind. For example, the Rocky Mountain Internet Users Group can be accessed through FTP, Gopher, and the World Wide Web.

Pssst... What Is FTP?

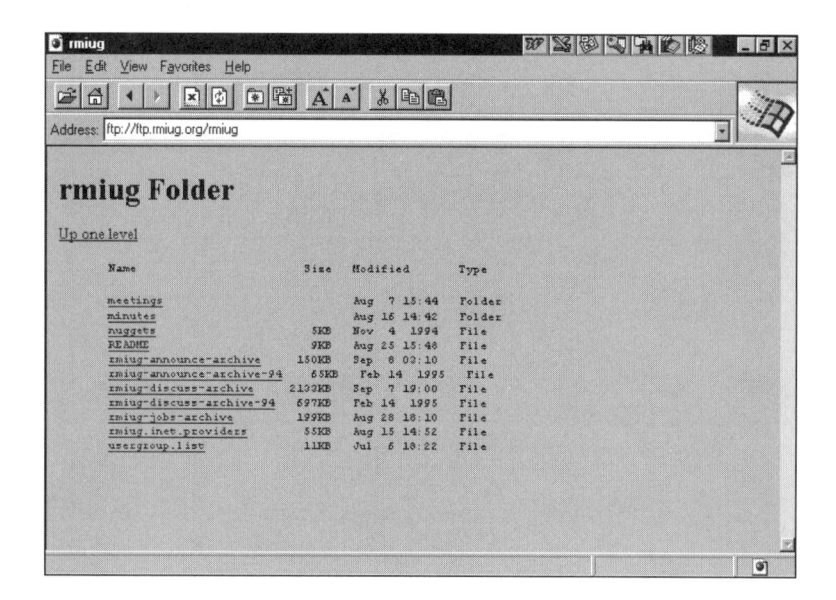

FTP stands for File Transfer Protocol. This system allows you to access other computer systems to retrieve designated files and download them to your system. To use this in a sentence you can say that you "FTPed (ef-tee-peed) a file—as in, 'I FTPed the Johnson's front yard on Halloween.'"

There are two types of FTP access—anonymous and restricted. Usually, you'll be accessing files anonymously. Like most places on the Internet, there is an etiquette to be used in this situation. Even though it is called anonymous FTP, you should use your screen name/Internet address when a password is requested. Some systems won't allow you in unless you comply with this minimal requirement. On other systems, you'll need to use the password **guest** rather than your screen name.

Restricted FTP requires that you be granted permission to be admitted. In some cases, you will be told the requirements for admission. In other instances, you'll need a contact to get in.

Through FTP you and I can access a wealth of shareware, utilities, and text files. File Transfer Protocol (FTP) is a program you use to copy files stored on computers around the globe. Games, software upgrades, pictures, and documents are yours to download using FTP.

* To use the FTP client, make sure you are connected using an MSN/Internet number.
* Click the Start menu, Run, and type **ftp**, then click OK.
* At the command prompt, type **open ftp.rmiug.org.**
* Once you've connected, you'll be prompted for a Member ID.
* Press **enter** or **anonymous** or **your full Internet electronic mail name** (depending on the system requirements). In this case, I used **anonymous** for my name and my full MSN Internet address for the **password.**

A few basic navigation commands are included in the following chart.

At the ftp> prompt, to get this result:	Type this:
ls	to list directories and folders at an FTP site
ls-l	to view more details about the current directory
cdup	to go back up a directory
binary	to switch from ASCII to binary transfer mode
ascii	to switch from binary to ASCII transfer mode
get *filename*	to transfer a file to your computer
disconnect	to disconnect from the host
quit	to stop using FTP

You can also use the browser to access most ftp sites. Type the address in the browser's address field, as in: **ftp://ftp.rmiug.org**

How Do You Find Out Where Files Are Stored on FTP Sites?

Sometimes, you'll spot a reference to a file when you're reading a newsgroup or bulletin board. They often mention FTP sites as a way to read important FAQs. Or you may see an FTP address in a book, magazine, newspaper, or even in an e-mail message. Once you find a site that you like, you may even find additional documents or files of interest at the same site.

Another place to try is Microsoft's own FTP site: **ftp.microsoft.com**

Searching for Gopher

There's no *Caddyshack*-like goofing around here. You can use Gopher to search for, view, and download documents, files, and other goodies. With its menu-driven simplicity, Gopher can turn you into an Internet star in addition to an Internet dynamo.

With Gopher, you need very little technical knowledge to become a hot shot user. As you browse a site's directories and subdirectories, you just enter the number that corresponds to your selection or just point-and-click.

From the browser's address field, enter the name of the gopher site you want to access:

```
gopher://gopher.rmiug.org/
```

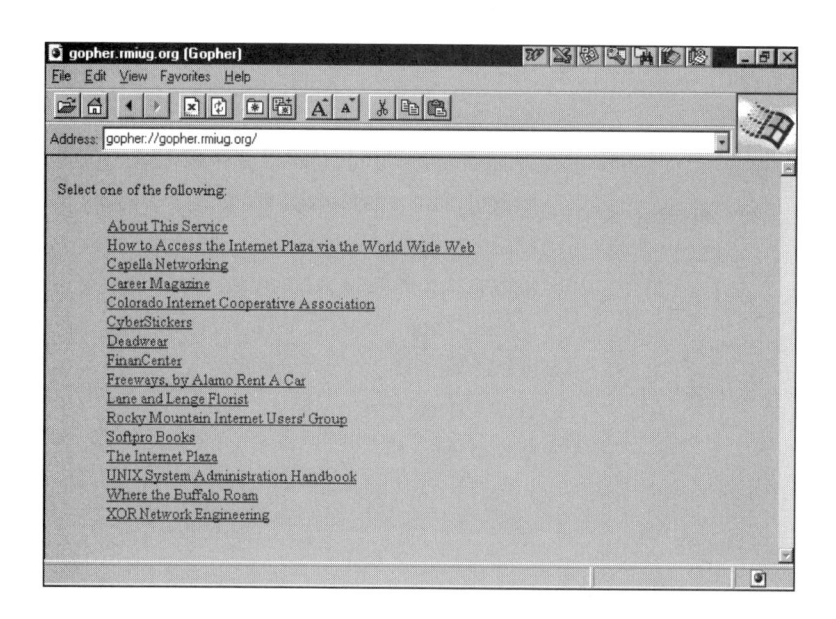

When you get there, follow the menus to the selections you prefer.

Another place to try is **gopher.microsoft.com**, where you'll discover the full searchable text of Microsoft Knowledge Base, along with scads of supporting files.

What Are All Those Addresses I See in the Newspaper That Begin with http:// ?

When you see an address beginning with http://, that means you've stumbled across a site on the World Wide Web.

The address is called a URL. Most people pronounce each letter, U-R-L, although a few people call them "Earls." In any case, depending on who you talk to in this business, the letters stand for either a Universal Resource Locator or a Uniform Resource Locator.

Type carefully and you'll connect to your desired Web site within seconds. Type a URL wrong, even just one character, and you'll be staring at a computer screen that's on the way to nowhere.

Some sites maintain different addresses so that people can use different protocols to access the site. For instance, some sites provide an FTP address, a Gopher address, and a Web address because not all users have access to all of these protocols. In any case, with a Web browser, like the Explorer, you can use virtually any protocol (provided that the address exists) in an address. Here's a good example:

Sample URLs	Rocky Mountain Internet Users Group
Web site	http://www.rmiug.org/
FTP site	ftp://ftp.rmiug.org/rmiug
Gopher site	gopher://gopher.rmiug.org/

You can use any of these addresses. They all take you to the same basic site; of course, the Web site will be more graphically appealing because FTP and Gopher protocols don't support graphics. Sites like this one provide multiple ways to access so that users who don't have a Web browser can still get in.

Any Tips for Keeping Track of URLs?

I have a stickies program on my computer and, whenever I find an interesting URL, I cut and paste it onto a sticky for further reference. You can do this with WordPad or your word processor, too. Of course, if my browser is open, I can add it the URL address to my Favorites list.

The Internet Explorer saves Web pages you've already viewed in an immense cache on your hard disk. This speeds navigation back to your favorite sites and it's only limited by the space you've designated on your hard disk.

When you return to sites, be sure to select Refresh from the View pull-down menu. This will update your screen if any changes have been made to the Web page.

URLs can also be saved as "objects" on your desktop. You can drag objects from the Explorer browser to the Windows 95 desktop and back to the Explorer. It's also simple to drag a hyperlink from a Web page to your desktop. The Explorer creates a URL shortcut to represent the hyperlink.

Even better (for fast navigation)—if you drop a shortcut icon onto the Internet Explorer icon, the Explorer reads the URL and loads its Web pages automatically.

> **FYI** *When you return to sites, be sure to select Refresh from the View pull-down menu. This will update your screen if any changes have been made to the Web page.*

What's the Fastest Way to Navigate?

To speed your return to favorite places, you can move URLs or Web addresses in the form of shortcuts. After I've saved a favorite site, I sometimes drag the site to my desktop, where it remains for use as a shortcut. From then on, I can launch from the shortcut and zoom directly to the selected URL.

It's easy to see that once you work with shortcuts, the line is blurred between what's on your computer and what's located elsewhere on MSN or the Internet.

How Do I Read a URL?

Let's take a look at the address for David Letterman's Top Ten list, as kept at CBS.

http://cbs-tv.tiac.net:80/lateshow/ttlist.html

http, shown here with the single underline, indicates the type of protocol being used. Those you'll see most often include *ftp* or *gopher* for retrieving files, *news* for accessing Usenet newsgroups or *http* for accessing Web hypertext-based sites.

Address. The portion of the URL that's double underlined is the address of the server where the file is located. Often, the server name includes the type of server. This portion of the URL is also called the "domain name."

The final destination, indicated by the dashed line, specifies the directory information for the file's location, which allows you to travel directly to a folder or directory that might be nested several levels deep within other folders. Each successive folder level is denoted by a slash in the URL.

If you've typed in a URL correctly but receive a message stating that the file was not found, it may mean that the particular file you are seeking has been moved or deleted. When this happens, remove the directory information (the portion with the dotted lines) and begin your search farther up the "food chain." For the previous example, you could try going to this address:

```
http://cbs-tv.tiac.net:80
```

That approach often works because, even if a particular file or folder has been deleted or renamed, the basic site address is probably still the same. You'll have to deal with a different starting point, but you'll usually be able to figure out how to navigate from this point to the particular file or information you're seeking.

It's also important to keep in mind that Internet connections come and go. If you get a message stating that a file wasn't found, it may be that your system's connection to the Internet has been severed. This can happen even if you're still connected to MSN. Sometimes it can be tough to determine whether you've entered a URL incorrectly, whether the URL is no longer valid, or whether you're Internet connection has dropped off. That's one of the downsides of spending life in the online lane.

> ***Super Sleuthing Dynamo Tips***
> - *Web addresses almost always end with the file name.*
> - *If the address ends with .htm, the server is running under Windows.*
> - *If the address ends with .html, the server is most likely running under Unix—or possibly a Macintosh.*
> - *How do I know? Prior to the introduction of Windows 95, file extensions could not be longer than three letters.*

You can use these tips to troubleshoot your own minefields. All Unix web addresses are case sensitive. If the address ends with .html and you are having problems connecting, make sure that you are typing the address exactly as written.

How Does the Web Differ from the Internet?

Every Internet author has to come up with a cute anecdote to answer this question. Should I relate the car to the engine? The earth to the solar system? Park Place to Monopoly?

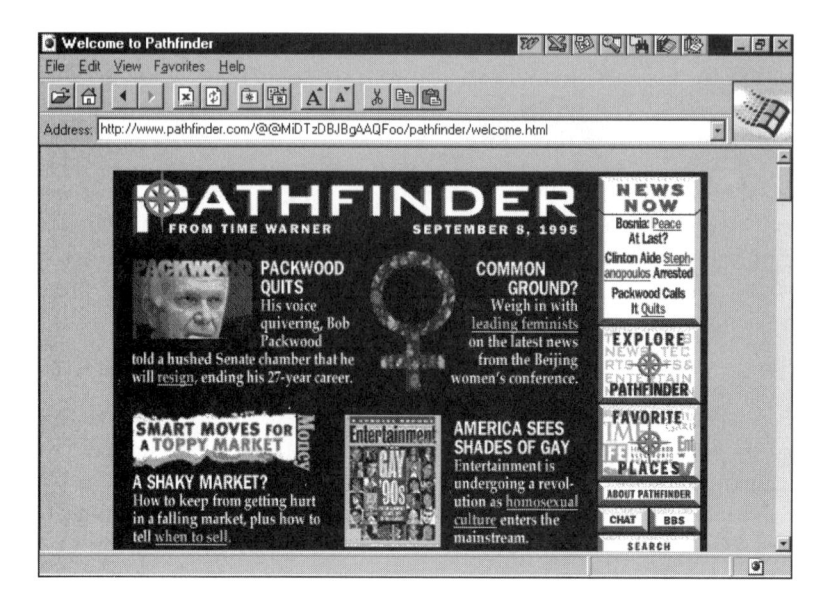

It's my turn now, so I'd like to bring the Jetsons in here. I've been thinking about George a lot lately. Do you remember George and Elroy? How about Astro? Well, I've wanted to use them in a book for a long time. In the high tech advanced age in which they live, all of their communication is done over the Internet. It comprises the entire system of electronic communications. George Jetson of 1995 no longer counts on the newspaper and television to keep him up to date. In the age of information, George uses his Internet browser to tap into the electronic World Wide Web. He may access Time Warner's Pathfinder to read the highlights of *Time*, *People*, and *Money*—in hypertext format.

The Internet is the massive network that comprises the data transmission for all e-mail, FTP, Gopher, Telnet, Newsgroups, and World Wide Web access. Therefore, the Web is just part of the Internet, and currently it's the most popular part due to its graphical interface and ever-creative possibilities.

When you use a browser for your online communication, it reads the HTML codes from electronic files and relays the graphic representation onto your screen. If you have colorful, attractive, graphic images on your screen, you are either connected to an online service or you are accessing the Web.

The Web is a subset of the Internet, but it is also the most rapidly growing and most consumer-aware portion. The Web's technology has brought commercialism to the Internet with unprecedented speed and growth.

Tip: You already know that you can use Favorite Places on MSN to store shortcuts to MSN's forums or services. You can also use Favorites in the Internet Explorer to store names (URLs) of Internet sites.

What's HTML?

Don't you remember? It's Hamburger, tomato, mayo, and lettuce at Burger King—it's a bit messy on the computer keyboard. Didn't we clear up this one in the FAQ section? HTML is the abbreviation for Hyper Text Markup Language—the dominant format for creating World Wide Web pages. You only need to know this if you are creating your own pages or if you want to understand every reference you see to html.

What's on a Web Page?

It's pretty rare to find spiders on a Web page, but you will usually find attractive graphics, icons, and hyperlinked text. That's what makes the Web so popular: its graphical nature. People like to be entertained, and that includes computer users. Web pages actively grab your attention and bring you into the action. You can select the marked text that links you to other areas and instantly leap to another part of cyberspace. Remember the Lay's potato chip commercial, "Betcha can't eat just one"?

Well, I find that Web surfing grabs my attention the same way. I just keep jumping from link to link. Soon I lose track of time and the whole bag of chips has disappeared. The only thing left is my greasy fingers.

Here's a good introduction to the Web: Launch the browser from the Internet desktop icon to go straight to the MSN home page:

http://www.microsoft.com/

Can I Create My Own Web Page on MSN?

Soon, very soon, I hope. One of Microsoft's goals for MSN is for members to be able to create their own Web pages. Of course, the Microsoft suite of products will be available to help you do this. The first two products to look for are MediaView and Blackbird.

Webbish Features

The World Wide Web is a collection of documents, graphics, videos, and other files scattered throughout the Internet and linked into hypertext documents on thousands of conceivable and inconceivable documents.

Microsoft's browser is based on the famed Mosaic interface. But there are several other browsers available. All are designed to recognize HTML codes and then convert the codes into an attractively laid-out Web page. But each browser reads and portrays HTML documents in a different fashion—mainly because some browsers don't understand some of the fancier HTML codes that are currently in use. If you and your brother Bob are viewing the same page with different browsers, the pages may not look alike.

The Silken Web

Web browsers, including the Explorer, are pretty darn smart. In fact, they'll try to figure out which address you're looking for even if you don't type the entire address. So, if you remember only a part of an Internet address, you can enter the portion you know in the address line of the browser. I typed in **pathfinder.com** and it reinvented itself on the screen as **http://www.pathfinder.com**.

Treasures of the Web

Over the past few weeks, I've collected an eclectic mix of my personal favorite Web sites, which I've decided to list here. One of my online friends, Michael from Alaska, gets credit here for his nominations.

Internet Couch Potato Headquarters

OK, NBC is on MSN, but you can also use the browser to catch the other networks. Seek and ye shall find ABC, Fox, CNN, and more.

http://www.cbs.com

At the Movies

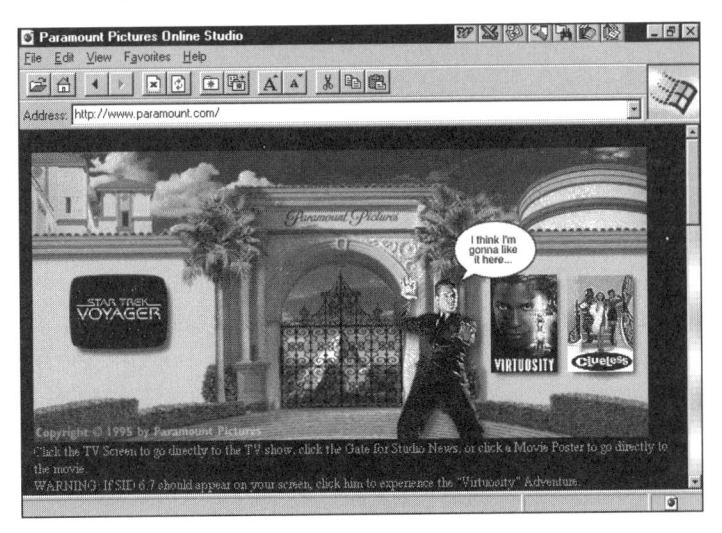

My local newspaper is filled with movie advertisements. And all the major studios are including the URLs for their Web sites in their ads. I guess that's what we get in L.A. Cool movie studios are using Web sites to promote hot properties and coming attractions.

```
http://www.paramount.com
```

Bookish Webbish Reads

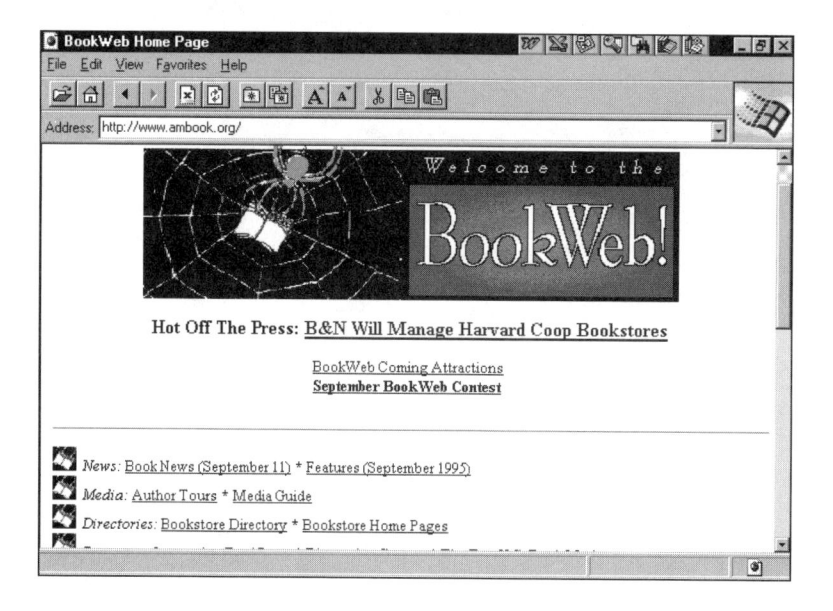

When you've had enough hyperactive media, you can take a refreshing break with the latest literary news. Two finds include the American Booksellers' Association's BookWeb and the Pulitzer Prize Board's list of winners.

```
http://www.ambook.org
http://www.pulitzer.org
```

Bring on the Locusts

This is the third time I've lived in California. Let's be honest—the Golden State has a bit in common with the State of Disaster. The disaster home page doesn't focus solely on the state of California, but sometimes I think it should. Earthquakes, fires, floods, hurricanes, and other tragedies are discussed here (at the home page that is).

```
http://www.disaster.org/
```

A Walkman for Your Computer

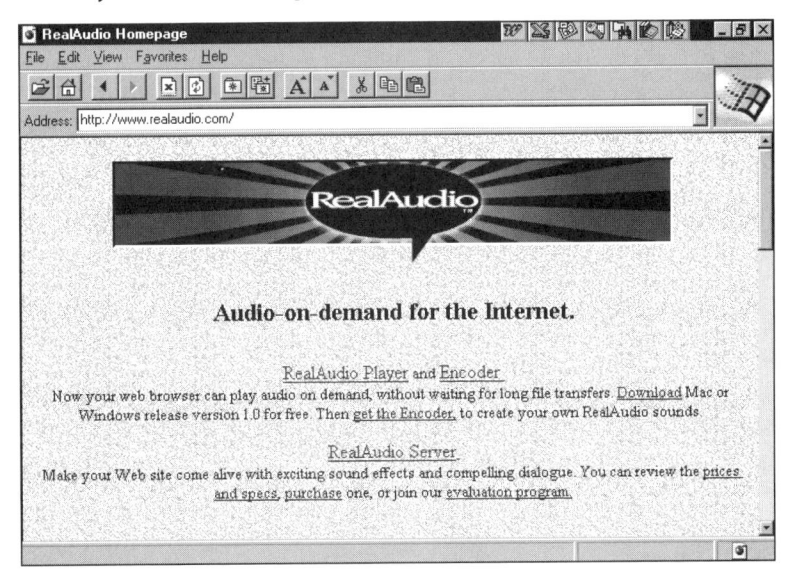

With the RealAudio Player, your Web browser can play audio on demand—without waiting for long file transfers. You can download the RealAudio Player for free from this site—or you can just stop by to listen to the news.

```
http://www.realaudio.com/
```

Bucky Bison

Simply because every writer gets to slip something personal into a book, I've chosen to include my alma mater's Web site. (And right now, it's better than my husband's alma mater's Web site.) Bucknell is in Central Pennsylvania, just off the banks of the Susquehanna River, and pretty far from just about anywhere important.

http://www.bucknell.edu/

Daily Dilbert

The daily Dilbert cartoon beats a dozen donuts when it comes to getting my day off to a good start. For that warm, good-morning smile, add Scott Adam's creation to your list of Favorites.

http://www.unitedmedia.com.comics/dilbert/todays_dilbert.gif

The Imperative Informer

Time/Warner captures the heartbeat of America better than any Chevrolet commercial. From Pathfinder, you have access to features from *Time, People, Money*, and more!

```
http://www.pathfinder.com
```

For more fun finds, check out the useless Web sites near the back of this book.

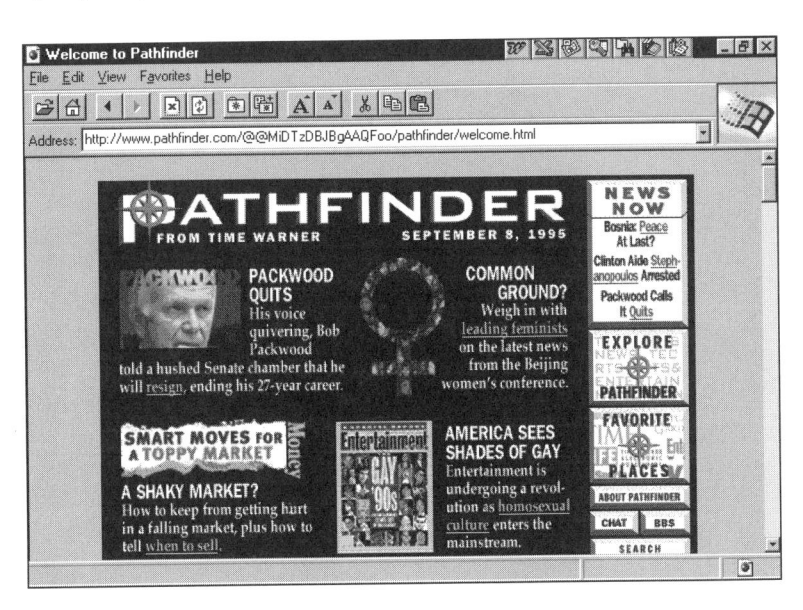

PART 5

Ten Fun but Useless Web Sites That Actually Work

Now is the time for all good men...to find those stupid and silly Web sites that you've probably heard about. I just don't have the patience to rip all the URLs out of the newspaper, so I trusted the various Web searchers to find them for me. Using words and terms like Bill Gates, silly, stupid, useless and cat, I prowled through Yahoo, Lycos, and InfoSeek to find the best (or maybe I should say the *worst*) for your browsing enjoyment.

Bill's House

So whaddya think of Windows 95? Can you keep up with the hoopla? Are you working more efficiently and earning more money due to the increased productivity? Is it as much fun as winning the lottery?

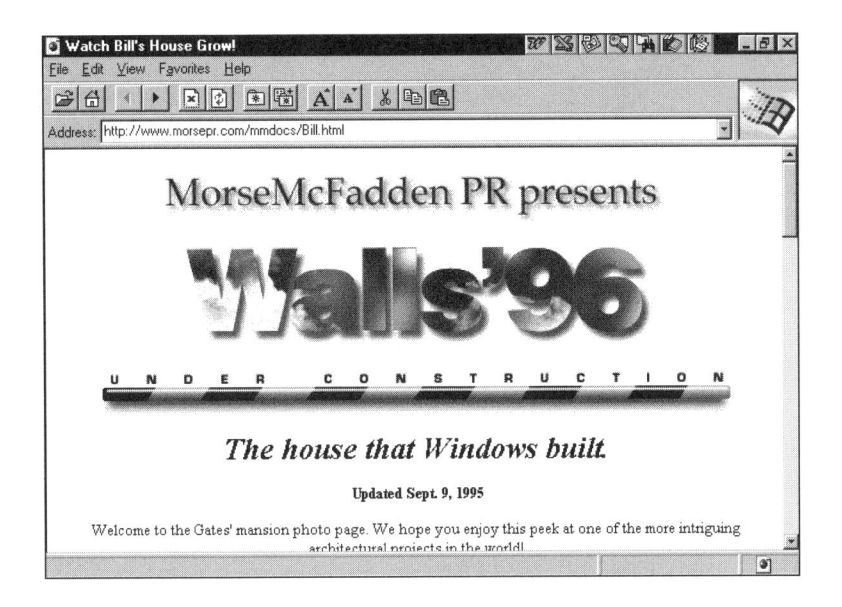

The cost of developing and launching Windows 95 barely put a dent in the coffers of Microsoft, as evidenced by this fun Web site. MorseMcFadden Communications has put up a site known as Bill's House, which follows the construction of Bill Gates' $50 million monumental lakeside home construction project. Your purchase of Windows 95 may have gone toward a light switch or toilet paper dispenser.

```
http://www.morsepr.com/mmdocs/Bill.html
```

San Diego Bay Cam

Having lived in San Diego, I really like this site. It isn't particularly useful, but it does carry me back to one of my favorite places in the world. Checking into the San Diego Bay Cam is a virtual vacation for me.

I wish I'd known about it when we lived there. I could have checked on the comings and goings of the Navy ships in the harbor. That would have allowed me to know if my husband was on his way home. Once I saw the ship cross the screen, I'd have had just enough time to drive from home to the pier to meet him. Just like in the movies.

When I'm missing San Diego a little too much, I check the link provides traffic reports at the junction of Interstates 5 and 805. That always cures my nostalgia.

    http://www.live.net/sandiego/

Trojan Room Coffee Machine

Hello, is anyone home here? Last time I visited, the lights were off and the pot was empty. When I checked the time, I realized it was not an ideal hour for coffee drinking computer fiends at Cambridge.

Back in 1991 a group of impoverished academics toiled to find a solution to their coffee dilemma. The advent of the coffee camera meant they no longer had to trek the stairs and navigate the corridors—only to find an empty pot. With its prominent position of lore on the Internet, the famous coffee pot is ready for your virtual cup.

    http://www.cl.cam.ac.uk/coffee/coffee.html

Foam Bath Fish Time

Putting up a wacky Web site is one way to get attention. This one is brought to you by an Internet book author—and it's not mine. (I'm still trying to decide if I need my own.) When I checked in, over 100,000 people had visited this site in its history.

The fish magically arrange themselves to the current time—and you can view the time in your zone by modifying the URL. I'm sure that for someone, somewhere, this is very useful. *Please let me know who you are...*In the meantime, I'll use the clock in my PC or Power Mac.

```
http://redwood.northcoast.com/cgi-bin/fishtime
```

Talk to My Cat

Meeowww...I first heard about this wacky site on Jaclyn Easton's Log-On USA radio show. A computer techie specializing in voice synthesis has created a program that speaks your words to his cat. Type your comments and the cat will hear them. It's too bad the cat's meow doesn't come back in Real Audio, but perhaps it will in the next update.

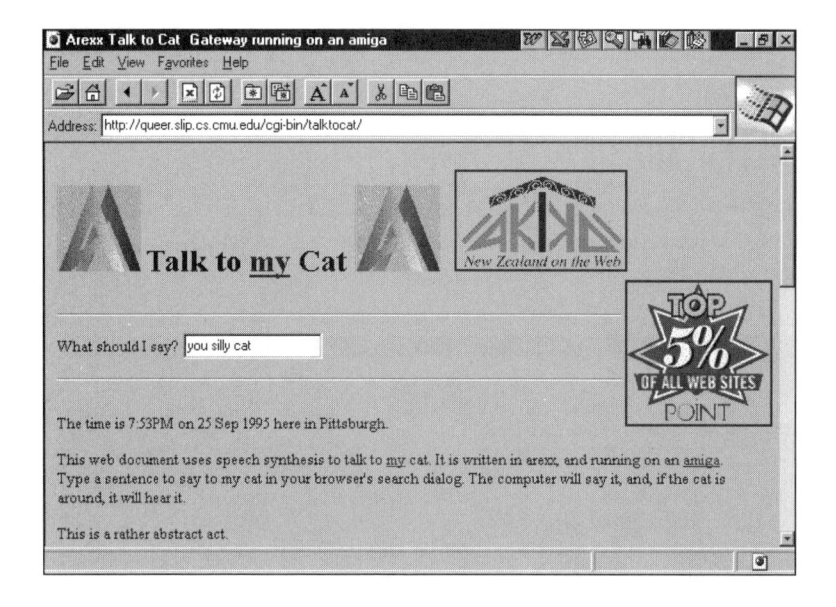

Since I'm not a cat lover, never had a dog, and once flushed my goldfish, I really don't understand this site, although I'm not sure anybody does. Anyway, I do appreciate participating from a distance because it doesn't stir up my cat allergy.

```
http://queer.slip.cs.cmu.edu/cgi-bin/talktocat/
```

What's in My Desk Drawer

Oh sure. *This* is a helpful site. Why would anybody want to know what's in this guy's desk drawer? Shall I covet his yellow Hi-Liter?

Perhaps this reflects the sheer imagination and talent of a college student. Or perhaps he was procrastinating and didn't want to work on his political science paper. Maybe he just can't get a date and this is how he spent his Saturday night.

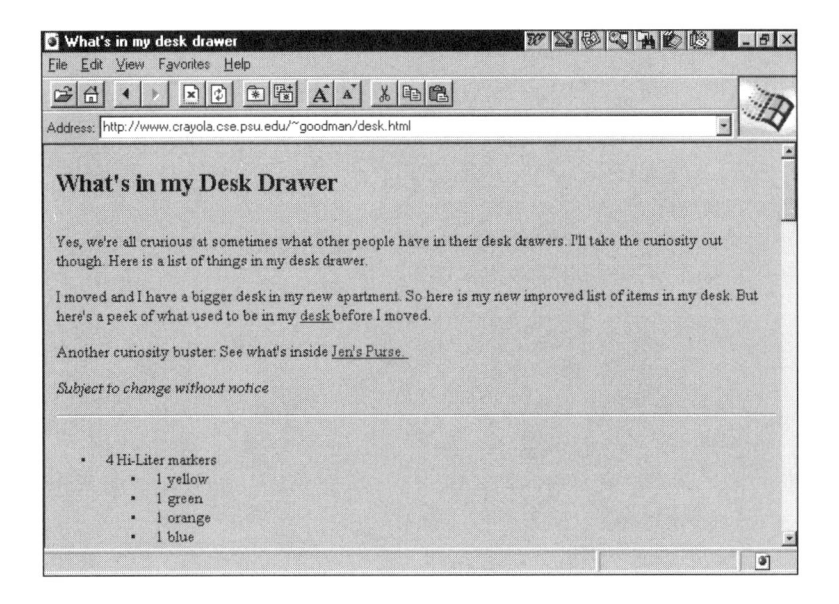

I just hope he has the time to keep it updated every time he uses one of his mechanical pencils.

```
http://www.crayola.cse.psu.edu/~goodman/desk.html
```

CD Player Gateway

If you've read any of my other books, you may already know that we were the last household in America to get a CD player. I'm still trying to figure out what all the buttons mean. Anyway, I'm stumped that a kind soul at MIT is willing to share his CD entertainment with me—and you.

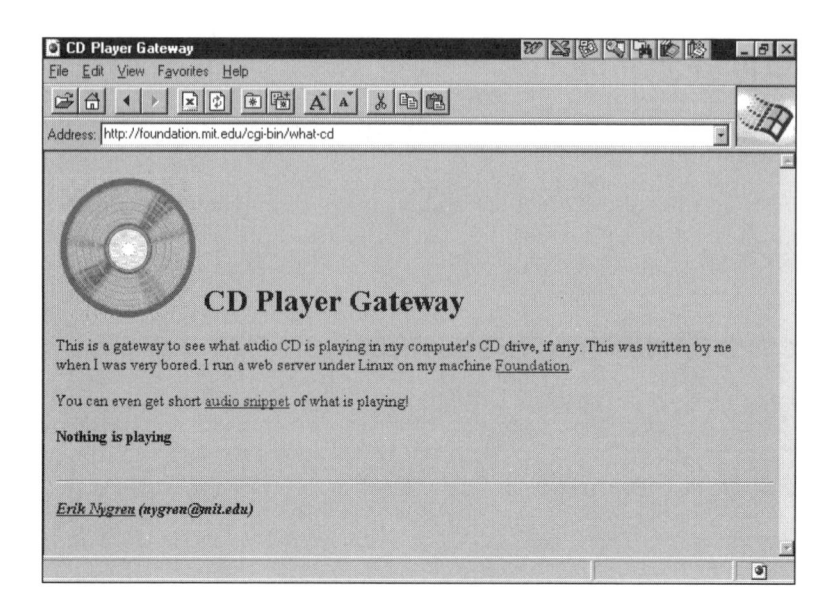

If Erik Nygren's CD player is in action, you can even get a short audio snippet for your own listening entertainment.

Can you imagine a conversation between two of his friends...

"Let's go bug Eric..."

"What if he's not home?"

"Let's check his CD Player Gateway."

"If we don't like what he's playing, can we go to Sam Goody's instead?"

```
http://foundation.mit.edu/cgi-bin/what-cd
```

RIT Computer Science House Drink Machine

Students at the Computer Science House at RIT (Rochester Institute of Technology) can grab a Coke, Mountain Dew, Hawaiian Punch, Country Time, or Jolt. Like all good student projects, this machine requires no cash. Rather, students run credit accounts. Maybe that'll help when they graduate and apply for American Express cards.

The students have worked hard to keep multiple machines operational and filled. You can even check to see what it's stocked with and how cold it is. I remember a fraternity that kept various brands of beer in an old soda machine. I'd better go look for that one too. Maybe it's on the Net now.

Until they find a way to transfer the beverage through my modem, I'll have to keep making the trek to my refrigerator and to the store.

`http://www.csh.rit.edu/proj/drink.html`

Cams Around the World

If you don't have the money or time to travel, you can at least use your Internet connection to become an armchair traveler, where you can take a world tour from your desktop. The output from a collection of cameras from around the world has been focused in one central location. When I checked in, there were scenes from Seattle, San Diego, San Francisco, and the campus of the University of Southern California.

Do be warned, though: This Web page take awhile to load, since it's so heavy with inline images, which are links to their related worldly Web pages.

A bit of a snooze waiting for the pictures, it's a highly recommended place when you can't think of anywhere else to go on the Net…and your passport has been confiscated.

`http://www.it.dtu.dk/~gonget/window.html`

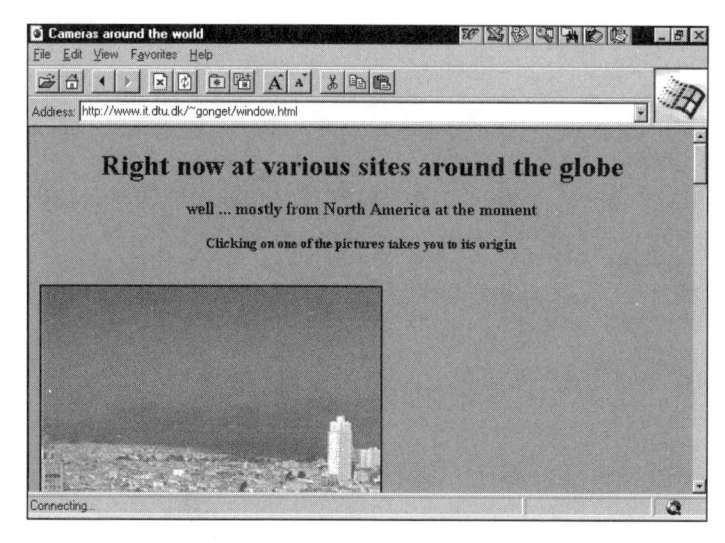

[Browser screenshot: "Cameras around the world" — Right now at various sites around the globe, well ... mostly from North America at the moment. Clicking on one of the pictures takes you to its origin.]

Steve's List of T-Shirts

A college friend, prowling in my basement, recently found my high school diaries. He couldn't believe that I wrote down what I wore each day, so that I wouldn't wear the same outfit too often. I'm surprised he didn't find an inventory of my clothes and their mix-and-match possibilities.

Now that I've become a mom, I no longer have the time nor the inclination to keep a diary or inventory of my clothes. Apparently Steve shares my old interest because he keeps a list of T-shirts on the Web to entertain us all.

```
http://www.chaco.com/~stev0/shirts.html
```

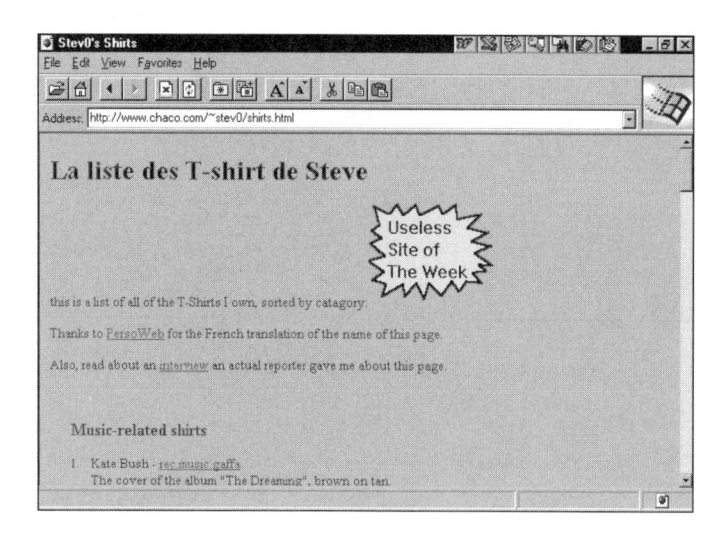

[Browser screenshot: "Stev0's Shirts" — La liste des T-shirt de Steve. *Useless Site of The Week.* this is a list of all of the T-Shirts I own, sorted by catagory. Thanks to PersoWeb for the French translation of the name of this page. Also, read about an interview an actual reporter gave me about this page. Music-related shirts: 1. Kate Bush - rec.music.gaffa. The cover of the album "The Dreaming", brown on tan.]

PART 6

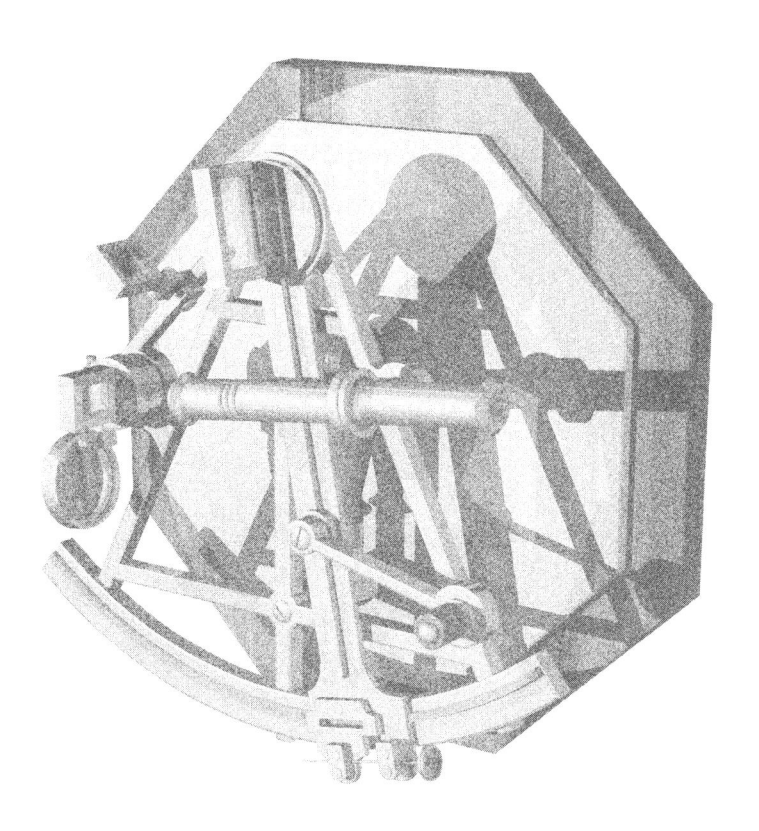

Webs of the World

The Web is truly an international affair. I'm writing this from the U.S., but I certainly acknowledge that a majority of Internet and Web users are outside of the U.S. So, toward this end, I've included a selected list of Web sites around the world. If you're looking for something local, and if local means something that most people think of as foreign, then you'll want to look here. I've included sites in virtually every "corner" of the globe.

Africa

Cape Town

http://www.cs.uct.ac.za/UCT.html

University of Cape Town Computer Science Department

Johannesburg

http://www.is.co.za/

Johannesburg

Witwatersrand

http://www.cs.wits.ac.za/

University of the Witwatersrand, Computer Science Department

http://www.rau.ac.za/

Rand Afrikaans University

Asia and Oceania

Australia

http://www.agsm.unsw.edu.au/Welcome.html

Australian Graduate School of Management

http://werple.apana.org.au/apanahome.html

Australian Public Access Network Association

http://www.cs.su.oz.au/

Basser Department of Computer Science, University of Sydney

Beijing

http:/ihep.html

China Institute of High Energy Physics

Hong Kong

http://www.air.org/

The Association for Internet Resources

http://www.cuhk.hk/

The Chinese University of Hong Kong

India

http://iucaa.iucaa.ernet.in/welcome.html

Inter-University Centre for Astronomy and Astrophysics

Japan

http://www.huie.hokudai.ac.jp/

Hokkaido University

http://www.hirosaki-u.ac.jp/index.html

Hirosaki University

http://www.sendai-ct.ac.jp/welcome.html

Sendai National College of Technology

http://www.tia.ad.jp/welcome.html

Tohoku internet Association

http://www.u-aizu.ac.jp/

The University of Aizu

http://ks001.kj.utsunomiya-u.ac.jp

Utsunomiya University

http://www.atom.co.jp/

Minato-ku

Korea

http://silla.dongguk.ac.kr

Dongguk University

http://www.cs.usm.my/

Universiti Sains Malaysia, Penang

New Zealand

http://icair.iac.org.nz/

International Centre for Antarctic Information and Research

http://hmu1.cs.auckland.ac.nz/

The University of Auckland

Singapore

http://biomed.nus.sg:80/

National University of Singapore

Taiwan

http://peacock.tnjc.edu.tw/NEW/WELCOME.HTML

Tung Nan Junior College of Technology

Thailand

http://emailhost.ait.ac.th:80

Asian Institute of Technology

EUROPE

Austria

http://info.uibk.ac.at:80/

Innsbruck

http://www.ifs.uni-linz.ac.at/home.html

Johannes-Kepler-University, Linz

http://www.tcs.co.at/

TechConsult, Fremdenverkehrs informations system

Belgium

http://www.bekaert.com/

ÜjÜŒBekaert

http://www.belnet.be/

Belgian National Research Network

http://info1.vub.ac.be:8080/index.html

Free University of Brussels

http://pespmc1.vub.ac.be/

Free University of Brussels

Croatia

http://tjev.tel.etf.hr/zzt/zzt.html

University of Zagreb

http://wwws.irb.hr/

Rudjer Boskovich Institute

http://animafest.hr/

World Festival of Animated Films, Zagreb

Czech Republic

http://www.cuni.cz/

Charles University

Denmark

http://www.dd.dk/

Damgaard International

http://gopher.ku.dk/

University of Copenhagen

Estonia

http://www.eenet.ee/english.html

Estonian Research and Education Network

Finland

http://honeybee.helsinki.fi/index.html

Faculty of Agriculture and Forestry

http://www.hut.fi/English/www.english.html

Helsinki University of Technology, Espoo

http://www.tky.hut.fi/

Helsinki University of Technology, Espoo, Student Union

http://www.tky.hut.fi/.publish/tf/

Teknologföreningen, the Swedish Student Union

http://www.uwasa.fi/

University of Vaasa

http://www.freenet.hut.fi/

Freenet Finland

http://www.pcuf.fi/

PC-Users of Finland

http://www.fuug.fi/

Finnish Unix User's Group

http://www.jyu.fi/~otto/42.html

Jyväskylä Science Fiction Club 42

http://www.funet.fi/pub/doc/telecom/phonecard/afpc/

Association of Finnish Phonecard Collectors

France

http://www.calvacom.fr/

Paris

http://www.cert.fr/

Toulouse

http://www.ciril.fr/CIRIL/

Lorraine

http://cirm.univ-mrs.fr

Marseille

http://www.ipl.fr/

Lyon

http://www.fdn.fr

Paris

http://www.sct.fr

World-Net

Germany

http://www.augusta.de/

INGA, Internet-Gruppe des ACF e.V

http://www.chemie.fu-berlin.de/adressen/berlin.html

Berlin

http://www.artcom.de/

ART+COM

http://www.cnb.compunet.de/

CompuNet

http://www.contrib.de/

Contributed Software

http://www.dfn.de/home.html

Deutsches Forschungsnetz

http://www.dhzb.de/OpeningPage.html

Deutsches Herzzentrum

http://www.zblmath.fiz-karlsruhe.de/

Fachinformationszentrum Karlsruhe

http://www.fta-berlin.de/HOME-PAGE.html

Forschungs- und Technologiepark Berlin-Adlershof

http://www.chemie.fu-berlin.de/index.html

Fachbereich Chemie

http://www.chemie.fu-berlin.de/index_e.html

Fachbereich Kommunikationswissenschaften

http://www.inf.fu-berlin.de:80/~weisshuh/infwiss/

Arbeitsbereich Informationswissenschaft

http://www.math.fu-berlin.de/

Fachbereich Mathematik und Informatik

http://www.chemie.fu-berlin.de/tmp/phil/philos.html

Fachbereich Philosophie und Sozialwissenschaften

http://www.rz-berlin.mpg.de/

Fritz-Haber-Institut der Max-Planck-Gesellschaft

http://www.rz.hu-berlin.de/inside/rz/

Rechenzentrum

http://www.netcs.com/

netCS

http://sun24.tfh-berlin.de:8000/

Technische Fachhochschule

http://www.cs.tu-berlin.de/

Fachbereich Informatik

http://www.math.tu-berlin.de/

Fachbereich Mathematik

http://keynes.fb12.tu-berlin.de/

Fachbereich Verkehrswesen und phys. Ingenieurwissenschaften

http://www.prz.tu-berlin.de/

Prozessrechnerverbund-Zentrale

http://www.tu-berlin.de/zrz/index.html

Zentraleinrichtung Rechenzentrum

http://duplox.wz-berlin.de/

Technik - Arbeit - Umwelt/Organisation und Technikgenese

http://www.nordwest.germany.eu.net/

POP NordWest

http://www.techfak.uni-bielefeld.de/blfd/blfd.html

Bielefeld

http://peel.lili.uni-bielefeld.de/foebud/foebudHome.html

FoeBud e.V

http://www.hrz.uni-bielefeld.de/

hochschulrechenzentrum

http://www.ep1.ruhr-uni-bochum.de/

Experimentalphysik 1

http://wti.tp4.ruhr-uni-bochum.de/www/html/homepage.html

Physik / Education Server WTI2000

http://speckled.mpifr-bonn.mpg.de:8001i/home/spckle/ms/html/bonn.html

Bonn

http://orade.ora.com/home.html

O'Reilly International Thomson Verlag

http://www.rhein.de/

Regionalnetz Bonn/Rhein.DE

http://opalr2.physik.uni-bonn.de/

OPAL Group

http://www.rhrz.uni-bonn.de/index.html

Regionales Hochschulrechenzentrum

http://sfb350.ipb.uni-bonn.de/

Sonderforschungsbereich 350

http://www.cs.tu-bs.de/

Fachgebiet Informatik

http://ramz.ing.tu-bs.de/

Rechenanlage des Mechanikzentrums

http://asterix.ipmi.uni-bremen.de/fb7home.html

Fachbereich Wirtschaftswissenschaft

http://www.ins.de/

Inter Networking Systems

http://www.tu-chemnitz.de/home/ins/chemnitz.html

Chemnitz-Zwickau

http://www.rz.tu-clausthal.de/

Rechenzentrum

http://www.heim2.tu-clausthal.de/

Wohnheime I und II

http://www.th-darmstadt.de/darmstadt.html

Darmstadt

http://www.igd.fhg.de/

haus der Graphischen Datenverarbeitung

http://zgdv.igd.fhg.de/

Computer Graphics Center

http://www.th-darmstadt.de:/

Technische Hochschule

http://tutor.oc.chemie.th-darmstadt.de/

Tutorenzentrum Chemie

http://www.dvs1.informatik.th-darmstadt.de/

Datenverwaltungssysteme 1
Fachbereich Maschinenbau

http://www.dik.maschinenbau.th-darmstadt.de/

Datenverarbeitung in der Konstruktion

http://venus.muk.maschinenbau.th-darmstadt.de/

Maschinenelemente und Konstruktionslehre

http://www.physik.th-darmstadt.de/

Fachbereich Physik

http://www.fibronics.de/

Fibronics GmbH

http://www.germany.eu.net/

EUnet Deutschland GmbH

http://www.informatik.uni-dortmund.de/EXUG/EXUG.html

European X User Group

http://jwd.ping.de/

Windows Programmer's Group

http://www.chemie.uni-dortmund.de/index.html

Fachbereich Chemie

http://www.informatik.uni-dortmund.de/

Fachbereich Informatik

http://www.venture.net/

VentureNET

http://www.nacamar.de/rheinmain.html

Dreieich

http://www.nacamar.de/

Nacamar

http://www.tu-dresden.de/dresden/dresden.html

Dresden

http://radon.uni-duisburg.de/

Fachbereich Chemie

http://ateg.uni-duisburg.de/

Fachgebiet Allgemeine und Theoretische Elektrotechnik

http://sent5.uni-duisburg.de/Welcome.html

Fachgebiet Nachrichtentechnik

http://www.fb9-ti.uni-duisburg.de:8080/

Fachgebiet Technische Informatik

http://hlt3.uni-duisburg.de/

Halbleitertechnologie

http://WWW.thp.Uni-Duisburg.DE/

Theoretische Physik

http://www.novell.de/

Novell European Support Center

http://www.fho-emden.de/

Fachhochschule Ostfriesland

http://www.rrze.uni-erlangen.de/docs/Erlangen/

Erlangen

http://pctc.chemie.uni-erlangen.de/fakultaet/chemie.html

Fachbereich Chemie

http://www.lte.e-technik.uni-erlangen.de/

Lehrstuhl Technische Elektronik

http://www.rrze.uni-erlangen.de/

Regionales Rechenzentrum

http://www_win.rrze.uni-erlangen.de/

WiN-Labor

http://www.franken.de/

Kommunikationsnetz Franken e.V.

http://callisto.fsag.rhein-main.de/

Free Software Association of Germany

http://www.omnilink.net/

Omnilink GbR

http://hpfrs6.physik.uni-freiburg.de/

Physik

http://www.psychologie.uni-freiburg.de/

Psychologisches Institut
Fraunhofer-Gesellschaft

http://www.freinet.de/

Freinet

http://http.hq.eso.org/eso-homepage.html

ESO, European Southern Observatory

http://www.ipp-garching.mpg.de/rzg.html

Plasmaphysik

http://www.physik.tu-muenchen.de/tumphy/d/einrichtungen/wsi/

Walter Schottky Institut

http://www.gkss.de/Geesthacht.html

Geesthacht

http://www.gkss.de/

GKSS Forschungszentrum

http://www.med-stat.gwdg.de/

Abteilung Medizinische Statistik

http://risc350b.mdv.gwdg.de/jura/welcome.html

Fachbereich Rechtswissenschaften

```
http://www.uni-geochem.gwdg.de/docs/
home.htm
```
Geochemisches Institut

```
http://www.physik.uni-greifswald.de/
general/greifswald.html
```
Greifswald

```
http://www.physik.uni-greifswald.de/
```
Fachbereich Physik

```
http://www-kommsys.fernuni-hagen.de/
welcome.html
```
Fachgebiet Kommunikationssysteme

```
http://www.uni-halle.de/HALLE/HAL-
Home.html
```
halle

```
http://www.mathematik.uni-halle.de/
```
Fachbereich Mathematik und Informatik

```
http://www.uni-hamburg.de/Hamburg/
HH_homepage.html
```
hamburg

```
http://info.desy.de:80/
```
Deutsches Elektronen-Synchrotron

```
http://dxhra1.desy.de:80/hERMES-Experiment
http://www.dkrz.de/
```
Deutsches Klimarechenzentrum

```
http://nda.net/nda/
```
Norddeutsche Datenautobahn

```
http://idom-www.informatik.uni-hamburg.de/
external-entry.html
```
Arbeitsbereich Datenbanken und Informationsysteme

```
http://www.math.uni-hamburg.de/math/
```
Fachbereich Mathematik

```
http://www.econ.uni-hamburg.de/
```
Fachbereich Wirtschaftswissenschaften

```
http://energie1.en.tu-harburg.de/
AB_Energietechnik.html
```
Arbeitsbereich Energietechnik

```
http://abnt2.et2.tu-harburg.de/
Welcome.html
```
Arbeitsbereich Nachrichtentechnik

```
http://www.tu-harburg.de:80/sde/
```
Fachschaftsrat Elektrotechnik

```
http://bashir.ti1.tu-harburg.de/home.html
```
Technische Informatik I

```
http://www.ix.de/
```
iX-Redaktion, Heise-Verlag

```
http://www.urz.uni-heidelberg.de/city-
info/index.html
```
Heidelberg

```
http://www.dante.de/
```
DANTE, Deutschsprachige Anwendervereinigung TeX e.V

http://www.dkfz-heidelberg.de/index.html

DKFZ, Deutsches Krebsforschungszentrum

http://iris02a.inet.dkfz-heidelberg.de/

Abteilung Histodiagnostik und Pathomorphologische Dokumentation

http://mbi.dkfz-heidelberg.de/

Abteilung Medizinische und Biologische Informatik/Bildverarbeitungsgruppe

http://www.embl-heidelberg.de/

EMBL, European Molecular Biology Laboratory

http://www.oci.uni-heidelberg.de/index.html

Axels Experimenteller Server

http://www.astro.uni-jena.de/

Staub in Sternentstehungsgebieten

http://www.uni-kl.de/Stadt/

Kaiserslautern

http://klinfo.unix-ag.uni-kl.de/de/kl_server

Unix-AG

http://uklirb.informatik.uni-kl.de/

Fachbereich Informatik

http://www.uni-kl.de/

Regionales Hochschulrechenzentrum

http://klinfo.unix-ag.uni-kl.de/

UNIX-AG

http://www.ba-karlsruhe.de/KA/KA.html

Karlsruhe

http://www.ba-karlsruhe.de/

Berufsakademie

http://www.zblmath.fiz-karlsruhe.de/

Fachinformationszentrum Karlsruhe, Abt. Mathematik und Informatik

http://www.fzi.de/

Forschungszentrum Informatik

http://www.xlink.net/

NTG/Xlink

http://www.ask.uni-karlsruhe.de/welcome.html

Akademische Software Kooperation

http://www.nic.de/

DEutsches Network Information Center

http://www.cls.de/

Commercial Link Systems

http://www.fh-kiel.de/

Fachhochschule

http://www.netuse.de/

NetUSE GmbH

http://rhodesit.min.uni-kiel.de/Welcome.html

Mineralogisch-Petrographisches Institut und Museum

http://www.uni-koblenz.de/local/CityGuide/index.html

Koblenz

http://sunny.metaworks.de/

MetaWorks GmbH

http://www.fh-konstanz.de/

Fachhochschule, Rechenzentrum

http://imperia.fh-konstanz.de/

Imperia

http://www.lake.de/

Lake.de

http://www.roka.net/

roka EDV und Datenkommunikationsberatung GmbH

http://hiris.anorg.chemie.tu-muenchen.de/AAL/

Astronomische Arbeitsgruppe Laufen e.V

http://www.uni-leipzig.de/leipzig/

Leipzig

http://rzws01.grz.fh-lueneburg.de/

Fachhochschule Nordostniedersachsen

http://www.tu-magdeburg.de/~schroede/mdstadt.html

Magdeburg

http://www.nacamar.de/city/mainz/g_mainz.html

Mainz

http://radbruch.jura.uni-mainz.de/

Fachbereich Rechtswissenschaft

http://www.ba-mannheim.de/

Berufsakademie

http://www.uni-mannheim.de/users/ddz/index.html

Dokumentations- und Datenbankzentrum

http://WWW.Informatik.Uni-Mannheim.DE/

Fachbereich Mathematik und Informatik

http://www.mathematik.uni-marburg.de/

Fachbereich Mathematik/Informatik

http://www.physik.uni-marburg.de/

Fachbereich Physik

http://www.wiwi.uni-marburg.de/

Fachbereich Wirtschaftswissenschaften

http://i53s.ifi.th-merseburg.de/menu/Merseburg1.html

Merseburg

http://www.nonlin.tu-muenchen.de/chaos/chaos.html

Chaosgruppe e.V.

http://www.cycom.de/

CyberWebCommunications

http://www.ecrc.de/

European Computer-Industry Research Center GmbH

http://www.isar.de/

I.S.A.R Netzwerke GbRmbH

http://www.lrz-muenchen.de/Lrz/homepage_ge.html

Leibniz-Rechenzentrum

http://www.bl.physik.tu-muenchen.de/

Beschleunigerlaboratorium

http://www.mch.sni.de/welcome.html

Siemens Nixdorf Informationssysteme AG

http://www.physik.tu-muenchen.de/tumphy/d/einrichtungen/wsi/

Walter Schottky Institut

http://www.uni-muenster.de/math/

Fachbereich Mathematik

http://aquila.uni-muenster.de/

Astronomisches Institut

http://www.uni-muenster.de/WiWi/

Fachbereich Wirtschaftswissenschaften

http://smurf.noris.de/

Noris Network GbR

http://pid.da.op.dlr.de/

DFD - Deutsches Fernerkundungsdatenzentrum

http://www.informatik.uni-oldenburg.de/~xray/Oldenburg_index.html

Oldenburg

http://www.hrz.uni-oldenburg.de/fb9.html

Fachbereich Chemie

http://www.informatik.uni-oldenburg.de/index.html

Fachbereich Informatik

http://www.physik.uni-oldenburg.de/welcome.html

Fachbereich Physik

http://www.hrz.uni-oldenburg.de/hrzhome.html

hochschulrechenzentrum

http://www.north.de/

OLIS - Oldenburger Informationssysteme

http://esther.mathematik.uni-osnabrueck.de/

Fachbereich Mathematik / Informatik

http://godard.oec.uni-osnabrueck.de/

Fachbereich Wirtschaftswissenschaften

http://www.uni-paderborn.de/paderborn.html

Paderborn

http://www.uni-paderborn.de/pcpc/pcpc.html

Paderborn Center for Parallel Computing

http://www.sni.de/

Siemens Nixdorf Informationssysteme AG

http://pooh.uni-paderborn.de/

heinz Nixdorf Institut

http://www.uni-paderborn.de/

Informatik

http://math-www.uni-paderborn.de/
Mathematik

http://www.fmi.uni-passau.de/passau/uebersicht.html
Passau

http://www.gfz-potsdam.de/
GeoForschungsZentrum

http://www.pik-potsdam.de/
Institute for Climate Impact Research

http://excalibur.rz.uni-potsdam.de/homepage.htm
Geisteswissenschaften

http://www.ba-ravensburg.de/
Berufsakademie

http://www.fh-reutlingen.de/index.html
Fachhochschule

Rheinstetten
Rheinstetten

http://jil.informatik.uni-rostock.de:8000/index.html
Fachbereich Informatik

http://www-dbis.informatik.uni-rostock.de/
Lehrstuhl Datenbank- und Informationssysteme

http://hp710.math.uni-rostock.de:8001/home.html
Fachbereich Mathematik

http://www.saar.de/index.html
Internet Privat e.V

http://ps-www.dfki.uni-sb.de/
Forschungsbereich Programmiersysteme

http://www.jura.uni-sb.de/
Server der Rechtsinformatik

http://www.gmd.de/
GMD German National Research Center for Computer Science

http://www.uni-stuttgart.de/Ist/Ist.html
Stuttgart

http://www.belwue.de/belwue.html
BelWue

http://www.mpi-stuttgart.mpg.de/
Max-Planck-Institute

http://192.253.114.31/
Patch American High School

http://www.pem.com/
PEM GmbH

http://www.uni-stuttgart.de/Cis/cis.html
Campus Informationssystem

http://www.uni-stuttgart.de/
Regionales Rechenzentrum

http://www.uni-trier.de/trier/trier.html
Trier

http://www.trier.fh-rpl.de/

Fachhochschule Rheinland-Pfalz, Rechenzentrum

http://fsai.trier.fh-rpl.de/

Fachschaft Angewandte Informatik

http://www.informatik.uni-trier.de/

Informatik / Computer Science

http://www.uni-trier.de/urt/urt.html

Rechenzentrum

http://greco.gris.informatik.uni-tuebingen.de/

Arbeitsbereich Computer-Graphik

http://sunwww.informatik.uni-tuebingen.de:8080/

Arbeitsbereich Datenbanken und Informationssysteme

http://www-pu.informatik.uni-tuebingen.de/

Arbeitsbereich Programmierung

http://aorta.tat.physik.uni-tuebingen.de/

Theoretische Astrophysik und Computational Physics

http://www.mathematik.uni-ulm.de/stadtulm/ulm.html

Ulm

http://www.nacamar.de/city/wiesbaden/g_wiesbaden.html

Wiesbaden

http://www.ploenzke.de/

Ploenzke AG

http://www.fh-wolfenbuettel.de/rz/

Rechenzentrum

http://w3.worms.fh-rpl.de/

Rechenzentrum

http://tkz-220.tkz.fh-rpl.de/

Telekommunikations-Zentrum

http://www.uni-wuppertal.de/misc/wuppertal/welcome.html

Wuppertal

http://wmwap1.math.uni-wuppertal.de/pub/Mosaic/Mathematics_WWW.html

Fachbereich Mathematik

http://www.uni-wuppertal.de/fachbereiche/FB8/welcome.html

Fachbereich Physik

http://www.uni-wuppertal.de/welcome.englisch.html

Rechenzentrum

http://www.ifh.de/

DESY-IfH

Greece

http://www.ics.forth.gr/

Foundation for Research and Technology Hellas - Institute of Computer Science

http://www.cc.uch.gr/
University Of Crete Computer Center

http://www.duth.gr/
Demokritos University of Thrace

http://iris.di.uoa.ariadne-t.gr/
Department of Informatics, University of Athens

Hungary

http://www.fsz.bme.hu/hungary/budapest/budapest.html
Budapest

http://www.fsz.bme.hu/bme/bme.html
Technical University of Budapest

http://www.univet.hu/
University of Veterinary Science

http://www.lib.klte.hu/
Kossuth Lajos University of Sciences

http://www.abc.hu/
Agricultural Biotechnology Center

http://gold.uni-miskolc.hu/
University of Miskolc

http://woland.iit.uni-miskolc.hu/
Multimedia Archive of the Maniacs

Iceland

http://www.isnet.is/
ISnet

http://www.isnet.is/iceuug/
The Icelandic Unix Systems User Group

http://www.hafro.is/welcome.e.html
Marine Research Inst./Directorate of Fisheries

http://www.rhi.hi.is/
University of Iceland

Ireland

http://star.arm.ac.uk/planet/planet.html
Armagh Observatory

http://www.cis.ie/
Cork Internet Services

http://curia.ucc.ie/
CURIA Irish Literature archive

http://147.252.133.152/
Dublin Institute of Technology

http://granuaile.ieunet.ie:80/
IEunet Networking Information regarding Ireland, and Links to the rest of Europe

http://www.iol.ie/IOL-HOME.html
Ireland Online

http://www.regiodesk.ie/
Regiodesk Ireland

http://www.hq2.telecom.ie/
Museum of Communications

http://www.tcd.ie/
Trinity College Dublin

http://www.ucc.ie/webentry.html
University College Cork

http://www.ucd.ie
University College Dublin

http://www.webnet.ie/
WebNet

Italy

http://cstv12.to.cnr.it/
Centro di Studio per la Televisione

http://sun01.iigb.na.cnr.it/
Istituto Internazionale di Genetica e Biofisica

http://www.iasi.rm.cnr.it/../WelcomeIASI.html
Istituto di Analisi dei Sistemi ed Informatica

http://www.esrin.esa.it/htdocs/esrin/esrin.html
ESRIN - European Space Research Institute

http://www.ist.unige.it/Welcome.html
Istituto Nazionale per la Ricerca sul Cancro - CBA Centro Biotecnologie Avanzate

http://rea.ei.jrc.it/
Environment Institute

http://www.saclantc.nato.int/
Undersea Research Center

Latvia

http://www.vernet.lv/ Latvia OnLine
The Latvia Home Page

http://www.riga.lv/ LVNet-Teleport
Beautiful Riga Map

http://www.latnet.lv/LU/lu.html
University of Latvia

http://www.latnet.lv/LATNET/head.html
LATNET

Lithunia

http://neris.mii.lt
Lithuania WWW

Luxembourg

http://www.echo.lu/
I'M-EUROPE

http://www.restena.lu/
RESTENA, the National Network for Education and Research

Netherlands

http://www.caos.kun.nl/
CAOS/CAMM Center, the Dutch National Expertise Center for Computer Aided Chemistry and BioInformatics

http://colibri.let.ruu.nl
Colibri language, speech, logic and information

http://www.cwi.nl/index.html
Center for Mathematics and Computer Science, Amsterdam

http://www.icce.rug.nl
ICCE, State University of Groningen

http://kviexp.kvi.nl/
Kernfysisch Versneller Instituut

http://www.ripe.net/ripe/default.html
European IP group

http://www_trese.cs.utwente.nl/
The TRESE Project at the SETI

http://www.twi.tudelft.nl/welcome.html
Delft University of Technology

http://www.cca.vu.nl
Vrije Universiteit Amsterdam

Norway

http://www.service.uit.no/homepage-no
Norway

http://ananse.irv.uit.no/trade_law/nav/trade.html
Ananse International Trade Law

http://www.bibsys.no/bibsys.html
BIBSYS

http://www.ii.uib.no/
Department of Informatics, University of Bergen

http://www.uio.no/
University of Oslo

http://www.uib.no/
University of Bergen

http://www.idt.unit.no/
University of Trondheim

http://www.dhhalden.no/
Ostfold Distriktshogskole

http://www.odh.no/
Oppland Distriktshogskole

http://www.aid.no/homepage-aid.html
Agder Ingenior- og Distriktshogskole

http://harpe.tdh.no/tdh.html
Telemark Distriktshogskole

http://www.hsr.no/
Hogskolen i Stavanger

http://www.ludvigsen.dhhalden.no/
The Ludvigsen Residence

http://www.oslonett.no/
Oslonett, Inc.

http://www.service.uit.no/homepage-uit.no
University of Tromsoe

http://www.odh.no/
Oppland College

http://www.unik.no
Center for Technology at Kjeller

http://www.mogul.no/
Mogul Media

http://www.datametrix.no/
DAXNET

http://info.cern.ch/hypertext/WWW/People/howcome/NorskeLover.html
Norwegian Laws

http://www.bbb.no/ Bergen By Byte A/S
BBS / Commercial Internet provider

http://www.eunet.no/nuug/nuug.html
Norwegian Unix systems User Group

http://www.uit.no/npt/homepage-npt.en.html
The Northern Lights Planetarium

Poland

http://info.fuw.edu.pl/pl/poland.html
Poland

http://www.if.uj.edu.pl/
Physics Department, Jagiellonian University

http://www.pg.gda.pl/pg.html
Computer Centre, Gdansk Technical University

http://www.gliwice.edu.pl/
Silesian Technical University, Gliwice

http://zsku.p.lodz.pl/
Technical University, Lodz

http://www.umcs.lublin.pl/
Maria Curie-Sklodowska University, Lublin

http://www.amu.edu.pl/welcome.html
Adam Mickiewicz University, Poznan

http://www.ncac.torun.pl
Nicolaus Copernicus University, Torun

http://www.cc.uni.torun.pl/
Torun home page

http://info.ippt.gov.pl/Welcome.html
Warsaw

http://www.astrouw.edu.pl/
Astronomical Observatory, Warsaw University

Portugal

http://s700.uminho.pt/homepage-pt
Portugal Home Page

http://www.uminho.pt
Universidade do Minho

Russia

http://www.mnts.msk.su

Russian House for International and Technological Cooperation

http://www.jinr.dubna.su/JINR Welcome

Joint Institute for Nuclear Research, Physics

http://top.rector.msu.su/

Moscow State University

http://www.kiae.su/www/wtr/

Window-to-Russia

Slovakia

http://www.tuzvo.sk/

Slovakia Home Page

http://turing.upjs.sk/

University of Pavol Jozef Safarik

Slovenia

http://www.ijs.si/slo.html

Slovenia Home Page

Spain

http://www.uji.es/

Department of Education, Universitat Jaume

http://dftuz.unizar.es/

University of Zaragoza

http://www.uniovi.es/

Universidad de Oviedo

Sweden

http://www.abc.se/

ABC Computer Club

http://www.jmk.su.se/Aftonbladet.kultur/home.html

Aftonbladet Kultur

http://www.algonet.se/

AlgoNet

http://www.pi.se/as-sayf/

As-Sayf

http://www.astrakan.hgs.se/

NuclearWar Mud and Astrakan Computer Club

http://www.cd.chalmers.se/

Computer Society at Chalmers University, Gothenburg

http://europen.swip.net/europen

Swedish Unix Users Group

http://www.gu.se/

Göteborg University

http://www.svt-falun.sr.se/

Gold of Gaia

http://www.nordic.ibm.com/

IBM Nordic Information Network

http://www.ideon.lth.se/

IDEON Research Park in Lund

http://www.island.lysator.liu.se/

Industrial Engineering and Management, LiTH

http://www.ids.se/

Information Dimensions Scandinavia

http://www.sb.gov.se/

Information Rosenbad

http://www.wblab.lu.se/itl/

Informationsteknologi i Lund

http://www.mm.se/interakt/home.html

Interakt, Interactive art and media magazine

http://www.pi.se/ivo.html

Internet Venture Organization

http://www.lu.se/

Lund University

http://www.forv.mh.se/

Mid Sweden University

http://www.kth.se/

Royal Institute of Technology

http://www.su.se/

Stockholm University

http://www.sunet.se/ SUNET

Swedish University Network

http://www.uu.se/

Uppsala University

http://www.bmc.uu.se

Biomedical Centre of Uppsala

http://www.csd.uu.se/

Computing Science Department

http://www.cmd.uu.se/

Center for Human-Computer studies

http://xray.uu.se/

X-Ray Server

http://www.surfchem.kth.se/

YKI - Institute for Surface Chemistry

Switzerland

http://info.hasler.ascom.ch/Web/mosaic-home.html

Ascom Tech WWW Server

http://www.cern.ch/

CERN

http://delinfo.cern.ch/Delphi/

DELPHI Experiment

http://info.cern.ch/

The server for the World-Wide Web initiative

http://www.cim.ch/

CIM Action Programme Switzerland

http://www.ethz.ch/
ETHZ Main WWW Server

http://rock0.ethz.ch/
Institute of Geotechnics at the Swiss Federal Institute of Technology

http://www.math.ethz.ch/
International Congress of Mathematicians

http://www.math.ethz.ch/~zari/
European Aviation Server

http://www.unige.ch/crystal/crystal_index.html
European Crystallography Committee

http://www.eunet.ch/top.html
Official WWW server for EUnet Switzerland

http://beta.embnet.unibas.ch/embnet/info.html
European Molecular Biology Network information

http://www.eunet.ch/GenevaGuide
The Geneva International Guide

http://www.zurich.ibm.com/
IBM Zurich Research Laboratory

http://heiwww.unige.ch/
Graduate Institute of International Studies

http://www.ifh.ee.ethz.ch
Lab. for Electromagnetic Fields Theory and Microwaves Electronics

http://www.ntb.ch
Neu-Technikum Buchs

http://www.osilab.ch/
OSILAB

http://www.psi.ch/
Paul Scherrer Institut

http://www.ping.ch/
Ping Switzerland

http://www.policom.ch/Customers/POLICOM
POLICOM WWW Server

http://www.rs.ch/
RadioSuisse Services

http://www.isbe.ch
School of Engineering Bern HTL

http://zoo4.isburg.ch
School of Engineering of Burgdorf

http://www.switch.ch/
Swiss Academic and Research Network

http://www.ubilab.ubs.ch/
UBS Information Technology Laboratory

http://iamwww.unibe.ch/index.html
Institute for Informatics and Applied Mathematics

http://www.unil.ch/
University of Lausanne

http://www-imt.unine.ch
Institute of Microtechnology, Research activities at IMT,Neuchatel

http://www-iwi.unisg.ch
Institute for Information Management

http://www.unizh.ch/
University of Zurich

http://www.who.ch/
World Health Organization

Turkey

http://www.bilkent.edu.tr/
Bilkent Main Web Server

http://www.ege.edu.tr
Ege University Unix Web Server

http://www.itu.edu.tr
Istanbul Technical University Web Server

http://www.tubitak.gov.tr
Tubitak Main Web Server

http://www.tcmb.gov.tr
Central Bank Web Server

http://gopher.bilkent.edu.tr:7001/1s/inet-hotel/tmd/
Turkish Mathematical Society

http://gopher.bilkent.edu.tr:7001/1s/inet-hotel/yad/
Operational Research Society of Turkey

http://gopher.bilkent.edu.tr:7001/1s/inet-hotel/tuba/
Turkish Academy of Sciences - TUBA

http://www.ee.bilkent.edu.tr/~ieee/ieee.html
IEEE Turkey Section Web Server

http://dec002.cmpe.boun.edu.tr/
Boun CS Web server

United Kingdom

http://www.abdn.ac.uk/
University of Aberdeen

http://www.dct.ac.uk/
The University of Abertay Dundee

http://www.dct.ac.uk/www/steps.html
The Steps Theatre Cinema Programme

http://www.dcs.aber.ac.uk/
Aberystwyth, University of Wales

http://www.ihi.aber.ac.uk/index.html
Institute for Health Informatics

http://star.arm.ac.uk/
Armagh Observatory

http://www.aston.ac.uk/home.html
Aston University

http://www.bubl.bath.ac.uk/BUBL/home.html
Bulletin Board for Libraries Information Service

http://www.bath.ac.uk/home.html
University of Bath

http://www.bbk.ac.uk/
Birkbeck College, University of London

http://web.dcs.bbk.ac.uk/ukuug/home.html
UKUUG-UK Unix User Group

http://www.bham.ac.uk/
The University of Birmingham

http://sun1.bham.ac.uk/acs/home_page.html
Academic Computing Service

http://sun1.bham.ac.uk/ctimath/home_page.html
CTI Centre for Mathematics and Statistics

http://ugsun1a.ph.bham.ac.uk:3006/
Cloud 9 at Birmingham University

http://wcl-rs.bham.ac.uk/GamesDomain
Games Domain

http://www.brad.ac.uk/
University of Bradford

http://www.bton.ac.uk/
University of Brighton

http://www.bris.ac.uk/
University of Bristol

http://www.icbl.hw.ac.uk/bcs/bcsmain.html
The British Computer Society

http://ub.nmh.ac.uk/
British Geological Survey

http://http1.brunel.ac.uk/
Brunel University

http://www.cam.ac.uk/
University of Cambridge

http://www.cup.cam.ac.uk/
Cambridge University Press

http://www.cl.cam.ac.uk/coffee/coffee.html
Coffee Machine

http://svr-www.eng.cam.ac.uk/
Speech, Vision & Robotics Group

http://web.city.ac.uk/
The City University, London

http://www.ucl.ac.uk/home.html
University College, University of London

http://www.cs.ucl.ac.uk/misc/uk/intro.html
Guide to the UK

http://info.cf.ac.uk/
College of Cardiff, University of Wales

http://www.cm.cf.ac.uk/Movies
Cardiff's Movie Database Browser

http://www.cm.cf.ac.uk:80/CLE/
The Eiffel Page

http://www.cranfield.ac.uk/

Cranfield University

http://www.dl.ac.uk/

Daresbury Laboratory

http://www.dmu.ac.uk/0h/www/home.html

De Montfort University

http://gotwo.dundee.ac.uk/

University of Dundee

http://forteana.mic.dundee.ac.uk/ft/

Fortean Times, The Journal of Strange Phenomena

http://www.dur.ac.uk/

Durham University

http://cpca3.uea.ac.uk/welcome.html

University of East Anglia

http://www.cru.uea.ac.uk/ukdiving/index.htm

UK Diving

http://www.sys.uea.ac.uk/MacSupporters.html

Mac-Supporters

http://www.uel.ac.uk/

University Of East London

http://www.ed.ac.uk/

Edinburgh University

http://www.chemeng.ed.ac.uk:80/ecosse/

The Ecosse Group

http://www.dcs.ed.ac.uk/staff/jhb/whisky/

The Scotch Malt Whisky Society

http://www.vet.ed.ac.uk/

The Royal School of Veterinary Studies

http://tardis.ed.ac.uk/

Tardis Public-Access Service

http://www.ucs.ed.ac.uk/Unixhelp/TOP_.html

Hypertext of helpful information for new users of the UNIX operating system

http://www.essex.ac.uk/

University of Essex.

http://www.essex.ac.uk/law/human-rights/

On line human-rights information

http://www.dcs.exeter.ac.uk/

Department of Computer Science, University of Exeter

http://www.gla.ac.uk

University of Glasgow

http://www.stats.gla.ac.uk/home.html

Department of Statistics

http://www.gold.ac.uk/

Goldsmiths College, University of London

http://www.gre.ac.uk/

University of Greenwich

http://www.cee.hw.ac.uk/index.html

Department of Computing & Electrical Engineering, Heriot-Watt University http://www.efr.hw.ac.uk/EDC/Edinburgh.html

Tourist Guide to Edinburgh

http://micros.hensa.ac.uk/

Higher Educational National Software Archives

http://www.hull.ac.uk/homepage.html

University of Hull

http://gea.lif.icnet.uk/

Imperial Cancer Research Fund, Reference Library DataBase

http://www.ic.ac.uk/

Imperial College, University of London

http://euclid.tp.ph.ic.ac.uk/

Theoretical Physics Group

http://src.doc.ic.ac.uk/

SunSITE Northern Europe

http://src.doc.ic.ac.uk/bySubject/Computing/Overview.html

The World-Wide Web Virtual Library: Computing

http://src.doc.ic.ac.uk/gnn/GNNhome.html

Global Network Navigator

http://src.doc.ic.ac.uk/req-eng/index.html

Requirements Engineering Newsletter Index

http://src.doc.ic.ac.uk/all-uk.html

United Kingdom Based WWW Servers.

httpp://cen.ex.ac.uk/economics/ICAEW/accweblib.html

Institute of Chartered Accountants of England and Wales, Accounting Information Service.

http://www.ioppublishing.com

The Institute of Physics

http://sunrae.uel.ac.uk/palaeo/index.html

International Organisation of Palaeobotany

http://www.keele.ac.uk/

Keele University

http://www.ukc.ac.uk/

University of Kent at Canterbury

http://ee016.eee.kcl.ac.uk/vrlhome.htm

Department of Electronic and Electrical Engineering, Kings College, University of London

http://www.kingston.ac.uk/

Kingston Universtity

http://www.lancs.ac.uk/

Lancaster University

http://www.leeds.ac.uk/

The University of Leeds

http://www.le.ac.uk/

University of Leicester

http://www.linux.org.uk/

Information about Linux, the Unix-like operating system for PCs

http://www.liv.ac.uk/
The University of Liverpool

http://www.lbs.lon.ac.uk/
London Business School

http://www.lpac.ac.uk/SEL-HPC/
London & South East High Performance Computing Centre

http://info.lut.ac.uk/
Loughborough University of Technology

http://info.mcc.ac.uk/UofM.html
The University of Manchester

http://www.mdx.ac.uk/
Middlesex University

http://server.nrs.ac.uk/NRS/
NRS Central Database

http://ncet.csv.warwick.ac.uk/
National Council for Educational Technology

http://www.ncl.ac.uk/
University of Newcastle

http://www.unl.ac.uk/
University of North London

http://www.nott.ac.uk/
University of Nottingham

http://www.doc.ntu.ac.uk/index.html
Department of Computing, Nottingham Trent University

http://hcrl.open.ac.uk/ou/ouhome.html
The Open University

http://www.ox.ac.uk/
University of Oxford

http://linux1.balliol.ox.ac.uk/fax/faxsend.html
The Oxford Internet Fax Server

http://www.brookes.ac.uk/
Oxford Brookes University

http://dan.see.plym.ac.uk/
The Network Research Group

http://www.port.ac.uk/
The University of Portsmouth

http://www.qub.ac.uk/
Queen's University of Belfast

http://www.dcs.qmw.ac.uk/
Department of Computer Science, Queen Mary and Westfield College, University of London

http://www.rdg.ac.uk/
University of Reading

http://www.rfhsm.ac.uk/
The Royal Free Hospital School of Medicine

http://www.rhbnc.ac.uk/
Royal Holloway, University of London

http://www.roe.ac.uk/
Royal Observatory, Edinburgh.

http://www.salford.ac.uk/
University of Salford

http://www.salford.ac.uk/os2power/os2power.html
Page for OS/2 users

http://www2.shef.ac.uk/
The University of Sheffield

http://www2.shef.ac.uk/chemistry/collegiate/collegiate-home.html
Sheffield Collegiate Cricket Club

http://pine.shu.ac.uk/
Sheffield Hallam University

http://www.sbu.ac.uk/
South Bank University

http://www.sbu.ac.uk/
Department of Architecture & Civil Engineering

http://avebury.arch.soton.ac.uk/
Department of Archaeology, University of Southampton

http://warp.dcs.st-and.ac.uk
Warp: systems group, University of St. Andrews

http://www.stir.ac.uk/
University of Stirling

http://www.strath.ac.uk/
University of Strathclyde

http://orac.sunderland.ac.uk/
University of Sunderland

http://www.surrey.ac.uk/
University of Surrey

http://www.ee.surrey.ac.uk/Personal/sf.html
Science Fiction TV series Guides

http://www.surrart.ac.uk/
Surrey Institute of Art and Design

http://www.swan.ac.uk/
Swansea University

http://www.ulst.ac.uk/
University of Ulster.

http://www.bangor.ac.uk/
University of Wales, Bangor.

http://www.csv.warwick.ac.uk/default.html
Warwick University

http://www.csv.warwick.ac.uk/WWW/law/default.html
CTI Law Technology Centre.

http://www.maths.warwick.ac.uk/
Mathematics Institute.

http://www.csv.warwick.ac.uk:8000/default.html
WWW Service for Nurses

http://www.csv.warwick.ac.uk:8000/midwifery.html

Midwifery page.

http://www.westminster.ac.uk/

University of Westminster.

http://www.wlv.ac.uk/

University of Wolverhampton.

http://www.york.ac.uk/

University of York

Central America

Costa Rica

http://ns.cr/

Costa Rica's Research Network

North America

Alberta

http://www.arc.ab.ca/

Alberta Research Council

http://www.nofc.forestry.ca/

Canadian Forest Service

http://www.tcel.com/index.html

Telnet Canada Enterprises

http://web.cs.ualberta.ca/UAlberta.html

University of Alberta

http://inuit.phys.ualberta.ca/

Center for Subatomic Research

http://www.ucalgary.ca/Welcome.html

University of Calgary

British Columbia

http://www.aurora.net/

auroraNET

http://www.camosun.bc.ca/camosun.html

Camosun College

http://www.cdnair.ca/

Canadian Airlines International

http://www.col.org/

Commonwealth of Learning

http://www.env.gov.bc.ca/

Ministry of Environment Lands &Parks

http://hrbwww.env.gov.bc.ca/

Human Resources Branch

http://www.cg94.freenet.victoria.bc.ca/

Ministry of Small Business, Tourism and Culture

http://kh.botany.ubc.ca/welcome.htm

Haughn/Kunst Laboratory

http://www.island.net/
Island Internet

http://bbs.sd68.nanaimo.bc.ca:8001/welcome.html
Nanaimo School District

http://cadc.dao.nrc.ca/CADC-homepage.html
Canadian Astrophysical Data Center

http://spanky.triumf.ca/
Spanky Fractal Database

http://pine.pfc.forestry.ca/
Advanced Forest Technologies Program

http://sol.uvic.ca/nami
North American Institute - Canada

http://freenet.unbc.edu/
Prince George Free-Net Association

http://www.seawest.seachange.com/
Sea Change Corporation

http://www.sfu.ca/
Simon Fraser University

http://view.ubc.ca/
University of British Columbia

http://www.uvic.ca/
University of Victoria

http://www.wimsey.com/~bmiddlet/vampyre/vampyre.html
Vampyres Only

http://freenet.vancouver.bc.ca/
Vancouver Regional FreeNet Association

http://freenet.victoria.bc.ca/vifa.html
Victoria Free-Net

http://interchange.idc.uvic.ca/
Westcoast Interchange

http://www.eitc.mb.ca/eitc.html
Economic Innovation and Technology Council

http://www.umanitoba.ca/
University of Manitoba

New Brunswick

http://www.gov.nb.ca/
Government of New Brunswick

http://www.mta.ca/
Mount Allison University

http://degaulle.hil.unb.ca/UNB.html
University of New Brunswick

Nova Scotia

http://www.acadiau.ca/
Acadia University

http://www.cfn.cs.dal.ca/
Chebucto FreeNet

http://ac.dal.ca/
Dalhousie University

http://www.stmarys.ca/
Saint Mary's University

http://www.tuns.ca/index.html
Technical University of Nova Scotia

Ontario

http://tourism.807-city.on.ca/
807-CITY

http://www.canadorec.on.ca/index.htm
Canadore College of Applied Arts and Technology

http://www.canadorec.on.ca/northbay.htm
City of North Bay

http://www.lakeheadu.ca/menu.html
Lakehead University

http://www.carleton.ca/
Carleton University

http://debra.dgbt.doc.ca/cbc/cbc.html
Canadian Broadcasting Corporation

http://www.chin.doc.ca/
Canadian Heritage Information Network

http://www.magi.com/
MAGI Data Consulting Inc.

http://ai.iit.nrc.ca/home_page.html
Knowledge Systems Laboratory

http://www.emr.ca/
Natural Resources Canada

http://ccm-10.ccm.emr.ca/
Canada Centre for Mapping

http://info.queensu.ca/index.html
Queen's University

http://mango.genie.uottawa.ca/Welcome.html
Multimedia Communications Research Laboratory, University of Ottawa

http://www.physics.brocku.ca/
Department of Physics, Brock University

http://www.netpart.com/che/brochure.html
Canadian Himalayan Expeditions

http://www.ists.ca/Welcome.html
Institute for Space and Terrestrial Science

http://www.eol.ists.ca/Welcome.html
Earth Observations Laboratory

http://www.sal.ists.ca/Welcome.html
Space Astrophysics Laboratory

http://www.lambton.on.ca/index.html
Lambton College

http://www.physics.mcmaster.ca/
Department of Physics and Astronomy, McMaster University

http://www.utoronto.ca/uoft.html
University of Toronto

http://www.scar.toronto.edu/
Scarborough College

http://csclub.uwaterloo.ca/

Computer Science Club, University of Waterloo

http://phobos.astro.uwo.ca/

Department of Astronomy, University of Western Ontario

http://turner.lamf.uwindsor.ca/

Science OnLine, University of Windsor

http://www.yorku.ca/

York University

http://www.crafts-council.pe.ca/vg/index.html

Prince Edward Island Tourism

http://www.upei.ca/index.html

University of Prince Edward Island

http://www.meteo.mcgill.ca/welcome.html

Centre for Climate and Global Change Research, Montreal

http://www-vlsi.concordia.ca/HomePage.html

VLSI Design Laboratory, Concordia University

http://www.ee.mcgill.ca/efc/efc.html

Electronic Frontier Canada/ Frontiere Electronique Canada

http://www.mcgill.ca/

McGill University

http://www.usask.ca/

University of Saskatchewan

http://www.cfht.hawaii.edu/

Canada-France-Hawaii Telescope

Mexico

http://info.pue.udlap.mx/

Universidad de las Americas

http://www.udg.mx/

Universidad de Guadalajara

http://www.mty.itesm.mx/

ITESM Campus Monterrey

http://www.dsi.uanl.mx/

Universidad Autonoma de Nuevo Leon

http://infux.mxl.cetys.mx/

Centro de Ensenanza Tecnica y Superior

http://bufa.reduaz.mx/

Universidad Autonoma de Zacatecas

http://info.main.conacyt.mx/

Consejo Nacional de Ciencia y Tecnologia

http://sparc.ciateq.conacyt.mx/homeciateq.html

CIATEQ, AC

http://kin.cieamer.conacyt.mx/

CINVESTAV-IPN Unidad Merida

http://www.ccu.umich.mx/

Universidad Michoacana

http://www.labvis.unam.mx/
Laboratorio de Visualizacion, UNAM

http://sunulsa.ulsa.mx/home-page.html
Universidad La Salle A.C.

http://www.astroscu.unam.mx/
Instituto de Astronomia, UNAM

http://tonatiuh.uam.mx/
Universidad Autonoma Metropolitana

http://www.ucol.mx/
Universidad de Colima

http://www.cicese.mx/DOCUMENTOS_CICESE/CICESE.html
Centro de Investigacion Cientifica y de Educacion Superior deEnsenada

http://dch.mty.itesm.mx/
Tec de Monterrey

http://www.lania.mx/
Laboratorio Nacional de Informatica Avanzada, A.C.

http://axp1.iiecuer.unam.mx/
Instituto de Investigaciones Electricas

http://cronos.sgia.imp.mx/General.html
Instituto Mexicano del Petroleo

http://www.ugto.mx/
Universidad de Guanajuato

http://www.ibt.unam.mx/
Instituto de Biotecnologia. UNAM

Puerto Rico

http://www.naic.edu/
National Astronomy and Ionosphere Center

http://hpprdk01.prd.hp.com/
Puerto Rico WWW

United States of America

http://sgisrvr.asc.edu/index.html ASN
Alabama Supercomputer Network

http://www.auburn.edu/
Auburn University

http://138.26.184.4/stumedia.htm
The StuMedia WWW Server

http://info.uah.edu
The University of Alabama in Huntsville

http://tdcems.tdc.redstone.army.mil/micom/home.html
U.S. Army Missile Command, Technology Development Laboratory

http://www.af.mil/
USAF Web Server

http://www.arsc.edu
Arctic Region Supercomputing Center

http://www.amug.org/index.html
Arizona Macintosh Users Group WWW Server

http://www.asu.edu/Welcome.html

Arizona State University

http://info.ccit.arizona.edu/

University of Arizona information

http://www.tucson.ihs.gov/

Indian Health Service

http://www.indirect.com/

Internet Direct

http://www.sibylline.com/

Sibylline, Inc.

http://161.31.2.29/

College of Business,
University of Central Arkansas

http://emerson.netmedia.com/IMS/rest/ba_rest_guide.html

Bay Area Restaurant Guide, Palo Alto

http://www.election.ca.gov

California Election Results, Sacramento

http://smaug.ucr.edu/Quakes/quake_page.html

Earthquake Information, Riverside

http://www.hotelres.com

Hotel Information and Reservations, San Francisco

http://www.northcoast.com/unlimited/unlimited.html

Redwood Country Unlimited, Eureka

http://www.cccd.edu/ski.html

Southland Ski Server, Costa Mesa

http://sailfish.peregrine.com/surf/surf.html

Surfing reports, Carlsbad

http://www.cts.com/~health

Center for Anxiety and Stress Treatment, San Diego

http://www.clarinet.com/

ClariNet Communications, San Jose

http://www.dvts.com/

daVinci Time & Space, Los Angeles

http://www.northcoast.com/

Evergreen Technologies, Eureka

http://www.lp.org/lp/ca/lpsc.html

Libertarian Party, San Jose

http://www.mojones.com/motherjones.html

Mother Jones, San Francisco

Appendix

Independent Content and Solution Provider Directory for the Microsoft Network

3Com Corp.
3M Office Markets Center
7th Level Forum
21st Century Online
A2S2 Digital Projects, Inc.
Acer America
ACES TeleRecruiting
Activision
Adaptec
Adventure Media Inc. (Travelon)
Adobe Systems Incorporated
Albion Books (The Netiquette Center)
Alcom the LanFax Company
AMA Health and Medical Forum
American Greetings
American Business Information, Inc.
American Management Association (WorkSmart)
American Venture Capital Exchange (Business Exchange)
Amos Press
Ansett Airlines
Apricot Computers Ltd.
Arcada Software Inc.
Arrow Associates Inc. (WinTrak, The Online Interactive Financial Planning Game)
AST Computers
Attachment Corp.
AutoMall Online Inc.
Automotive Information Center (AutoNet)
Baker, Thomsen Associates Insurance Services Inc.
Best Friends Animal Sanctuary (Animal Net)
BIG Entertainment (TeknoComix Forum)
Blackhurst (Guitar Network)
Books That Work
Borland International Inc. (Smooth Sailing)

Broderbund Software
Brother International Corp.
Business Listing Services Inc. (Relocatable Business)
Byron Preiss Multimedia Company Inc.
CarSource
CCH Business Owner's Toolkit
Charles Schwab & Co., Inc.
Chase Manhattan Bank (ChaseDirect Online)
Cheyenne Software Inc.
Claris Corp.
The Cobb Group (Cobb's PC Productivity Center)
Commonwealth Bank of Australia
The Company Corporation
Computer Associates International, Inc.
Cooking Light Magazine
Corbis Corp.
Corel Corporation
Court TV Law Center
Cowles Business Media (Media Central Plus)
Cristal Software Inc.
The C-SPAN Networks
Data Broadcasting Corp.
Davidson & Associates Inc.
Decision Point
Dell Computer Corp.
Deloitte and Touche Online
DFI
Diamond Multimedia Systems, Inc. (Diamond Online)
The Digital Foundry Inc./Toy World Inc. (GameGallery Online)
Digital Mystix Inc.
Disclosure Inc.
The Domain Group (Involved Christian Network)
Dun & Bradstreet Information Services
Dymocks
Economic Research Institute (ERI)
Eddie Bauer
Edmark Corp.
Educational Edge Inc. (Accounting Office)
Emerging Markets Information Inc. (Max's Investment World)
Entrepreneur Magazine's Small Business Network (BizNET)
Epson America Inc.
Equifax Credit Information Services
Everyday Communication AB (Modern Times Group)
Fantasy Sports Properties, Inc.
Faulkner & Gray Specialty Business Publishers

Fawcette Technical Publications (WinDX Forum)
Federal Express
Fidelity Investments
Flashman Trading
Future Domain
Galley Books
Gateway 2000 Inc.
Gauthier & Gilden Inc.
GE Information Services Inc. (Electronic Data Interchange (EDI))
Global Network for Environmental & Technology (GNET)
Governet/Q&A Communications
Green Light Communications Inc. (The Marketing Store)
Greenfield Online Research Center
Hayes Microcomputer Products Inc.
Handman & Associates Food Group Inc. (Encyclopedia Cuisines)
Health Publishing Inc. (Healthline)
Hearst New Media & Technology (Home Arts Online)
Hogia AB
Hollywood Online Inc.
Home Office Association of America (Home Office Network)
Home Office Computing Magazine
Home Shopping Network
HSN Interactive Inc.
Humongous Entertainment
ICL
IAM Online Inc. (Martial Arts Network)
IAM Online Inc. (Collectors Direct Network)
IN SYNC, INC. (Screenwriters Studios)
Individual Inc. (*iNews*)
Information Access Company (IAC Business Intelligence Forum)
Infotel Inc.
Ingenius Online
IntelliCom Digital Solutions Forum
Intergraph Corp.
International Culinary and Nutrition Network
International Fire Service Network Inc. (INFERNO)
International InsureNet Corp.
Iomega Corporation
J&H Communications Group Ltd. (HR OnLine)
JCI Technologies (World Match)
Kaplan Educational Centers
KidStar Online
Kodalux Digital Imaging (Kodalux Online)
The Komando Corporation (The Komputer Klinic)

Landmark Corporation (The Weather Channel, The Travel Channel, Collectors Online)
The Law Office Inc. (The Law Forum)
The LEXIS-NEXIS Small Business Service
Lexmark International Inc.
Lotus Development Inc.
Macromedia
Maestro
Magnet Interactive Studios Inc.
Mainstream Online
The MapInfo Forum
Matrix Software (The New Age Forum)
Maxis
Maxtor Corp.
McAfee Network Security & Management
McDonald's Corporation (McFamily)
Mediatrends, Inc.
MetaBridge Inc.
METZ Software Inc.
Microcom Inc.
Micrografx
Micron Computer Inc.

Microsoft
Microsoft Consumer Division
Microsoft Developer Network
Microsoft Office
Microsoft Online Institute
Microsoft Services
Microsoft TechNet
Microsoft WindowsÆ 95

Mind Garden, Inc.
Mindscape Inc.
Minority Business Network (Minority BizNet)
MLC
Monotype Font and Typographic Resource
Multi-Player Games Network (MPG Net)
Music Pen Inc.
Mustang Software Inc.
N2K Inc. (Jazz Central Station)
NBC SuperNet
The National Parenting Center
National PTA (Children First)
NCR Microelectronic Products

NEC Technologies
NET - Political NewsTalk Network
NewMedia/HyperMedia Communications
The New Republic Magazine
The New York Times Magazine Group (Sports/Leisure Magazines Online)
Newsbytes News Network
Nokia
Novell Inc.
Now Software
Nustar International (Home Guide)
OfficeMax Inc.
Olivetta SPA
Online Games Inc. (Online Sports Games and Online Fantasy & Strategy Games)
Ontrack Data Recovery and Ontrack Computer Systems
Orbis Broadcast Group (America's House Call Network)
PalCom Hospitality Corporation (THE INNterREST Global Food-Service & Lodging Industry Forums)
Paramount Television ("Star Trek" and "Entertainment Tonight")
Paranet Information Services Inc.
Parent Council
Patriot Services Inc. (Mortgage Online/Patriot System)
Paul Budde Communications (Superhighway News)
PC World Communications, Inc.
Peterson's Guides Inc. (Peterson's Education and Career Headquarters)
PhotoDisc Digital Photography Forum
Pinkerton Services Group
PlanetOut
Planet Youth
Planetel (The Telecom Forum)
Pont Securities
Portsmouth Trading Company Ltd. (Online Gourmet)
Poulton Associates Inc. (Insurance & Risk Management Central)
PowerSoft Corporation
Practical Peripherals
The Princeton Review
QVC Interactive Shopping/Marketplace
The Reference Press Inc. (Hoover's Business Resources)
Reuters NewMedia Online
Rocknet, Inc.
SAS Institute
Saber Software Corp.
Sendai Interactive (NUKE +)
SeniorNet
Shapeware Corp.

Sharp Electronics Corp.
Shaq World Online
Shepard's
Siemens Nixdorf Informationssysteme AG
U.S. Small Business Administration
Smithsonian Magazine/Air & Space Smithsonian Magazine
SoftSource
Splash Studios Inc. (Splash Kids)
SportsTicker Enterprises, L.P.
Stac Electronics Corp.
Starfish Software
Starlog Entertainment
Starwave Corp. (ESPNET SportsZone)
Starwave Corp. (Family Planet)
Starwave Corp. (Mr. Showbiz)
Starwave Corp. (Outside Online)
Success Magazine
Supra Corp.
SWMG Productions Inc. (Nonline — The Non Profit Network)
Symantec Corp.
Telstra Multimedia Services
Thomson Financial Services (MarketEdge)
Toshiba Computer Systems Division (Toshiba PC Forum)
Toy World Inc. (GameGallery Online)
TRW Business Information Services
Traveling Software Inc.
TV Key
Twenty First Century Municipals Inc. (Bonds Online)
United Airlines (United Connection)
United Parcel Service
USA Today
U.S. Healthcare
VideoLogic Inc.
The Village Software Store
Visio Corp.
Wall Data Inc.
WeatherLabs Inc.
Western Digital Corp.
WinWay Corporation (WinWay Career Forum)
Wire Networks Inc. (Women's Wire)
Yoyodyne Entertainment
Xircom
Zenographics Inc.
Ziff Davis Net
Zycon Inc. (Global Real Estate Services)

GLOSSARY

Access Number   The phone number, dialed by your computer, that you use to reach the online system. It may be a free call or a toll call.

Accounts, Individual   All MSN accounts are set up as individual accounts—for one person. Each account is billed separately and has only one *screen name* or *member ID* assigned to it.

Address Book   A database used by the e-mail system (Microsoft *Exchange*) to record user names and electronic address information.

Adult Content   Selected forums and newsgroups that are off limits to members until they submit an e-form requesting admission to areas with adult content. The Sexuality Forum is an example of a forum with adult content.

Anonymous FTP   A simple technique for downloading files from an Internet-based *FTP* site for which you do not have a user ID. Many FTP servers make their file archives accessible to all Internet users, which means you can access the site by using the ID "anonymous."

Area   This term is used interchangeably with *category* and *site* to refer to a forum, BBS, or Internet location.

ASCII   The American Standard for Computer Information Interchange provides a numeric code for all the characters available on a standard keyboard. Data in ASCII format is compatible with virtually all computer systems.

ASCII Text   Textual data represented internally as ASCII codes, which are converted to and displayed as text. Most e-mail is ASCII text (also "plain text") and is compatible with a variety of machines. *Text files* are the same as ASCII text files.

Attachment (to e-mail)   MSN allows you to attach computer files—graphics, text, animation, and sound—in the form of an object or shortcut. Icons (shortcuts) representing *Favorite Places* or *URLs* can also be attached to e-mail.

Baud Rate   This is an industry-accepted method of modem speed. One baud refers to one bit transmitted per second. There was a time when 2,400 baud modems were state-of-the-art. Today 14,400 is considered a minimum speed and

28,800 is the going rate. The faster your modem, the speedier your connection to MSN, and the less time you will spend waiting for images to appear on your screen.

BBS   A bulletin board service (BBS) is any central system accessed via modem and phone lines and where data is posted for transmission and sharing among the BBS users. MSN is essentially a very large BBS. Typically BBSs are much smaller and many cover only one specialized topic. MSN also uses the term *BBS* in place of *Message Boards*.

Blind Courtesy Copy (bcc)   MSN provides the capability to send a blind courtesy copy, which is a copy of an e-mail message sent to someone other than the primary recipient—without the recipient being aware of the copy.

Browser   In connection with the World Wide Web, any graphical interface that uses *HTML* to display and find information on the Internet. Microsoft's Internet *Explorer* is the browser used in this book. Other browsers include Netscape and Mosaic.

Bulletin Board   See *Message Board* and *BBS*.

Courtesy Copy (cc)   Just like a memo, e-mail correspondence can be copied to someone other than the primary recipient. In this case, the primary addressee is aware of any courtesy copies sent. See also *Blind Courtesy Copy*.

Categories   MSN has 16 Categories that provide the top level of content. The categories are Arts & Entertainment; Business & Finance; Computers & Software; Education & Reference; Health & Fitness; Home & Family; Interests, Leisure & Hobbies; News & Weather; People & Communities; Public Affairs; Science & Technology; Special Events; Sports & Recreation; Internet Center; MSN Passport; and Chat World.

Chat   A chat is the electronic conversation that occurs when two or more members are communicating in a chat room. Chats occur in real time—that is, as soon as one person types in his or her message, it appears on the recipient's screen. In this way, an ongoing dialog can be held.

Chat Room   Chat Rooms are designated areas where MSN members gather to participate in real time conversations, where their fingers do the talking. Chats may be moderated or unmoderated and some likely fall under the heading of adult content.

Click   A single mouse click.

Client Usually a system attached to a network that accesses shared network resources.

Client-Server Any network-based system where information is stored in a centralized location (the server computer) for access by multiple users (who are said to be the clients). On MSN, the information for most categories, ICPs, e-mail, and chats is stored centrally on MSN's server system. Individual MSN subscribers are considered to be clients of the MSN server and must go to the server to view and download information. On the Internet, the system where a Web site's information is stored is called a Web server, while the system where an FTP site's files are stored is called an FTP server.

Compressed Files Most files available for download have been compressed to save disk space and transfer time. Your copy of MSN should be able to decompress virtually all files upon arrival, but it's always a good idea to keep a compression program, like WinZip, on your hard drive.

Connect Time This is the time for which you are actually online and connected to MSN. Connect time is first deducted from your monthly allotment and then you are billed for time beyond this allotment. While you are accruing connect time, the virtual cash register is running.

Desktop This is the main Windows 95 operating screen. It contains icons or objects representing files or shortcuts. The MSN icon rests there too.

Directory What we now call *Folders* were previously called Directories under Windows 3.1.

Domain A portion of a URL address that identifies a host system or a part of the system dedicated to a specific user group. The domain description provides a human language technique for specifying a host system's address. For MSN members, **msn.com** is the domain portion of your e-mail address.

Double Click Two rapid clicks of the mouse.

Download The process of retrieving or pulling a file down from MSN or from the Internet. The term is used as both noun and verb. You can download (v.) a file or the file itself can be referred to as a download (n.). See also *upload* and *retrieve*.

Download Libraries See *File Libraries*.

Glossary

Drag This is the action of moving an object around your desktop or screen. Left-click, and move the mouse while still holding the left button down.

Drag-and-Drop The ability to move objects from one part of your desktop and drop them onto another part of your desktop.

E Form Electronic form. This is a standardized electronic form generally used for a submission to MSN or one of the forum providers. Simply fill in the blanks or check the boxes and send the submission off.

Electronic Mail (E-mail) Electronic mail is private mail sent from one computer to another. Copies can be sent to multiple recipients. Multiple *courtesy copies* and *blind courtesy copies* can also be sent. Mail can be sent within MSN or across the Internet.

Explorer In all likelihood, there are two Explorers on your system. The first is Windows Explorer, which allows you to search and navigate through folders. The second is the Internet Explorer, which is MSN's Web *browser*.

Ezine A magazine that is available online—either on MSN, the Internet, or some other online service.

Favorite Your favorite *URLs*. See also *Favorite Places*.

Favorite Places Just as with Explorer above, there are two types of favorites to be discussed. Favorite Places are those special MSN sites that you've added to your Favorite Places list. A separate list of *Favorites* can be maintain by your Web *browser*, Explorer.

File A file is a computer file (text, graphics, program, sound, animation) that is intended to be downloaded by a member for review offline. Files may be attached to *e-mail* or stored in *file libraries*.

File Compression See *Compression*.

File Libraries These are also known as *download libraries*. Found in forums, file libraries hold files that you download and generally utilize offline.

File Sharing The ability for two or more users to access the same file. Shared files can typically by read by many users at a time, but only one user can write to the file at a time. ICPs stores information within text and graphic files, all of which can be shared and viewed by multiple subscribers simultaneously. However, only the

ICP's supervisors can write (add, modify, or delete) information in these files, and only one supervisor at a time can make any changes.

Find Function   Accessed from the MSN icon in the lower right corner of your screen, Find is a great key to content on MSN. You can use the find function to search for topics, forums, newsgroups, and more. The *Index function* is related to the Find function.

Folder   A logical "place" that allows the user to group any collection of items such as files. Folders are also known as directories. See *Directory*.

Forum(s)   Forums are areas where people with similar interests gather to exchange ideas, comments, and files. Most forums include *message boards* or *BBSes, file libraries, chat rooms,* and *kiosks*. Each forum has a particular theme to attract people who share common interests.

FTP   File Transfer Protocol, which defines the communications standards used to upload and download files to and from an Internet FTP server. See also *Anonymous FTP*.

GIFs   Files in the Graphic Interchange Format, a highly compressed format for storing and transferring images. Created by CompuServe, it is also the most widely used graphic format on the Internet.

GO Words   GO Words, also known as Go To references, are speedy jumps to specific destinations within MSN. To use a GO Word, right-click on the MSN icon in the lower corner of your screen or use the Go To command found under the Edit pull-down menu.

Gopher   A text search and retrieval system named after the mascot at the University of Minnesota, where Gopher was created. A Gopher server treats the hierarchy of Internet databases, directories, and files as a series of menus, which you can browse through to find specific information.

Guidebooks   Guidebooks are editorial works produced by Microsoft. Each guidebook covers a single topic and introduces the user to the forums related to that topic on MSN. You can think of them as electronic magazines (E-zines) on MSN.

Highlight   Selecting an item on screen so that it changes color or brightness. This *selects* the item in preparation for the next action.

Home Page   The starting point or first screen of a Web page.

Host The computer to which your computer connects. Generally it is MSN, but at other times it will be the "host" of whatever Web site you are visiting. See also *server*.

Hotlink An underlined or highlighted word, phrase, or address that you can click on to jump to other information about the linked phrase or to a related Web page. *Smart Link* essentially means the same but hotlink is used more often.

HTML Stands for Hyper Text Markup Language, which is a standardized method for defining formatting, links, and other special handling of text images, and objects within a Web page. You need to learn HTML only if you are planning to create your own Web page.

http Stands for hyper text transfer protocol. This is the protocol that tells your Web browser that the address you are about to specify (as in **http://www.coriolis.com**) is a site that uses HTML. When you specify an address in a Web browser, you need to begin with a protocol because browsers are capable of recognizing and accessing multiple protocols. For instance, if you want to connect to an FTP site, you need to begin the address with the **ftp://** protocol. If you want to connect to a Gopher site, you begin with the **gopher://** protocol. To connect to a Usenet newsgroup, you need to begin the address with the **news:** protocol.

Icon(s) A pictographic representation of a command, shortcut, or object. Usually, you can click an icon with your mouse, and the computer will take the action designated by the icon.

ICP Independent Content Provider. *USA Today* is an example of a forum provider that fits this definition. See also *Third Party provider*.

Index You'll find the Index function when you locate the *Find function* on MSN. Both are search tools for finding content and solutions on MSN. See also, *Find function*.

Internet The Internet is a worldwide network of computer networks. The Internet is maintained by the National Science Foundation, but is not really "owned" by anyone. As a member of MSN, you have access to the Internet, and to its graphical interface called the World Wide Web. See also *World Wide Web*.

JPEGs Stands for Joint Photographic Experts Group, which defined a standard compression format for high-resolution color images. Most images stored or displayed on the Internet and World Wide Web are either JPEGs or GIFs.

Kiosk Like the newsstand at a village square, kiosks provide information on forums, their topics, the name of the forum manager, special events, and answers to frequently asked questions.

Library Generally used as *File Library*, libraries are the areas where files are stored for ready access.

Listserv This is an electronic discussion forum that arrives in your mailbox. A listserv is conducted by *e-mail* and appears as a forum where messages arrive in your mailbox.

Member ID Your member ID is the name that you are known as on MSN. In my case, it is LuanneO. Each member ID is unique. It's also known as a *screen name*. Unlike other online services, MSN allows only one Member ID per account.

Menu Bar The horizontal bar at the top of the screen showing the names of pull-down menus.

Message Board Also known as a *BBS* in MSN terminology, a message board is like a cork bulletin board where members post messages to ask or answer questions in an ongoing conversation. These are also called *Bulletin Boards*.

Messages Messages are posted on *Message Boards* or *BBSs*. They are generally part of a running conversation and are available for public viewing.

Multitasking An operating system feature (included with Windows 95) that allows several independent programs to run concurrently.

Netiquette This is etiquette for the Internet. It refers to the proper behavior and customs for chat rooms, forums, BBS postings, and e-mail.

Network A group of computers connected in order to transmit information from one to another. A network can be created locally by using cables or can be created using phone lines, as is the case with MSN and the Internet.

Newsgroups Usually referred to as Usenet newsgroups. These are bulletin boards on the Internet. At last count there were 18,000 newsgroups with hundreds of thousands of postings each day. See also *Usenet*.

Object An object encapsulates both data and access methods, some or all of which may be used by another application. An object can be inserted into e-mail, and in that case, may be a *file* or a *shortcut*.

OLE Object Linking and Embedding, a Microsoft-owned technology that allows users to link files to multiple applications so that any update to one link is made to all applications. For example, you can link an Excel spreadsheet to a Microsoft Word document, where it is embedded and displayed. Then, if you make a change to the spreadsheet from within Word, the change is automatically updated within the spreadsheet linked to and embedded within the Word document.

Online You are online when you are connected to MSN and can exchange e-mail or navigate through the system. You are billed for your online time. You can save money and conserve online time by composing messages offline and then connecting to MSN when you're ready to send your mail. See also *session*.

Password This is your secret code that prevents anyone else from accessing your MSN account without your permission. Each *member ID* has a single password that only the member can modify. Change your password often.

Plug and Play The specification for hardware and software architecture that allows automatic device identification and configuration. Plug and play hardware makes it easy for users to add multimedia devices, such as video and sound cards, CD players, cameras, microphones, and others.

Postmaster This is the person to contact if you have trouble with incoming or outgoing mail.

Progress Bar This is the bar that fills like a thermometer when you are waiting for a file to download. It fills to indicate the proportion of data that has been transferred.

Property This is an attribute of an object. The term is used widely throughout Windows 95 to described the properties or attributes of an object, forum, or whatever.

Property Sheet A Windows 95 dialog box intended to allow the convenient grouping of an object's properties in a single place.

Retrieve The process of downloading files is also known as retrieving files.

Rich Text Text information that includes formatting features such as font, layout, and other properties. Rich text is saved in rich text files (RTF). Rich Text is a format agreed-upon by many different software vendors and allows files to be exchanged and read by different programs. For instance, Ami Pro, Microsoft Word, and WordPerfect can all read the same RTF file. The text formatting descriptions are converted back to the word processor's own proprietary codes when the file is opened.

Right-Click See *Click*. Use right mouse button.

Save History Along with the command Save History As, this function can be used to save a "recording" of a chat.

Screen Name MSN prefers the term *Member ID*. Screen names are the names used by members to identify themselves online.

Select Use your mouse and mouse button to make a selection as you navigate on MSN. See also *highlight*.

Server Essentially means the same as *host*; however, in cyberspace the term "server" has taken on another connotation, in which "server" is preceded by an adjective that identifies the type of Internet service it provides—for instance, you can connect to a Web server, an FTP server, or a Gopher server.

Service Provider In this case it is Microsoft Network, because that's who you pay for online time.

Session The duration of each *online* period is a session. For example, my sessions average an hour each.

Shareware Shareware is software that's typically posted on online services for distribution by download straight to the user. Payment for shareware is voluntary, but it does operate on an honor system. Freeware and postcardware are variations on shareware.

Shortcut A technique that allows the use of an alternative name to refer to an object. Many shortcuts can be defined as a single *object*. In their history, shortcuts have also been known as links or aliases.

Sig (Signature) A sig is a short message at the bottom of an e-mail message that identifies the sender. Large signatures are considered to be poor netiquette as they waste readers' time.

Site Site is sometimes used in place of area or *category* when describing a forum on MSN. More commonly it is used to describe an Internet location. See also *Host*.

Smart Link See *Hot Link*

Start Menu The most obvious place to start in Windows 95 is that button with the pop-up menu in the lower left hand corner of your screen.

Status Bar Appears at the bottom of every MSN window, and displays such information as quick start icons, the time, or information about the screen being displayed.

Taskbar You'll find this along the bottom of your Windows 95 screen. It includes the Start Button and shows all currently running programs or forums in MSN.

Telnet A utility that allows your computer to emulate a terminal connected to a particular network. Telnet allows you to log into a network and run programs and other services available on the network.

Text File See ASCII text.

Third Party Content This refers to forums and information provided by organizations other than Microsoft. See also *ICP*.

Thread, Message Board This term is used to describe a group of messages on a BBS that all pertain to the same subject.

Title MSN uses "title" the way you and I use the word screen. By now you may have seen the little message that says "waiting for title." It'll build in a few seconds, but it may feel like minutes.

Title Bar Windows 95 features titles bars in the top of each open window. Generally the title bar carries the name of the application or file, and it works the same way on MSN.

Upload Uploading refers to the transfer of files from your computer to MSN. Uploaded *files* may be attached to e-mail or uploaded to a file library, where they will be available to the membership of MSN. See also *download*. You can also use MSN's FTP feature to upload files to the Internet.

URL Stands for Uniform Resource Locator (also called Universal Resource Locator). A URL is essentially the address and path the browser uses to find an addressable site. See also *favorites*.

Usenet A massive networked collection of *newsgroups*, which in turn refers to special-interest forums where Internet users gather to discuss their special interests.

User Account A database of information, accessed via the user's network logon name, that defines the user's access. See also *user name*, *screen name*, and *Member ID*.

User Name See *Member ID*.

Virus A computer virus is a program that travels from machine to machine via floppy disks, networks, or telecommunications services. Viruses are unwelcome intruders and may be destructive. When you *download* files, you should protect your system by running a virus checker prior to opening the new file.

Web Browser See *Browser*.

Web Page Typically used to refer to a site on the Internet that uses *HTML* as the interface. Web pages can only be viewed with an HTML-based browser, like Microsoft's Internet *Explorer*.

World Wide Web A hypertext based system for linking databases, servers, and pages of information available across the Internet. A Web site displays graphical and multimedia information, unlike other Internet sites, which can only display text. As a member of MSN, you can access the Web through Internet Explorer.

Index

9-Puzzle, 117
@Play
   Cruising World, 148
   Golf Digest, 148
   Golf World, 148
   Sailing World, 148
   Snow Country, 148
   Tennis Magazine, 148

A

ABC Television, 177
Access
   changing number, 56
   Internet, 77, 84-85, 156-158
   MSN/Internet 158, 161
   to content, 53
   worldwide, 67-68
Access Charges, 50-51, 90
   See also Membership Plans.
   hourly, 49, 84
   Internet, 50, 84-85, 156, 158
   MSN, 50, 158
   MSN/Internet, 50, 158
   phone, 50, 158
Accounting Today, 98
Activision, 102-103
Add to Favorite Places command, 41
Add to Favorites command, 40-41
Address book, 55
   changing your profile, 55
   command, 40
   finding members, 76

Adobe, 102-103
Adoption forum, 121
Adult content, 54, 85
Advanced Research Projects Agency (ARPA), 153
Advertising, 5, 161
Air & Space/Smithsonian, 143
Ale & Lager Beerbrewing forum, 120
Alien Encounters and UFOs forum, 128
America Online, 47, 54, 57, 69
America's Cup, 144
American Bookseller's Association Web site, 177
American Greetings Personal Cardshop, 126
American Management Association, 98
Amusement parks. *See* Theme Parks! Forum.
Andreessen, Mark, 157
Andrews, Julie, 89
AnimalNet, 116
AP News Summary, 132
Archaeology. *See* History & Archaeology.
Archived Files. *See* File compression.
Architecture, 91
Armed Forces forum, 139
ARPANET, 153
Arts & Crafts, 123
Arts & Entertainment, 12-13, 91
Association of Shareware Professionals, 108

Astrology forum, 128
Astronomy & Space, 141-142
Attachments, 22-23, 68
   paperclip icon, 22
   to e-mail, 68, 70-71
   to files, 22
Audio
   CD Player Gateway, 189-190
   MIDI & Electronic Music Forum, 105-106
   Real Audio Web site, 179
Austin Chronicle, 94-95
Australia, 128
Australia Today, 68
Automotive forum, 124

B

Back command, 40
Basketball. *See* Sports & Recreation.
BBS. *See* Bulletin boards.
Beer, 120
Ben & Jerry's Homemade, Inc., Web site, 87
Bermuda, 128-129
Best Friends Animal Net, 116
Biochemistry. *See* Chemistry & Biochemistry.
Biology & Life Sciences, 141
Books. *See* American Booksellers Association Web site.
Bookshelf forum, 28-29, 112
British Grand Prix, 144
Broderbund, 102-103
Browser, 3, 35, 38-40, 85, 87-88, 90, 157-159, 161-162, 166, 172. *See also* Microsoft Explorer.
   Launching, 3, 172
   Open Start Page command, 40
   Open Favorites command, 40
Bucknell University Web site, 180
Bulletin Boards, 77-81, 163
   missing messages, 78
   posting messages, 78
   reading offline, 80
   tools, 41
Busch, 128-129
Business & Finance, 96-101
   Decision Point, 100-101
   Federal Express, 98-99
   Fidelity Online, 101
   Hoover's Business Resources, 59, 99-100
   Mainstream Career Center, 96-97
   Small Office Home Office, 97-98
   UPS, 99
   WinWay Career Forum, 97

C

Cams Around the World, 191-192
California
   Disaster Information Web site 178-179
Careers
   Mainstream Career Center, 96-97
   WinWay Career forum, 97
   Women's Wire, 138
Cars. *See* Automotive forum.
Cats. *See* Talk to my Cat.
Categories, 6-7, 10-11, 35, 89-90
Category tools, 41
CBS Television
   Letterman's Top Ten List, 172
   Web site, 177

Index 247

CD Player Gateway, 189-190
CD-ROM. *See* Multimedia & CD-ROM forum.
Chat
    etiquette, 42
    gavels, 43
    parental tip, 151
    participants, 42
    rooms, 77
    saving contents of session, 79-80
    sessions, 79-80
    spectacles, 43
    tools, 41
Chat World, 42-43, 150-151
    Lobby, 150
Chemistry & Biochemistry, 141
Chicago Reader, 94-95
Children First, 121-122
Children's areas
    Children First, 121-122
    Family Planet, 121
    Ingenius Online, 118-119
    Kidstar Online, 118
    National PTA, 121-122
    parenting/kids newsgroups 167
    Splash Kids, 117-118
Cigars. *See* Wine, Beer, Spirits, & Cigars Forum.
Cinemania Collection, 93-94
Clinton, Bill, 32
CNN, 177
Cobb's PC Productivity Center, 105
Coffee machine online, 186-187
Cola machine online, 189-190
Collecting, 125
College prep
    Kaplan Online, 113
    Princeton Review, 112-113
Columbia Healthcare WWW link

Comic Strip. *See* Dilbert Web site.
Comics, 91
Communications technology, 141
Complaints, 65
CompuServe Information Service, 47, 57, 69
Computer books, 110
Computer Games forum, 106-107
Computer Gaming World, 105
Computer Life, 105
Computer Science. *See* RIT Computer Science House Drink Machine.
Computer Shopper, 105
Computers & Electronics, 141
Computers & Software, 102-110
    Computer Games forum, 106-107
    Computer Periodicals, 102
    Desktop Publishing forum, 107
    Komputer Klinic, 110
    Maxis, 107-108
    Microsoft Knowledge Base, 108-109
    Microsoft Windows 95, 109
    MIDI & Electronic Music forum, 105-106
    Multimedia & CD-ROM, 106
    NewMedia, 104-105
    Newsbytes, 103
    Online Service Providers, 110
    PC World Communications, Inc., 104
    Shareware, 108
    Software Companies, 102-103
    ZD Net, 105
Content, 36-37, 156
    locating 36-37
Conversations View command, 41
Cooking
    Ale & Lager Beerbrewing forum, 120

Fast & Easy Recipes, 120
In the Kitchen, 120
Kidstar Kitchen, 118
Pathfinder's Kitchen, 120-121
SeniorNet, 136
What's Cooking Online, 120
Wine, Beer, Spirits, and Cigars forum, 120
Copy command, 40-41
Corel, 102-103
Cost. *See* Access charges.
Court TV, 92
Crafts. *See* Arts & Crafts.
CreataCard Online, 126
Credit, requesting, 66
Credit cards. *See* Security.
Crossword puzzle, 131
Cruising World, 148-149
Customer profiles. *See* Profiles.
Cut command, 40-41
Cyberspace, 153

D

Decision Point, 100-101
Delete command, 40
Deliver Now command, 40
Demos. *See* Shareware.
Desk. *See* What's in my desk drawer.
Desktop Publishing forum, 107
Details command, 41
Dilbert Web site, 180-181
DisAbilities forum, 114
Disaster Information Network Web site, 178-179
Disney
  BBSes, 22-23
  Disney World, 122
  library, 22-23
  Theme Parks! Forum, 22-23, 115-116, 128-129
Domain name, 172
Download, 22-23, 81-83
  and Open command, 22
  destinations, 82-83
  File command, 22
  libraries, 77
Downloading Files, 22-23, 81-82
  attachments, 22-23
  in the background. See Multitasking.
  transfer and disconnect, 81-82
Drawer. *See* What's in my desk drawer.
Drink Machine. *See* RIT Computer Science House Drink Machine.
Dun & Bradstreet Information Services, 98

E

Easton, Jaclyn, 188
Eddie Bauer, 63
Edinburgh Festival, 144
Edit menu. *See* Menus.
Education & Reference, 111-113
  Encarta Encyclopedia, 111-112
  Bookshelf forum, 112
  Princeton Review, 112-113
  Kaplan Online, 113
Educational Software Cooperative, 108
EForm, 63
Electronics. *See* Computers & Electronics
E-mail, 6-7, 26-33, 68-77, 81. *See also* Microsoft Exchange.
  American Greetings Personal Cardshop, 126

Index

attachments, 70-71
backup copies, 73
Blind Courtesy Copy (bcc), 73
Composing offline, 74
Courtesy Copies (cc) 70
Delivery Receipt, 32-33, 76
faxing with E-mail, 73
folders, 26-27
from word processor, 71
icons, 68, 70-71, 73-74
including a file, 70
incoming mail, 26, 75
Internet E-mail, 68, 77
mailing lists, 159, 163-165
New Message command, 40-41
postmaster, 77
problem solving, 76-77
Read Mail, 26, 31
Read Receipt, 32-33, 76
reading offline, 74-75
Reply to All command, 40
Reply to Sender command, 40
rich text, 59
saving messages, 76
shortcuts, 28-29, 70-71
Signature Art, 126
sorting, 30-31
status, 76
System Administrator, 33
to other online services, 69
tools, 40
transmission time, 69
UUENCODED attachments, 70
writing from within a forum, 81
Encarta Encyclopedia, 111-112
Entertainment, 91-95
    Cinemania Collection, 93-94
    Court TV, 92
    Mr. Showbiz, 92
    Music Central, 94
    TV Host, 93
Entrepreneur magazine, 98
Equifax, 98
Error messages, 44-45
ESPN, 147-148
    SportsZone, 147-148
Etiquette. *See* Netiquette.
Europe
    England, 128-129
    Friends of Europe forum, 133, 136-137
e-world, 69
Exclamation point icon, 73-74
Exchange. *See* Microsoft Exchange.
Exercise & Physical Fitness, 113
Explorer mode, 60
Explorer View, 8-9

F

Family PC, 105
Family Planet, 121
Family Travel forum, 122
Family. *See* Home & Family.
Fantasy Sports Games, 146
FAQ, 165
Fashion & Shopping, 138
Fast & Easy Recipes, 120
Flipper, 118
Favorites (Web sites)
    command, 40-41
Favorite Places, 6-7, 50, 61
    add to Favorite Places, 11, 18, 62-63
    add to Favorite Places command, 41
    command, 41
    Go to Favorite Places command, 40

Faxing with E-mail, 73
Federal Express, 98-99
Fee. *See* Access charges.
Ferguson, Mark L., 28-29
Fidelity Online Investor Center
File
   compression, 83
   libraries. See Download Libraries.
   sound, 84
File Menu. *See* Menus.
File Transfer Protocol. *See* FTP.
File View command, 41
Find
   command, 40
   function, 34-37, 57-58, 160, 166
Finger, 159
Fitness. *See* Health & Fitness.
Flipper, 118
Foam Bath Fish Time, 187-188
Font commands, 40
Forums, 37-38, 77-81, 156, 161. *See also* Bulletin Boards.
   BBS tools, 41
   chat buttons, 79
   finding GO Words, 79
   kiosks, 78
   managers, 78
   properties, 79
   reading message boards offline, 80
Forward command, 40
Fox Network, 177
Frequently Asked Questions. *See* FAQ.
Friends of Europe. *See* Europe.
FTP, 87-88, 159, 162, 167-171, 174
Full Access EForm, 166

G

Games forum, 125-126. *See also* Computer Games forum.
Gardening forum, 119-120
Gates, Bill, 183, 185
   House Web site, 185
Gavels. *See* Chat.
Gays & Lesbians, 134
Genealogy, 133-134
Geology & Geography, 130-131
GIFs, 83
Gifts, 126
Go to Favorite Places Command, 40
Go to MSN Central command, 40-41
GO Word Directory, 58
GO Words, 44, 50, 57-58, 61, 79, 90
Golf Digest, 148-149
Golf World, 148-149
Gopher, 159-160, 162, 167-171, 174
Gourmet GiftNet, 126-127
GoverNet, 140
Grand Prix. *See* British Grand Prix.
Guidebook. *See* MSN Guidebooks.

H

Hawk, Gary, 99
Hazel, 118
Health & Fitness, 113-115
   Medicine Forum, 114-115
Healthcare Professionals forum, 114
Help, 63-64
Help Command, 40
Help menu. *See* Menus.
Help topics, 36-37

Index

Contents, 36-37
Find, 36-37
Index, 36-37
History & Archeaology, 133, 137-138
HIV/AIDS test, 122
Hobbies. *See* Interests, Leisure & Hobbies.
Home & Family, 115-122
   Best Friends AnimalNet, 116
   Children First, 121-122
   Gardening, 119-120
   In the Kitchen, 120
   Ingenius Online, 119
   Kidstar Online, 118
   Lanier Travel Guides, 122-123
   Parenting, 121
   Pathfinder's Kitchen, 120-121
   Photography, 116-117
   Splash Kids, 117-118
   Theme Parks!, 115-116
Home Office Computing, 98
Home Zone. *See* Microsoft Home Zone.
Hoover's Business Resources, 59, 99-100
Horoscope. *See* Astrology forum.
HTML, 87, 157, 174, 175
Human Sexuality BBS, 113
Hyper Text Markup Language. *See* HTML.
Hypertext, 157
   links, *157, 172*

I

Icons, 68
   Large icons command, 24, 41
   Small icons command, 24, 41
Icons, menu. *See* View Menu.
ICP, 50, 63, 160

Ignore (members) command, 41
Images, formats, 83
Illusions. *See* Magic and Illusions forum.
In the Kitchen, 120
Inbox command, 40
Independent Content Provider. See ICP.
Index, 34, 36-37
InfoSeek, 160, 183
Ingenius Online, 119
Inspirational quotes. *See* Mind Garden.
Interactive Week, 105
Interests, Leisure & Hobbies, 123-129
   Alien Encounters and UFOs, 128-129
   Arts & Crafts, 123-124
   Astrology, 128
   Automotive forum, 124
   Collecting, 125
   CreataCard Online, 126
   Games forum, 125-126
   Gourmet GiftNet, 126
   Magic and Illusions, 127
   Travel, 128-129
Internet, 77, 153-192 *See also* membership plans.
   Access, 77, 84-85, 156, 158
   browser, 3, 35, 38-39, 85, 87
   E-mail. See E-mail, Internet.
   Finger, 159
   FTP, 87-88, 159, 162, 167-171, 174
   Gopher, 159-160, 162, 167-171, 174
   HTML, 87, 157, 174, 175
   Icon, 3
   InfoSeek, 183, 160
   Lycos, 183, 160
   Mailing Lists, 88, 159, 163-165
   Telnet, 159, 160, 162, 167-168, 174
   tools, 40
   Usenet newsgroups, 77, 85-86, 159, 162-163, 165-167, 174

WAIS, 159
World Wide Web, 38-39, 86-87, 156-162, 171-181, 177-192
Yahoo, 160, 183
Internet Center, 148-149, 153, 166
finding Usenet newsgroups, 166
Internet Explorer. *See* Microsoft Explorer.
Internet Service Provider, 166
Investing
Decision Point, 100-101
Fidelity Online Investor Center, 101
Schwab Online, 101

J

Jazz Central Station, 91
Jetsons, 174
Jobs. *See* Careers.
Journalism. *See* Pulitzer Prize Web site.
JPEGs, 83
Junk Mail, 75
avoiding, 75

K

Kaplan Online, 113
Kids. *See* Children's areas.
KidStar Online, 118
Komando, Kim, 110
Kitchen. *See* Cooking.
Knitting Mailing List, 88
Knowledge Base. *See* Microsoft Knowledge Base.
Komputer Klinic, 110

L

Languages, 67
Lanier Travel Guides, 122
Large Icons command, 24, 41
Leisure. *See* Interests.
Lesbians. *See* Gays & Lesbians.
Letterman, David
Top Ten List, 172
Life Sciences. *See* Biology & Life Sciences.
List command, 41
List view command, 41
Listserv. *See* Mailing Lists.
Locusts. *See* Disaster Information Web site.
Log-On USA, 188
Los Angeles LA Weekly, 94-95
Lycos, 183

M

Macintosh
access, 66
servers, 173
Magazines, 91. *See also* Pathfinder.
Accounting Today, 98
Air & Space, 143
Best Friends, 116
Black Belt Magazine, 146
Computer Gaming World, 105
Computer Life, 105
Computer Periodicals, 102
Computer Shopper, 105

Index

Cruising World, 148-149
Entrepreneur, 98
Family PC, 105
Golf Digest, 148-149
Golf World, 148-149
Home Office Computing, 98
Interactive Week, 105
Karate/Kung Fu Illustrated, 146
Martial Arts Training Magazine, 146
Multimedia World, 104
Natural Pet, 116
New Media, 104
PC Computing, 105
PC Magazine, 105
PC Week, 105
PC World, 104
Sailing World, 148-149
Smithsonian, 143
Snow Country, 148-149
Tennis Magazine, 148-149
Venture, 97
Windows Sources, 105
ZD Net, 105
Magic and Illusions forum, 127
Mail. *See* E-mail.
Mailing Lists, 88, 159, 163, 165
   finding, 163-165
   help command, 164
   knitting, 88
   Publicly Accessible Mailing Lists Web page, 164-165
   subscribing, 163-164
Mainstream Career Center, 96-97
Marfer. *See* Ferguson, Mark L.
Market & Securities Research, 101
Martial Arts Network, 146
   Black Belt Magazine, 146
   Karate/Kung Fu Illustrated, 146
   Martial Arts Training Magazine, 146

Massachusetts Institute of Technology. *See* MIT.
Math & Physics, 141
Maxis
McDonalds, 5, 85
   advertisement, 5
Medicine, 114, 141
   Health Care Professionals, 113, 114
   Medicine forum, 114
   Preventive Medicine, 114
   Public health, 114
Mental Wellness & Counseling, 113
Member
   Assistance, 6-7, 14-15, 56
   Lobby, 14-15
   Properties command, 41
   Support bulletin board, 14-15
Members
   locating, 65, 76
Membership
   Family Accounts, 53
   Individual Accounts, 53
   Plans, 49
Menus
   Edit, 24-25, 60
   File, 11, 18, 24-25
   Help, 24-25, 36-37
   Tools, 6, 24-25
   View, 12-13, 20-21, 24-25
Message Boards. *See* Bulletin Boards.
Michael from Alaska, 176
Microsoft
   FTP site, 170
   Gopher site, 171
   Web site, 176
Microsoft Bookshelf. *See* Bookshelf forum.
Microsoft Exchange, 50, 73
   See also E-mail.

Inbox, 73
Read Mail, 26, 31, 76
Receipt Options, 32-33, 76
tools, 40
Microsoft Explorer, 38-39, 157-159, 162, 172. See also Browser.
   Open Favorites command, 40
   Open Start Page command, 40
   Refresh command, 172
   tools, 40, 85, 87
Microsoft Home Zone, 112
Microsoft Knowledge Base, 108-109
Microsoft Office, 5
Microsoft Plus! 85, 87, 158
Microsoft Windows 95. See Windows 95.
Microsoft Word, 28
MIDI & Electronic Music forum, 105-106
Mind Garden, 133, 136-137
Minesweep, 117
MIT, 189-190
Money Magazine, 174, 181
MorseMcFadden Communications, 185
Motorcycling forum, 124
Move Item command, 40
Movies, 91. See also Paramount.
   Cinemania, 93-94
   Paramount, 177-178
   Mr. Showbiz, 92
Mr. Potato Head, 117
Mr. Showbiz, 92
MSN
   icon, 2-3, 60-61
   Customer Service, 77
MSN Central, 6-7
   tools, 40
MSN Executives. See Siegelman, Russell.
MSN Guidebooks, 16-17
   MSN Computing, 16-17

MSN Home & Family, 16
MSN Kids & Co., 16
MSN Life, 16
MSN SOHO, 16
MSN Spectrum, 16
MSN Sports & Recreation, 16
MSN News, 129-130
MSN Passport, 149-150
MSN plus Internet, 35
MSN Today, 4-5
   omit from startup, 4, 57
Multimedia
   & CD-ROM forum, 106
   Multimedia World, 104
   NewMedia, 104-105
Multitasking, 63, 81, 82
Music, 97. See also Jazz Central Station.
Music Central, 94
   Newsstand, 94-95
My Computer, 61

N

National Center for Supercomputing Applications (NCSA), 157
Navigation, 50, 60-61, 85, 172-173. See also Go Words.
NBC, 63, 177
   NBC News, 130-131
   NBC Sports, 147
   NBC Supernet, 132
NET Political Network, 140
Netiquette, 42
New Age forum, 134-135
New Message command, 40-41
New York Times Magazine Group. See @Play.

New York Village Voice, 94-95
NewMedia, 104-105
News & Weather, 129-132
    AP News Summary, 132
    MSN News, 129-130
    NBC News, 130-131
    NBC Supernet, 132
    The Weather Lab, 130-131
    Time Warner's Pathfinder, 130
    USA Today, 34-35, 130-132
Newsbytes, 103
Newsgroups. *See* Usenet newsgroups.
Newspapers, 91
Novell, 102-103
Nursing forum, 115. *See* also Pregnancy, Labor and Nursing Forum.
Nutrition, 113

O

Objects, 172
Online
    charges. See *Access charges*.
    services, 47, 52, 54, 57, 69
    service providers, 110
Open Command, 40
Open Containing Folder, 59
Open Favorites command, 40
Open Start Page command, 40
Options Command, 24

P

Packwood, Bob, 138
Paperclip icon. *See* Attachments.
Paramount Studios Web site, 177-178

Parenting, 121
    Parenting in the 90s forum, 121
Passport. *See* MSN Passport.
Paste command, 41
Pathfinder, 174, 181
Pathfinder's Kitchen, 120-121
PC Computing, 105
PC Magazine, 105
PC Week, 105
PC World Communications, 104
Pegs, 117
People & Communities, 133-140
    Armed Forces forum, 139
    DisAbilities forum, 134-135
    Friends of Europe, 133, 136-137
    Gays & Lesbians, 134
    Genealogy, 133-134
    GoverNet, 140-141
    History & Archaeology, 133, 137-138
    Mind Garden, 133, 136-137
    NET Political Network, 140
    New Age forum, 134-135
    Public Affairs, 138-139
    SeniorNet, 134, 136
    Women's Wire, 133, 138
People Magazine, 174, 181
Pet forum, 116
Pets. *See* Talk to My Cat.
Phone Charges. *See* Access Charges.
PhotoDisc Digital Image forum, 117
Photography forum, 116-117
Physics. *See* Math & Physics.
PICTs, 83
Politics. *See* Public Affairs.
Political memorabilia, 125
Postmaster, 77
Pregnancy, Labor and Nursing Forum, 121

Preventive Medicine, 114.
Price. *See* Access charges.
Princeton Review, The, 112-113
Print command, 40
Printing tips, 84
Prodigy, 69
Profiles, 52-53
Properties, 57-58, 79
   command 24, 41
Puck, Wolfgang, 144
Public Affairs, 138-139
   Armed Forces forum, 139
   GoverNet, 140-141
   NET Political Network, 140
Public health, 114
Publicly Accessible Mailing Lists Web page, 164-165
Pulitzer Prize Web site, 178

R

Radio, 91
Reading forum, 91
Real Audio Web site, 179
Recipes. *See* Cooking.
Recreation. *See* Sports & Recreation.
Reference. *See* Education & Reference.
Refresh command, 40, 172
Reply to All command, 40
Reply to Sender command, 40
Reuters, 59
Rich text, 59, 68
RIT Computer Science House Drink Machine, 190-191
RIT, 190-191
Rochester Institute of Technology. *See* RIT.

Rocky Mountain Internet Users Group, 168
ROT13 Encoding/Decoding 167-171
Runner's World Prefontaine Classic, 144
RTF files. *See* Rich text.

S

Sailing World, 148-149
San Diego Bay Cam Web site, 185-186
San Francisco Bay Guardian, 94-95
Santa Claus, 33
Save command, 41
Schwab Online, 101
Science & Technology, 141-144
   Astronomy & Space, 142
   ScienceFair, 142-142
   Smithsonian and Air & Space, 143
ScienceFair, 141-143
Scotland, 128-129
   Edinburgh Festival, 144
Scuba Online, 147
Sea World, 115-116
Seattle Rocket, 94-95
Security, 64-65
SeniorNet, 134-136
Sessions. *See* Chat.
Sexuality Forum, 54, 113
ShaqWorld Online, 144-145
Shareware, 59-60, 84, 108-109
   Shareware forum, 108-109
   Association of Shareware Professionals, 108
   Educational Software Cooperative, 108
Shortcuts, 18-19, 28-29, 50, 52, 61-62, 77
   creating, 18, 172

Index

moving, 28-29, *172*
launching, *172*
Show/Hide Folder List command, 40
Siegelman, Russell, 32-33, 55, 65-66
Sign Out command, 40-41
SimCity. *See* Maxis.
Six Flags, 115-116, 128-129
Small Business Administration, 98
Small Icons command, 24, 41
Small Office Home Office (SOHO), 97-98
Smithsonian and Air & Space, 143
Snow Country, 148-149
Software, 102-103. *See also* Computers & Software.
Sound files, 84, 156. *See also* Audio.
Space. *See* Astronomy & Space.
Special Events, 144
  America's Cup, *144*
  British Grand Prix, *144*
  Edinburgh Festival, *144*
  Puck, Wolfgang, *144*
  Runner's World Prefontaine Classic, *144*
Spectacles. *See* Chat.
Spirits. *See* Wine, Beer, Spirits, & Cigars Forum.
Splash Kids, 117-118
Sports & Recreation, 144-148
  ShaqWorld Online, *144-145*
  Fantasy Sports, *146*
  Online Games, Inc., *145-146*
  Martial Arts Network, *146*
  Scuba Online, *147*
  Sports Media, *147-148*
Sports Illustrated, 147
Sports Media, 147-148
  @Play, *148-149*
  ESPN, *147-148*
  NBC Sports, *147*

Sports Illustrated, *147*
USA Today, *132*, *147*
Status bar, 7, 61
Steve's List of T-shirts, 192
Stop command, 40
Subscriptions. *See* Membership Plans.
Suggestions, 65
Swatch World, 125
Symantec, 102
System Administrator, 33, 74

T

T-Shirts. *See* Steve's List of T-Shirts.
Talk to my Cat, 188
Taskbar, 39
TCP/IP, 155-156, 167
Technology. *See* Science & Technology.
Telnet, 159, 160, 162, 167-168, 174
Tennis Magazine, 148-149
Text
  text file, 28
  text reader, 28
  text, saving, 79
Theatre, 91
Theme Parks! Forum, 19, 115-116
Third party content providers. *See* ICP.
Tic-Tac-Toe, 117
Time, 187-188
Time Magazine, 174, 181
Time Warner's Pathfinder. *See* Pathfinder.
Title, defined, 57
Toolbar Command, 24
Tools. *See* Menus.
Toronto Now, 94-95
Transportation, 141
Travel, 18-19

Family Travel forum, 122
Lanier Travel Guides, 122
SeniorNet, 136
Theme Parks! forum, 128-129
Trojan Room Coffee Machine, 186-187
TV Networks
   Web sites, 177
TV Host, 93

U

UFOs. *See* Alien Encounters and UFOs forum.
Uniform Resource Locator. *See* URL.
United Media Web site, 180-181
United Parcel Service. *See* UPS.
Universal Resource Locator. *See* URL.
UNIX (servers), 173
Up One Level command, 40-41
UPS, 99
Use Larger Font command, 40
Use Smaller Font command, 40
URL, 171
   domain name, 172
   how to read a, 172-172
USA Today, 34-35, 131-132, 160-161
Usenet newsgroups, 77, 85 86, 159, 162-163, 165-167, 174
   add to Favorite Places, 166
   FAQ, 165
   finding, 85-86
   restricted, 166

V

Venture magazine, 97
View Menu. *See* Menus.

View menu icons
   choose icon size 12-13
   icons, 20-21
Village Voice, 94-95
Von Trapp family, 89

W

WAIS, 159
Wave files. *See* Sound files.
Weather. *See* News & Weather
WeatherLab, The, 130-131
Web browser, 38-39, 157-159 *See also* World Wide Web.
What's Cooking Online, 120
What's in my desk drawer, 189
Whitestone, Heather, 135
Windows 95, 52, 71, 104, 109, 167, 172-173
Windows Sources, 105
Wine, Beer, Spirits, and Cigars forum, 120
Winnie the Pooh, 22-23
WinWay Career forum,
Women's Wire
Woodworking forum, 123-124
World Wide Web, 38-39, 86-87, 156-162, 168, 171-181, 183-192
   addresses, 173
   defined, 86-87
   Favorites, 88, 171
   finding things on the Web, 38-39, 88, 160
   InfoSeek, 160, 183
   Lycos, 160, 183
   navigating, 172
   refresh image, 172
   tools, 40

URL, 38, 171, 172
Yahoo, 160, 183
Writing forum, 91

Y

Yahoo, 160, 183

Z

ZD Net Magazines, 105
Ziff-Davis Publishing, 105